Shaped by
GOD's
Love

George Adrian

Shaped by

GOD's

Love

With Introductory Notes by D. Stuart Briscoe

From the Editors of *Decision* Magazine

World Wide Publications
Minneapolis, Minnesota 55403

Shaped by God's Love

World Wide Publications is the publishing ministry of the Billy Graham Evangelistic Association.

Unless otherwise indicated, Scripture quotations are taken from The Holy Bible, New International Version. Copyright © 1973, 1978, 1984 International Bible Society. Used by permission of Zondervan Bible Publishers.

Scripture quotations marked KJV are taken from the Authorized King James Version of the Bible.

Scripture quotations marked RSV are taken by permission from the Revised Standard Version Bible, © 1946, 1952, 1971, 1973 National Council of Churches of Christ in the U.S.A., New York, New York.

Scripture quotations marked NASB are from the New American Standard Bible, © 1960, 1962, 1963, 1968, 1971, 1972, 1973, 1975, 1977 The Lockman Foundation, La Habra, California.

Scripture quotations marked TLB or The Living Bible are taken from The Living Bible, © 1971 Tyndale House Publishers. Used by permission.

Individual chapters are taken by permission from *Decision* magazine, January 1987, February 1987, March 1987, May 1987, July-August 1987, September 1987, October 1987, November 1987, December 1987, January 1988, February 1988, March 1988, April 1988, May 1988, June 1988, October 1988, November 1988, January 1989, February 1989, April 1989, May 1989, June 1989, October 1989, December 1989. Copyright © 1987, 1988, 1989, the Billy Graham Evangelistic Association.

Illustration credits (by page): 13, Gustave Doré; 57, Gustave Doré; 101, © 1980 Augsburg Publishing House, Reprinted by permission of Augsburg Fortress; 111, Gustave Doré; 121, Bill Gregg/Messenger Corporation; 243, Briton Riviere/ Walker Art Gallery, Liverpool. The following illustrations are copyright © Billy Graham Evangelistic Association (used by permission): 23, Marvin Espe, 1989; 33, Marvin Espe, 1988; 43, Myron Sahlberg, 1987; 67, Eugene Christopherson, 1988; 77, Steven Paul Carlson, 1988; 87, Kenneth Spirduso, 1987; 131, David Beal, 1985; 145, Marvin Espe, 1989; 155, Joe Nordstrom, 1988; 165, Michael Hackett, 1987; 175, Lois Rosio Sprague, 1988; 189, Michael Hackett, 1989; 199, James Rownd, 1987; 209, Steven Paul Carlson, 1988; 219, Eugene Christopherson, 1987; 233, Steven Paul Carlson, 1989; 253, Lois Rosio, 1988; 263, Ken Spirduso, 1989.

Library of Congress Catalog Card Number: 90-070293

ISBN: 0-89066-197-9

Printed in the United States of America

90 91 92 93 94 / 5 4 3 2

Contents

■ ● ■

Introduction

■●■

I love books. Ask my wife, Jill, and she will tell you that our home is full of them. My mother used to say I would read brown paper if nothing else was available! Recently, I bought a book entitled, *The Lifetime Reading Plan*—an introduction to the "classics" of western literature. I admit that I'm a little old to be starting on a lifetime of reading but I wanted to check out the great books. In the introduction the author, Clifton Fadiman, wrote, "You will at once note omissions. I have not listed the Old and New Testaments. The Bible, of course, is more important than any book on the list, influencing constantly and deeply the lives of all Westerners. . . . I assume you own one." I'm sure Mr. Fadiman is right about the Bible. But if it is assumed that most people in the West own one, it would be foolish to assume that they read it. In actual fact, the Bible could be described as the world's least read best-seller.

One of the reasons for this anomaly is that many people try to read it but say they can't understand it. They are not at all like the man from Zimbabwe who, when he was offered a New Testament, said he would use the pages to roll cigarettes. The person giving him the Testament said that was alright provided he read each page before he smoked it. Fifteen years later the two men met again, but by this time the "smoker" had become a pastor. He explained, "I smoked Matthew, I smoked Mark, and I smoked Luke, but when I came to John 3:16 I finally understood." In my experience, people are more often like another man from Africa, the Ethiopian whom Stephen met in the desert. When asked if he understood the Scriptures he was reading he replied, "How can I unless someone explains it to me?" (Acts 8:31) This book is designed for those of us who relate more to the Ethiopian who was in a fog than the Zimbabwean who was going up in smoke. It has been carefully crafted to "explain" the Bible.

Everybody loves a good story—especially if it is about people. This book focuses on stories about people who live in the Bible, with particular reference to their relationship to God. Skilled Bible teachers writing short, bite-size chapters draw out the lessons these characters learned and show how we are remarkably like them and can learn from them. Then, to make sure we don't miss crossing the bridge of application to our own day and age, various people have written brief stories of how their everyday lives have been greatly enriched as they have applied the life stories of these "Bible people" to their own situations.

Another reason people give for not reading their Bibles is a shortage of time. I have a lot of sympathy for many people whose lives are so frantic and frenetic that they rarely have a quiet moment. However, while I am sympathetic about their stress-filled lives, I suspect their busyness may, in part, be symptomatic of a lifestyle that is less than systematic in balancing life's many facets. When this is the case there is often a shortfall in spiritual care and nurture. This book is designed for the busiest of people who need help in disciplining themselves to take their spiritual vitamins. The benefit of reading this book will be felt over a considerable period of time, particularly when you find yourself being drawn into the further meditation and study which it offers.

—Stuart Briscoe

Part I
Our Failure, God's Grace

———— ■●■ ————

When Oliver Cromwell sat for his portrait he told the artist, Mr. Lely, that he wanted "A picture truly like me." He insisted that his assorted pimples and warts be depicted, and he warned Mr. Lely that he would not get a farthing for his services if he did not comply. So Oliver Cromwell became known as the man who was painted, "warts'n all."

Most of the characters in the Bible were described "warts'n all." There are good reasons for this. First, because the Bible is true. It tells the truth about both God and man. And anybody who knows anything about anyone knows that we all have our warts. The recognition of this, even in the biblical heroes, gives a great sense of authenticity to the biblical story.

Another reason for putting the Bible characters under such a spotlight is to give hope and encouragement to those who are conscious of their own failure in life. To be shown that the great apostle Paul was formerly Christ's arch-opponent gives hope to some people. John Mark's cowardly flight from commitment was reversed eventually and he became most productive for the cause of Christ—read his Gospel! Jonah, unfortunately, betrayed an unpleasant tendency to racism and bigotry which led to outright disobedience; and, of course, we all know that King David, author of dozens of psalms, beloved of millions, fell dreadfully into adultery and worse. But they all came back and lived well, reminding us that in God's way of looking at things, failure does not have to be final.

Then, of course, we have to recognize that every description of sin and failure is designed to highlight the love and grace of God. It was "while we were still sinners, Christ died for us" (Romans 5:8). It has always been that wherever "sin increased, grace increased all the more" (Romans 5:20). A word of caution is appropriate at this point. Some people, reading of the failures and warts of the heroes of the faith, have settled down in their own failure feeling perfectly justified and content.

Some years ago, when I was preaching through Genesis, a man stopped me in church and said, "Stuart, I haven't been in church in years but I started coming here a couple of months ago and I wouldn't miss it. I love Genesis. You know why? Because all these guys, Esau, Isaac, and Jacob, are worse than me! I feel great!" It took some time for him to see that the stories of "these guys" are not given to encourage sin and failure, but to encourage sinners to come to repentance and faith and discover life that is productive, not destructive. He eventually did see, did come to faith, and is living for God's glory.

Paul:
New Beginnings

■●■

William V. Crockett

Paul—I
A Haunting Past
■ ● ■

Christ Jesus came into the world to save sinners—of whom I am the worst (1 Timothy 1:15).

We all do things we would rather forget, but Paul's behavior has little parallel. In the early days of the church he hunted its members relentlessly, bringing them to dishonor, injury, and even death. Later in his ministry he often wished he had never heard the name Saul. He remembered how his single-minded cruelty had done great harm to Christ's church (Galatians 1:13–17).

Paul recognized the evil he had done. He had been so zealous for the law and so angry with those who preached Jesus as Messiah that he ignored his esteemed teacher, Gamaliel, who counseled toleration of the new sect. "You will only find your-selves fighting against God," Gamaliel had said (Acts 5:33–39).

None of this deterred the zealot Saul. His extreme hatred of Christianity drove him mercilessly. With no particular remorse he watched Stephen die, voted death for others, callously delivered men and women to prison, and persecuted Christians in cities other than Jerusalem (Acts 7:54–60; 22:2–5; 26:9–11).

He even tried to make believers blaspheme the name of Jesus. At a later date apostates and pagans would utter the phrase, "Jesus be cursed" to prove that they were not closet Christians (1 Corinthians 12:3). This phrase was known in Paul's day, and something like it may have been used by him to test believers.

Finally, on the Damascus road Paul found forgiveness, but the memories of his misguided zeal as a persecutor followed him to the end of his days, "I am the least of the apostles," he said, "unfit to be called an apostle, because I persecuted the church of God" (1 Corinthians 15:9, RSV).

William V. Crockett is Associate Professor of New Testament at Alliance Theological Seminary in Nyack, New York, and the author of *New Testament Survey*.

Paul—II
A Difficult Beginning
■ ● ■

*The man who formerly persecuted us is now preaching the faith
he once tried to destroy (Galatians 1:23).*

Like most Christians, Paul found that faith in Christ brought
peace and joy but not magical solutions to every problem.
Actually, following his Damascus road conversion, Paul discovered new problems. He faced strong opposition when he
tried to preach the gospel.

Shortly after God restored Paul's sight through Ananias,
Paul began preaching in the synagogues. His preaching so
angered the Jews and officials, such as Aretas IV, that Paul says
of his escape from Damascus, "In Damascus the governor
under King Aretas had the city . . . guarded in order to arrest me.
But I was lowered in a basket from a window in the wall and
slipped through his hands" (2 Corinthians 11:32–33).

After this, Paul went to Jerusalem and tried to join the
disciples, but they had little trust in the one who had caused so
much suffering. When he preached in the streets his old
associates, the Hellenists, saw him as a blasphemer and a
traitor; he barely escaped with his life (Acts 9:26–30).

Even when the disciples offered him the right hand of
fellowship, a group surfaced in the Jerusalem church who
opposed Paul and his gospel. They wanted Gentiles to obey the
Jewish law and to be circumcised. "This matter arose," said
Paul, "because some false brothers had infiltrated our ranks to
spy on the freedom we have in Christ Jesus and to make us
slaves" (Galatians 2:4). But in all these things, Paul remained
faithful to the truth of the gospel.

As Christians we sometimes talk of enduring trials for
Christ, but before we take ourselves too seriously, we might
recall the early days of Paul's ministry. He endured imprison-
ments, beatings, lashings, stonings, shipwrecks, lack of food,
water, and sleep.

Paul—III
A Confident Person
—— ■ ● ■ ——

For in him we live and move and have our being (Acts 17:28).

Paul had the ability to adapt himself to his audiences. At Athens he made his point by quoting a line from the poet Epimenides. To be sure, Epimenides intended something quite different from Paul when he said, "In him," but all the same, Paul was able to communicate to his audience that all men are God's creation and they accordingly are his "offspring" (Acts 17:28, KJV). In short, Paul was saying that all of us, whether or not we know it, are in God's hands.

As the offspring of God, neither we nor the men of Athens are guaranteed eternal life. That comes only to those who have "faith in Jesus" (Romans 3:26). But once we are in Christ, we can say with Paul, "Whether we live or die, we belong to the Lord" (Romans 14:8).

These were not idle words that Paul tossed around; they were words that he lived by. For Paul, being "in Christ," gave him great confidence in his ministry. Even at the worst of times, he knew that God was with him. In Asia, for example, he said, "We were so utterly, unbearably crushed that we despaired of life itself" (2 Corinthians 1:8, RSV). But then he goes on to say, "This happened that we might not rely on ourselves but on God, who raises the dead" (2 Corinthians 1:9).

All things are in God's hands, but sometimes God uses trials that come our way to remind us that in our natural strength we are helpless. Only then can we sense fully that "in him we live and move and have our being."

Paul—IV
A Glorious Future
■●■

Now there is in store for me the crown of righteousness, which the Lord, the righteous Judge, will award to me on that day— and not only to me, but also to all who have longed for his appearing (2 Timothy 4:8).

There are some who assume that Paul succeeded in his ministry by the sheer force of his personality. It is all very well, they say, for Paul to continue in the face of adversity—he had unique strength. But the truth of the matter is that Paul was no different from you or me. In fact, often his opponents saw him as a weak character. "His letters are weighty and forceful," they would say, "but in person he is unimpressive and his speaking amounts to nothing" (2 Corinthians 10:10).

The real strength of Paul was not his clever way with words or his bodily appearance, but his unshakeable belief in the gospel of Christ. Day after day he pursued his ministry with vigor and enthusiasm despite difficulties in his life because he knew that beyond this world was eternal glory. "We do not lose heart," he said. "For our light and momentary troubles are achieving for us an eternal glory that far outweighs them all" (2 Corinthians 4:16–17).

This is not unlike the description of Jesus we find in Hebrews 12:2–3. He faced his darkest hours, endured the cross, and scorned the shame because he knew of "the joy set before him" (Hebrews 12:12). This seemed also to be Paul's way of dealing with the inevitable unpleasantness of this life. "We fix our eyes," he said, "not on what is seen, but on what is unseen. For what is seen is temporary, but what is unseen is eternal" (2 Corinthians 4:18).

Some Christians may never face tragedy and suffering. But others like Paul, who have a long road ahead, need to "consider that our present sufferings are not worth comparing with the glory that will be revealed in us," (Romans 8:18). Ever since the Damascus road, Paul looked forward to (and is now experiencing) a glorious future with Christ.

Paul: How Does This Apply to Me?
Fresh Starts
■ ● ■
Sally Breedlove

Wedding night. Christmas Eve's eve. I had polished our furniture and the silverware until they shone like the candles that burned a warm glow from every point in the living and dining rooms. Soon our guests would arrive, and we would celebrate a recommitment marriage service for a couple whose marriage had been a pit of despair and pain for the last ten years.

One of the most liberating messages the Bible proclaims is that we can start over. Paul's conversion on the road to Damascus demonstrates how God gives new beginnings as people come to faith in Christ. Paul marveled at his own fresh start, "When the kindness of God our Savior and His love for mankind appeared, He saved us, not on the basis of deeds which we have done in righteousness, but according to His mercy" (Titus 3:4–5, NASB).

To whom was that kindness available? Did Paul think he qualified because somehow he had managed to get his life on a decent track? By his own affirmation, the answer is *no.* Paul declared himself to be the chief of all sinners. If a new beginning was available to Paul, God is certainly offering a new beginning to each of us.

But is this a reality in our Christian lives? Many of us live as if the new life that came to us with receiving Christ is too weak to carry us through.

Acknowledging that Jesus had a fresh start for us, many feel that the difference he initially made in our lives has not lasted. The same habits mock us as we move along in the ruts they have grooved into our lives. We continue to respond in the same way in the same damaged relationships.

For some of us, our faith in Christ is like the abandoned fallout shelters that once appeared in our country—great for an emergency, but no place to build a life in. We confess our shortcomings, pray for strength to change, then fail again, and

Sally Breedlove is a homemaker and has written and edited the curriculum for a Christian school system. Her husband, Steve, is head pastor at Tomball Bible Church. They have five children and live in Tomball, Texas.

confess again. And after awhile we become convinced that God must be tired of giving us new starts. Then we slowly move away from him; or, driven by our feelings of guilt, we flee the One whom we think is judging us.

Paul, however, cut through the cords that bind us to this way of thinking, pleading with us to see God as the One who is forever willing to offer us a fresh beginning. Paul relied on new beginnings that can change our lives today.

A relationship with Christ means that every day is a fresh start. For many people, each new day begins with all the unsettled problems and guilt from yesterday. It does not feel like a fresh day at all; it feels like an old day, weighted down by yesterday's pain and failures.

After Paul became a Christian, he sinned. Yet his failure did not destroy him. He knew that when he first responded to Christ, he had received forgiveness for more than his past. Being a Christian meant that he could ask God's daily forgiveness for whatever sins he committed as he lived out his Christian life.

Paul knew that God's daily disposition to him was one of forgiving love. If we realize that God feels the same way about us, we can rejoice at God's day-by-day forgiveness.

A destructive habit in my life was broken with God's help because I knew that his moment-by-moment forgiveness was available to me. I could take hope when I sinned, realizing that God still loved me and would forgive me. Because I know that he did not label me as a failure but continued to call me his child, I was more determined than ever to choose to do right in the area of my life that seemed to be destroying me.

Paul also knew that God could provide him with enough strength to live each day, no matter how great the difficulties or challenges. Consider the things Paul endured: dangers from people and circumstances, overwork, hardships, sleeplessness, physical pain, and want (2 Corinthians 11:23–30). Did he know at the beginning of his Christian life that he would face all of these things? Of course not! But as Paul trusted God on a daily basis, God proved how his mercies were new every morning, and how he could be more than a conqueror daily through the One who loved him.

In the past year I have been involved in the lives of several people as they have suffered through great physical or emotional pain. It has been a joy to watch them emerge victorious in spite of their difficulties. Their lives changed and they grew closer to the Lord, not because God promised them that tomorrow the problem would be easier, but because they recognized that what they needed in terms of strength, or perseverance, or joy was available from God in exactly the proportion their present need demanded.

During long car trips, a necessary part of each day's travel is to buy gasoline for the car. It is not possible to put enough gasoline for a two-thousand-mile trip into the gas tank before leaving. And we cannot move through our lives without making periodic and regular stops with the Lord Jesus Christ to draw again and again from his reservoir of strength to meet each day's needs.

Paul looked forward to the time when Christ would make the whole world and each Christian totally new. In 2 Corinthians 5:17, Paul speaks of a new man. No matter how much forgiveness we receive or how much strength God supplies to us daily, we still have a sense that we are not complete. However, a day is coming when God will provide a new beginning whose perfection will last forever. Fresh starts today are just a shadow of what is to come.

The beginning we experience with the Lord on a daily basis gives us a hunger for a beginning that we can enjoy forever. Paul longed for the same thing. In 2 Corinthians 5:4 (NASB) we read that he wanted what was mortal or temporary to "be swallowed up by life."

A new kind of life is coming that will never lose its freshness. In that life we will never be marred by sin, never lack in strength, never suffer from the limitations that we now endure.

Paul
Insights for Discovery
■ ● ■

1. Study Acts 22:1–21 and Acts 26:1–29. What are key elements to Paul's testimony? If you have never written out your personal story, prepare it now. Include what your life was like before coming to Christ, how you committed your heart to Christ, and how he has been changing your life since your conversion. Then pray for opportunities to witness clearly and boldly. Acts 17 is a good chapter to study for "tips" on evangelism from Paul's life.

2. Reflect on 1 Timothy 1:12–17. As Paul often reflected on the grace of God, take time to think about what God's grace means to you. Write a letter to God expressing your feelings of gratitude.

3. Study the Epistle to the Philippians and observe how circumstances (chapter 1); people (chapter 2); things (chapter 3); and worry (chapter 4) can rob us of joy. What does Paul recommend as solutions to each "thief"?

4. From Colossians 1:28–29 and 2 Timothy 4:1–8, what vision burned in Paul's heart throughout his ministry? How can this conviction be cultivated in your life? Now read 1 John 4 for a similar motivation for outreach.

5. Read Acts 15:36. What is the relationship between evangelism and Christian follow-up? See Acts 16:6–10 and pray that God will lead you to a specific ministry—at church, at work, at home, or in your neighborhood.

6. Throughout Paul's writing, the apostle stressed personal godliness and complete dependence upon the Holy Spirit. What observations can you make from Romans 8:1–17 and Titus 2 on living a disciplined, Spirit-filled life?

Jonah:
The Reluctant
Missionary
■●■
Stephen M. Hooks

Jonah—I
Running From God

■ ● ■

The word of the Lord came to Jonah son of Amitai: "Go to the great city of Nineveh and preach against it, because its wickedness has come up before me." But Jonah ran away from the Lord and headed for Tarshish (Jonah 1:1–3).

The book of Jonah is more than a "fish story." It is a "faith story." It is the saga of a reluctant missionary who was forced to confront the intolerance and personal prejudice which compromised his ministry and stood in the way of his spiritual service. In the process, the prophet learned some important lessons about God as the compassionate Father of all peoples, and about people as the objects of God's grace.

Jonah learned these lessons the hard way. Confronted with a commission he did not approve, he resisted the call of God. His orders were to go to Nineveh, the capital of Assyria— to warn its people of God's intention to judge them for their great evil. Instead, Jonah headed for Tarshish (perhaps the Tartessus of Spain) at the opposite end of the known world.

Jonah's attempt to defy God was futile. The Sovereign who made the sea used it as an arena of judgment. He summoned a tempest to its surface and a creature from its depths to frustrate the misguided mariner. Ironically, the ocean that Jonah saw as a means of escape became a threat to his existence.

So it is for those who try to run from God—it cannot be done. There is no place we can go to escape God's scrutiny: "Where can I go from your Spirit? Where can I flee from your presence? If I go up to the heavens, you are there; if I make my bed in the depths, you are there" (Psalm 139:7–8). The great message of the Bible is not that we have sought God, but that God has sought us. From its opening question, "Where art thou?" (Genesis 3:9, KJV) to its final invitation, "The Spirit and the bride say, Come" (Revelation 22:17, KJV), the Scriptures record the divine search for us. Our God comes calling. He calls us to our duty and destiny, and not until we answer his call will we find peace.

Stephen M. Hooks is Professor of Biblical Studies at Atlanta Christian College in East Point, Georgia. He and his wife, Katherine, have two children and live in Fayetteville.

Jonah—II
Running Toward God
------- ■●■ -------

From inside the fish Jonah prayed to the Lord his God. He said:
"In my distress I called to the Lord, and he answered me"
(Jonah 2:1–2).

This prayer by Jonah rose out of the circumstance and the
conviction that he had nowhere else to turn. From the depths
of the sea came a creature to rescue him from drowning and to
provide him with the most unique prayer closet in human
history!

The author of the book of Jonah seems to have anticipated
our incredulity that such a thing could ever happen. His
answer is that it did not just happen, but that it was the result
of divine intervention: "The Lord provided a great fish to
swallow Jonah" (Jonah 1:17). The author meant for us to
understand this event not naturally, but supernaturally. Jonah's
life was not controlled by circumstance; it was controlled by
Providence.

This was as clear to Jonah as it was to the superstitious
fishermen who at first had rowed so hard to get back to land
(Jonah 1:13–16). God was in charge. This was a time for Jonah
to realize God's will for his life. The Jonah who had run from
God now ran toward God. The prophet prayed with gratitude
to God and with confidence in him who hears the cries of his
children. In Jonah's confession is affirmation of Yahweh as the
only true God, who alone can save and is worthy of praise and
worship.

Near the end of his prayer Jonah supplies us with a timeless
truth: "Those who cling to worthless idols forfeit the grace that
could be theirs" (Jonah 2:8). This says as much about us as it did
about Nineveh. The idols of modern man are more sophisti-
cated than those of the ancients, but they are just as offensive to
God. As we bow before the gods of pleasure, power, and
wealth, we forfeit the grace that can be ours.

Jonah—III
Running With God
————— ■●■ —————

The word of the Lord came to Jonah a second time: "Go to the great city of Nineveh and proclaim to it the message I give you." Jonah obeyed the word of the Lord and went to Nineveh (Jonah 3:1–3).

The Lord is a God of second chances. He warns, threatens, and even judges to a limited degree. But behind these negative means is a positive end—that none should perish "but that all should come to repentance" (2 Peter 3:9, KJV). In Jonah 3, the prophet and the people of Nineveh became recipients of God's grace.

When Jonah's ordeal in the sea had ended, he received a second opportunity to fulfill his ministry. This time he complied with his commission and faithfully announced to Nineveh God's intention to punish them for their sins, "Forty more days and Nineveh will be overturned" (Jonah 3:4). The results of his proclamation were spectacular—a nation of more than one hundred and twenty thousand people, from king to commoner, repented at the preaching of Jonah.

Nineveh's repentance provides us with two important lessons. First, it was genuine. The people of Nineveh truly believed in God and sincerely repented of their sins. The gestures of fasting, wearing sackcloth, and sitting in ashes were ancient customs designed to demonstrate inner grief by means of outer discomfort. Second, Nineveh's repentance was theologically sound. They made no attempt to manipulate or obligate God by performing religious deeds. Instead, the people of Nineveh humbly submitted to God and threw themselves upon his mercy, hoping that "God may yet relent and with compassion turn from his fierce anger so that we will not perish" (Jonah 3:9).

God's Word is powerful and productive (Isaiah 55:11). So, too, are the lives of those who submit to it and faithfully communicate it to others.

Jonah—IV
Running Ahead of God
■ ● ■

The Lord said, "You have been concerned about this vine, though you did not tend it or make it grow. It sprang up overnight and died overnight. But Nineveh has more than a hundred and twenty thousand people. . . . Should I not be concerned about that great city?" (Jonah 4:10–11)

The last chapter of Jonah is often the least remembered, but it may be the most important in the book. In it we learn the reason for Jonah's negative response to God's call, and we learn an important lesson about God, who is no respecter of persons but offers grace to all who repent of their sins and believe in him.

Instead of rejoicing over the salvation of Nineveh, Jonah resented it because those people were his enemies. Jonah may have thought his participation in their deliverance constituted an act of treason against his own people. As far as Jonah was concerned, the people of Nineveh were unworthy of God's grace, and Jonah wanted no part in their salvation.

God's response to the prophet's intolerant attitude came in the form of a challenging question: "Have you any right to be angry?" (Jonah 4:4) Jonah did not. To demonstrate, God provided a plant to give Jonah shade, then just as quickly took away the plant. God then compared Jonah's attitudes over the loss of the plant and the salvation of Nineveh. Both attitudes were selfish and shameful. Jonah cared more about a plant than he did for people.

While exposing Jonah's intolerance, God also defended his own compassion. If Jonah cared about a plant, could he not understand God's great concern for a lost people?

Jonah ran ahead of God. The prophet dared to suggest who was and who was not worthy of God's grace. From Jonah's experience we learn that God does not permit this of his children. While we are called to participate in the redemptive process, we are not permitted to control it. We are evangels of Jesus Christ, and it is not our duty to determine who will receive God's truth. Our duty is to declare his truth.

Jonah: How Does This Apply to Me?
Sounds of Running
——— ■ ● ■ ———

Evelyn Meade

My friends and I sat in the concert hall enjoying the music of Shostakovich—at least I pretended to have a good time. Afterward we drove home and my friends dropped me off at my front door and waved good-bye. I sat on my bed and thumbed absentmindedly through the concert program. Tears blurred my eyes as waves of anger engulfed me as they had so many times before. I kicked off my high heels and tossed my dress in a heap in the corner. I pulled on my jeans and shirt, grabbed my jacket, and ran back out into the night.

The damp midnight air of the city wrapped around my shoulders like a shawl of lead. My heels thumped on the concrete sidewalk. The prophet Jonah had beat on the ribs inside a big fish. Surprising how the sounds of disobedience, whether on ribs or on a city sidewalk, are the same—the thump, thump, thump of running from God.

The hours whisked by as I walked down Houston's deserted streets. I pushed my hands deeper into my pockets and looked for a place to rest and find warmth from the cold night air. Suddenly, a door burst open. I stepped back into the shadows as a young couple came out and disappeared into the night. I pushed open the same dirty glass door of the bar.

Inside, smoke seemed to hang from the bar's ceiling like a stagnant storm cloud. Loud music from the jukebox penetrated my ears as I slid onto a bar stool. My body drank in the warmth, but inside I shook in chilled silence. My mind reached back into my past, and yet I denied why "I have been banished from your sight" (Jonah 2:4).

I was born into a Christian family. Some of the first words I heard were from nightly readings of the Bible. My earliest training was to believe in God. As a teenager I accepted Jesus Christ as my personal Savior, and during high school I sensed God calling me to work in the area of evangelism.

Back then, like Jonah, I prided myself in being one of God's

Evelyn Meade is a free-lance writer living in Moline, Kansas. She attends Moline Baptist Church. She chaired the Counseling Committee, Elk County Ralph Bell Crusade in 1990.

"elite." Jonah had felt his heritage gave him the right to demand that God destroy Israel's enemy. My own "religiousness" gave me a narrow, unbending view of God. When I was unable to place him in my corner and make him my property, I felt betrayed and angry. Like Jonah, I "ran away from the Lord" (Jonah 1:3).

To escape, I ignored God's calling and instead took a job with a major corporation after high school graduation. Before long I requested a transfer to Houston, Texas. In fact, I was so desperate to run that I went from working as a comptroller to being a mail-room clerk. But I was away from my small hometown, away from my Christian home and—I thought—away from God. My unforgiving spirit would no longer have to deal with a forgiving Lord.

In Houston my career advanced quickly—from mail-room file clerk to secretary to the executive vice president. I bought season tickets to the symphony, and enrolled in night courses at the University of Houston. My friends and I went to the beach and the opera. I vacationed in artist camps in New Mexico and faraway villages in Mexico. I thought I had everything!

But "those who cling to worthless idols forfeit the grace that could be theirs" (Jonah 2:8). The activities and possessions in my life were my worthless idols. My career and busyness were like Jonah's "deep sleep," but restfulness eluded me.

As I sat at the bar, my thoughts swirled. Like Jonah, I had built a barrier between God and me: my unforgiving spirit and sinfulness. Like Jonah, I judged myself guilty, ran away, and asked to be thrown overboard.

"Ya like another drink?" drawled the bartender, breaking into my thoughts. Startled, I shook my head, slipped off the bar stool, and trudged back into the night.

For the first time in years, I began to pray in the early hours of that cold morning. "In my distress I called to the Lord, and he answered me. From the depths of the grave I called for help, and you listened to my cry" (Jonah 2:2). I prayed for forgiveness and I decided to quit fighting God.

Of course, my life didn't change overnight. I attended church to listen to God's Word. I was hungry to know God and his will for my life.

The feelings and call to evangelism started to emerge again. But I knew I needed time to come back from the frenetic life I'd been living. Time alone with God was necessary to invest in my one-to-one relationship with him and to rediscover my self-worth in Christ.

A few years earlier I had bought a farmhouse and one hundred sixty acres of land near a ranching community in southeastern Kansas. The purchase was an investment; I never planned to live there. But one day, when I came home from work in Houston, I began to think about that land in Kansas. I decided not to renew the lease to the man who had been renting the land. I sensed God telling me that he wanted me to move there and live. It was as if he wanted to mold me and help me in my desire to obey him. I realized I needed to obey God if I were ever going to find contentment.

When I gave my boss a month's notice and told him I was moving to a farm in Kansas, he and the other people I worked with thought I had lost my mind. And it was tough to give up a steady job where I knew what I was doing and that I was good at, and move to Kansas to bale hay, and to raise hogs and cattle. But I did it because I felt that I was obeying God.

As Jonah had found dry land, so had I. Well, it wasn't exactly dry. I moved during March, and the water pipes under the house, exposed to below-freezing temperatures, erupted. I sat in the cold and muddy darkness under the eighty-year-old farmhouse, pipe wrench in hand, the maze of leaking pipes encircling me. Yet I felt warm! I knew God had forgiven me.

This was a healing time: a time to take off my running-away shoes, a time to give up my disobedience, a time to listen to God.

That was fourteen years ago. Since then, I've supported myself by doing odd jobs. My flexible schedule allows me time to witness to others. "Then the word of the Lord came to Jonah a second time: 'Go to the great city of Nineveh and proclaim to it the message I give you.' Jonah obeyed the word of the Lord and went" (Jonah 3:1–3).

My old pickup and I have logged more than one hundred thousand miles—down country roads and over brick-covered streets—to tell the story of Jesus. I communicate the gospel message through the stories, songs, and poems I write. I visit nursing homes, witness to friends, and speak and sing at community meetings. Anywhere God calls me, I go. The thump, thump, thump I hear now is the sound of running for God.

Jonah
Insights for Discovery
─────── ■ ● ■ ───────

1. Look carefully at Jonah's response to God's call in Jonah 1:1–3. Then read verses 4–16. Take note of Jonah's insight into the situation.

2. What hope does Jonah's prayer (Jonah 2:1–9) offer the disobedient believer? See also Hebrews 12:7–11.

3. Consider the power of the Word of God as it is preached by an obedient servant in Jonah 3:1–10. Examine a related thought in Hebrews 4:12.

4. Read Jonah 1:17 and Matthew 12:38–41. Notice how Jesus uses Jonah's experience?

5. After reading Jonah 4, compare and contrast Jonah's attitude with the attitudes he exhibited in previous chapters. Reflect on God's response to each attitude.

6. Since you have already studied Jonah's actions, what can you now learn from how Philip (Acts 8:26–40) and Paul (Acts 16:9–10) acted immediately upon God's call to preach the gospel?

7. In light of Romans 8:28 and Isaiah 55:8–11, think of God's sovereign plan for your life. Do you always obey God when he calls?

Mark:
The Man Who Made a
Comeback

Vernon D. Doerksen

Mark—I
A Man Who Failed
——————— ■ ● ■ ———————

Now Paul and his companions put out to sea from Paphos and came to Perga in Pamphylia; and John left them and returned to Jerusalem (Acts 13:13, NASB).

Isn't it strange that John Mark, a man who had such a promising beginning, gave up and returned home? That's precisely what he did! His experience serves as an example to help us avoid failing, and as an encouragement when we have failed.

John, who also went by his Greek name Mark, lived in the mainstream of the exciting activities of the early church in Jerusalem. It was in his widowed mother Mary's large home where the church fervently prayed for Peter (Acts 12:5, 12). Perhaps Mark himself was present at the time of Peter's miraculous release. It has also been suggested that the Last Supper took place in the large upper room of his home. It also may have been where the disciples gathered after the ascension.

In any case, Mark was obviously a privileged young man who lived at the hub of much of the social and religious activities of the early Jerusalem church. He was acquainted with many of Christ's followers, and perhaps even had sat under the teaching of Jesus.

When Barnabas and Paul came to Jerusalem on the famine visit, they may have stayed in the home of Barnabas's aunt Mary. Perhaps the excitement of travel motivated Mark to return to Antioch with his cousin Barnabas and Paul. When Barnabas and Paul embarked on their first missionary journey, it seemed natural that Mark went along as their helper (Acts 13:5).

Everything went well as they traveled through Cyprus. But when they crossed over to the mainland and entered the interior of Pamphylia, the rigors of the journey apparently became too much for Mark and he returned to Jerusalem. In spite of his good intentions and youthful zeal, Mark's commitment to the realities of harsh missionary service grew thin and Mark became a dropout—temporarily. Mark needed to learn the lesson of perseverance in the face of trials.

Vernon D. Doerksen is Executive Vice President and Chairman of the Department of Biblical Studies, Arizona College of the Bible. He and his wife, Josephine, have two sons.

Mark—II
Befriended by Barnabas
■●■

There arose such a sharp disagreement that they separated from one another, and Barnabas took Mark with him and sailed away to Cyprus (Acts 15:39, NASB).

Scripture doesn't say why Mark deserted. Perhaps he was fearful of dangers on the highway. Maybe he was homesick. The transfer of leadership from cousin Barnabas to Paul might have resulted in petty jealousy. Or perhaps the offer of free salvation to Gentiles, apart from the works of the law, grated against Mark's Jewish upbringing.

Whatever the reason or combination of reasons for desertion, Paul thought Mark's failure was serious enough to disqualify him from accompanying them on the second missionary journey. But God graciously intervened with Barnabas, the "Son of Encouragement" (Acts 4:36, NASB), to give Mark a second chance and restore him to ministry. Barnabas looked beyond the present failure and saw the potential of future usefulness. Just as he had earlier taken the risk of introducing Paul to the Jerusalem leadership, Barnabas was now willing to believe in Mark and give him the opportunity to redeem himself.

When Barnabas took a repentant Mark to Cyprus, they were venturing into an area known to Mark. It's possible that Mark, like his cousin, was actually a native of Cyprus who had immigrated to Jerusalem with his family. And Mark had ministered there with Barnabas and Paul before his failure and desertion from Perga. In this healing and restoration process, Mark was allowed to minister in familiar and friendly territory.

Through the compassionate encouragement of Barnabas, Mark learned the lesson of perseverance in ministry. A few years later, Paul referred to Mark as an "encouragement" (Colossians 4:11, NASB) and one of his "fellow-workers" (Philemon 24).

The church today has great need for individuals who serve as a "Barnabas" to those who desire restoration to fruitful ministry.

Mark—III
Reestablished by Peter
——— ■ ● ■ ———

She who is in Babylon, chosen together with you, sends you greetings, and so does my son, Mark (1 Peter 5:13, NASB).

One great need in the church is for spiritual fathers. Paul wrote the Corinthians that there were numerous tutors, but not many fathers (1 Corinthians 4:15). Peter served as a father to Mark. Exactly when Mark became a follower of the Lord we don't know, but evidently Peter played a significant part in Mark's conversion.

Peter's phrase, "My son, Mark," suggests that perhaps from the early days of the church Peter exercised a fatherly role in Mark's life. With the church meeting in Mary's home, likely Peter and Mark had numerous contacts. Peter knew firsthand the agony of failure and defeat. But he also experienced the ecstasy of forgiveness and restoration to ministry. He knew from bitter personal experience that there was hope for those who failed, and this served as an encouragement to Mark.

Mark's relationship with Peter lasted for many years. Ancient tradition indicates that Mark wrote his Gospel under the authority of Peter. Mark, the servant who had once deserted, became God's instrument in writing the second Gospel, the account which portrays the Lord Jesus as the perfect servant. Mark came to understand true servanthood. The vivid and fast-moving narrative of Mark's Gospel bears testimony to the closeness of Mark and Peter, and their common personality traits. Peter's willingness to share his experiences in a fatherly manner with Mark paid lasting dividends.

Mark—IV
Reaffirmed by Paul
■ ● ■

Only Luke is with me. Pick up Mark and bring him with you, for he is useful to me for service (2 Timothy 4:11, NASB).

Mark certainly had second thoughts about his desertion from Pamphylia, and when it came time for the second missionary journey he was anxious to redeem himself. But Paul was not willing to jeopardize the fruitfulness of the trip by taking along someone who had proved so unreliable (Acts 15:36–38). Paul's chilling, yet justifiable, rebuff must have pierced Mark to the core, making him acutely aware of the seriousness of his actions.

To Mark's credit, his heart did not become embittered. Barnabas was able to work with him and groom him for a successful future ministry. As only the Lord can, he took this bad experience and used it for good.

Nothing is known about Mark's activities for several years following his desertion. The next mention of Mark is by Paul during his first Roman imprisonment. By this time, Mark had redeemed himself and again earned Paul's confidence. In fact, Paul commended him to the Colossians, writing, "If [Mark] comes to you, welcome him" (Colossians 4:10, NASB). Mark is also spoken of as being an "encouragement" to Paul (Colossians 4:11). Finally, Mark is designated a "fellow-worker" by Paul. The split between Paul and Mark had been completely mended, and Mark became a trusted associate of the apostle.

Mark is a good example of a full return to ministry even after failure, and Paul is a good example of one who forgave, retaining no lasting grudge.

The apostle's dying testimonial to Mark was that he was "useful to me for service" (2 Timothy 4:11, NASB). Mark couldn't have asked for a more ardent reaffirmation.

We can learn much from Mark. There is hope for us when we fail. In spite of Mark's shortcomings, he chose to live in the company of godly men. He took seriously the sharp rejection by Paul, the friendly encouragement of Barnabas, and the fatherly example of Peter. In the end, Mark regained respect and usefulness.

Mark: How Does This Apply to Me?
A Second Chance
■ ● ■
Robert L. Poff

"Caught! Stealing a woman's purse," the officer said to me, with his hand on my shoulder.

"I don't know anything about a stolen purse," I said, trembling, unaware that he was referring to a purse that Jimmy had stolen. We were both twelve years old. Jimmy and I were in the movie theater when I was called out and questioned about the stolen purse. The truth was I didn't know anything about the purse.

I should have been suspicious of Jimmy's newfound wealth. He had money for the movies, popcorn, and candy bars. This was the same Jimmy who lived in a house with a dirt floor.

I liked this laughing, dark-haired boy a lot. I seemed able to steer him from trouble when I was with him. He had been in difficulty with the law before, but this time it was more than the usual pilfering from the drugstore.

This time he had stolen a woman's purse, and it was serious business in the small town in which we lived.

I never saw Jimmy again after that day. It was rumored that the state sent him to a correctional school for boys. Fifteen years later, I learned from my mother that this was not the case at all.

Long after I had moved away, Jimmy returned to town one day and visited Mom briefly. He related to her how he had graduated from college with a degree in social work. This poor kid from the wrong side of the tracks, who always seemed to be in trouble, was making a positive mark in society.

Instead of going to a correctional school as we had thought, Jimmy went to live with his married sister at her home in Washington, D.C. She brought some discipline into his life, and was a strong personality and friend when he needed help the most.

Mark was a Bible character who, like Jimmy, made a comeback. We read in Acts 13 that Mark, Barnabas's cousin, left him and Paul in Asia Minor on the first missionary journey and returned to Jerusalem.

Robert L. Poff is Assistant Attorney General for the Commonwealth of Virginia. He and his wife, Irene, have two children and live in Roanoke, Virginia.

We are not told the reason that Mark left. He may have simply grown tired of the long journey and the little provision made for them. He may have thought at the time that the task of spreading the gospel was just too big an order, or he may have thought he was personally unsuited for the work ahead.

Whatever Mark's reason, Paul refused to take Mark along on the second missionary journey. Paul chose Silas and went one way; Barnabas took Mark and went another (Acts 15:39).

When Mark returned to Jerusalem, he had a lot of time to think things over. Maybe God had not really called him to do the same kind of work to which he had called Paul and Barnabas. With Paul the great orator and Barnabas his faithful supporter, Mark might have wondered if he had anything of value to offer to God.

The odds are that most of us, like Mark, will fail at something during our Christian life. We may wonder if God can use our inferior talents. Perhaps when opportunity for service arises, we are inclined to give excuses. Fear of failure may keep many from serving God and encouraging others.

It is profitable to focus on what the reasons for failure may be. Are we too tired to finish the job? Isn't there enough in it for us? Or do we just not feel that we have the talent and are incapable of doing the job? Perhaps we simply do not devote enough time to the careful, thoughtful prayer, and preparation necessary for the task at hand.

God offers us many second chances and opportunities to renew ourselves with him. When we fail the Lord at some task he has given us and we ask his forgiveness, he lifts us up, wipes away our tears, and sends us back out again. It's as if God is saying to us, "I chose you on my first team, and no substitute will do."

When Mark made a mistake on Paul's first missionary journey, he needed a friend to help him get back on the right track. It was Barnabas who believed in Mark, who had a vision, and who gave that vision to Mark. Mark then pursued it to a godly end.

Often, behind a believer like Mark is a person like Barnabas, someone who makes the difference because he cares enough to discipline and to encourage. Just as Jimmy was cared for by his sister, we sometimes need the gentle touch and encouragement of a Barnabas to build up our confidence, someone who is good at teaching by example—and someone who sees the potential in us and won't give up until Christ's life shines through.

Simple encouragement is not a difficult job. It is kindness shown at the right time when someone is in the grip of depression; it is talking with a friend who has marital problems. It is God's Spirit who enables us to be encouragers when we may not feel like it. Encouragement is what allows us to work those extra hours when we thought we were too tired.

My adult Sunday school class sends notes and letters to members who have been absent, or hospitalized, or who have lost loved ones. We want to let them know that we are thinking of them and are praying for them. Many have come back to class testifying how much it meant to receive a note or a card during those times of distress. It takes only a few minutes to be an encourager. And those few minutes can mean a great deal to people in need of a spiritual lift by a kind word or prayer.

So much good can be done in the world. And you can be sure that whatever good the mind of man can conceive, the heart of God can empower to carry it out. God wants us to succeed and not to fail at his business. He doesn't promise us great riches. But he does promise us that quietly and resolutely, with internal confidence, we are empowered by his grace to carry out his objectives.

Mark discovered God's grace and, in spite of his previous failure, went on to become one of the great leaders of the early church. We know that the rift between Paul and Mark was healed by the time of Paul's final imprisonment. For Paul wrote, "Only Luke is with me. Take Mark, and bring him with thee: for he is profitable to me for the ministry" (2 Timothy 4:11, KJV).

What a beautiful tribute to Mark that Paul should ask for him and highly regard Mark's service during his last days.

Mark
Insights for Discovery
———— ■●■ ————

1. In Acts 13:1–6, read how Barnabas and Paul are commissioned for the special ministry to which God has called them and how Mark was their helper.

2. In Acts 13:6–12, contrast the proconsul's reaction to the teaching of God with that of the sorcerer and false prophet. (Note in Acts 13:13, after this account on Cyprus, Mark leaves Barnabas and Paul and returns to Jerusalem.)

3. Even though Barnabas and Paul suffered fierce persecution (Acts 13:50; Acts 14:2–6), including the stoning of Paul (Acts 14:19), in Acts 14:26–28, observe the encouraging report they presented to the church at Antioch. Think about their commitment to the grace of God, in Acts 14:26, and examine a related thought on God's grace, in Titus 2:11–14.

4. In Acts 15:36–41, Barnabas wanted Mark along to revisit the towns where he and Paul had proclaimed the gospel so that they could follow up the Christian believers. Though Barnabas and Paul disagreed strongly about who should go, Barnabas stuck by his cousin and sailed with him to minister on Cyprus.

5. Meditate on the restoration process that must have taken place for Mark to be mentioned by Paul in such a positive light (Colossians 4:10–11; 2 Timothy 4:11).

6. Compare and contrast Mark's failure yet subsequent comeback with the fall of Demas, who is mentioned only in Colossians 4:14; 2 Timothy 4:10; and Philemon 24.

David:
Loved by God

■ ● ■

Robert F. Ramey

David—I
The Pastor
■ ● ■

Now therefore, thus you shall say to My servant David,"Thus says the LORD of hosts, 'I took you from the pasture, from following the sheep, that you should be ruler over My people Israel'" (2 Samuel 7:8, NASB).

The story of David, second king of Israel, is prominent in the Bible. Although David lived a millennium before Jesus Christ, his name appears fifty-seven times in the New Testament. It is clear that David is pivotal in the sovereign plan of God.

Before David was anointed to be king, before anyone other than his own family knew him, God had characterized him as "a man after [my] own heart" (1 Samuel 13:14, NASB). In David, God found a man who would please him by obedience to his Word, by service to his people, and, supremely, by faith in his grace. David's life and government became standards of righteousness for all who would follow.

In view of David's prominence and divine importance, it may seem startling that his early life was obscure and humble. David was a shepherd. To be a shepherd in Bible times meant caring. A personal relationship between shepherd and sheep resulted in awareness of each animal's peculiarities and name.

Shepherding also meant commitment. No matter what the need, the weather, the dangers, the time of day or night—no matter what, the shepherd was responsible for his sheep.

Furthermore, shepherding meant cost. Whatever it required in terms of personal sacrifice of time, energy, or even life itself, the shepherd was willing. Another Shepherd later emphasized that a good shepherd, unlike an uncaring hired hand, never ran away if a wolf threatened the flock (John 10:11–13).

This was the man God chose to be Israel's king. God considered the leading of Israel to be shepherding work (2 Samuel 7:7–8). And the Bible makes it plain that David's early care of sheep was his apprenticeship for governing God's people.

Robert F. Ramey is Associate Editor of Academic Books at Moody Press. He lives in Carol Stream, Illinois, and attends Lombard Gospel Chapel (Plymouth Brethren).

David—II
The Penitent
■ ● ■

Then David said to Nathan, "I have sinned against the Lord."
And Nathan said to David, "The LORD also has taken away
your sin; you shall not die" (2 Samuel 12:13, NASB).

David became a tarnished disgrace to the names of Israel and
of God. The powerful sovereign was also the powerful sinner.
In David, the sublime and the sordid struggled for prominence.

Like all other people, David the king possessed a sinful
nature. One of his sins was polygamy, which eventually
involved eight wives and numerous concubines (2 Samuel
3:2–5; 5:13). This lifestyle broke the Law of God and nurtured
in David a moral laxity.

But of all David's recorded sins, the ones concerning Bathsheba and her husband, Uriah, are the most infamous (2 Samuel 11:1–27). One evening from his palace room David saw
Bathsheba and quickly effected a sexual liaison with her. From
this relationship Bathsheba became pregnant. According to
God's Law, David and Bathsheba were now under the penalty
of death (Leviticus 20:10). All this time Uriah was away
fighting with the Israelite army. David summoned Uriah home
and hoped to make it appear that Bathsheba's baby was actually by Uriah. When this scheme was unwittingly frustrated by
Uriah's devotion to duty, David arranged for Uriah's death in
battle. Today, nearly three thousand years later, David's name
is most commonly linked with either Goliath, one of his finest
victories, or Bathsheba, his most shameful defeat.

How could this sinful person be called a man after the heart
of God? How could God love this wicked man?

It is not, of course, David's wickedness in which our holy
God delights. Nor does God ignore it! Rather, it is in David's
general godliness and utter contrition when he realizes his sins
that God is pleased. For all repentant sinners, God's grace
provides forgiveness through the cleansing blood of Christ.

David—III
The Psalmist
■●■

Now these are the last words of David. David the son of Jesse declares, ... And the sweet psalmist of Israel, "The Spirit of the LORD spoke by me" (2 Samuel 23:1–2, NASB).

In David, the man of the earth soars and sings like a seraph of heaven. The tough outdoorsman, soldier, and king is also a tender confessor, lyricist, and singer. His physical lusts yield to lofty passions for God. By the Holy Spirit, David gives the world its choicest collection of literature for the heart.

Conservative scholars differ on the number and identity of David's psalms. Besides his songs recorded within his life story, about seventy-three psalms in the book of Psalms are attributed to David from internal evidence or long tradition. Other psalms are identified as David's because of external evidence. Some people believe David wrote more than eighty psalms.

Twenty-five of David's psalms are pleas for help uttered when he is distressed by enemies and troublesome circumstances. With respectful but bold faith, David urges God to "hurry up" with his aid. While confessing God's power, wisdom, and sovereignty, David pours forth his own impatience and desperation. Sometimes David's laments also have messianic significance, such as "My God, my God, why hast Thou forsaken me?" (Psalm 22:1, NASB)

Twenty of David's psalms are hymns of praise expressing his love and adoration for God because of his majesty, creation, and redemption. Although David repeatedly refers to God's presence in the sanctuary in Jerusalem, he envisions God's immensity and glory as far transcending the magnitude of all the natural order.

David's psalms have other recurring themes: exhortations to wisdom; expressions of trust; repentance from sin; and prayers for specifics. David's psalms have become the voice of people for three thousand years. And until the end of time, trusting hearts will echo David's sublime words: "The LORD is my shepherd" (Psalm 23:1).

David—IV
The Patriarch
——————— ■●■ ———————

"Brethren, I may confidently say to you regarding the patriarch David . . . that God had sworn to him with an oath to seat one of his descendants upon his throne" (Acts 2:29–30, NASB).

David was a father in more than one sense. He was father to many children, among them were Absalom and Solomon.

David was also the father to Israel's people. In a symbolic way, they look to David more than to any other patriarch for present and future paternal security.

David was the father of God's Messiah, the eternal King of Israel. This fact was promised to David himself in what has come to be called the Davidic covenant (2 Samuel 7:12–16). In this great prophecy, God graciously assured David of four provisions: (1) David would have a son who would succeed him, would build the Temple of God, and would be the object of God's abiding love. (2) David's house, i.e., his family, would be established forever. (3) David's kingdom would endure forever. Whatever its temporary interruptions or changing forms, the right to rule over Israel would always remain with David's dynasty. (4) David's throne would continue throughout the ages. The Lord would retain the power of earthly government over Israel for David's offspring.

Our Lord Jesus Christ is the ultimate fulfillment of these promises to David. He is called "the offspring of David" (Revelation 22:16), "the King of Israel" (John 1:49; 12:13), and "the Messiah" (John 1:41). The genealogies of Mary and Joseph carefully connect Jesus to David (Matthew 1:1–16; Luke 3:23–31). During the announcement of Jesus' birth to Mary, Gabriel said, "The Lord God will give him the throne of his father David, and he will reign over the house of Jacob forever; and His kingdom will never end" (Luke 1:32–33, NASB).

Although Christ now rules from the throne of God rather than the throne of David, he will assume this throne after the Second Coming at the beginning of his millennial kingdom (Matthew 19:28). Then David, loved by God and raised from the dead, shall lead all Israel and the world in exalting his great Son, the King of Kings and Lord of Lords.

David: How Does This Apply to Me?
Shaped by God's Love
■●■
Betty Douglas Street

The open casket was at the front of the sanctuary. Slightly afraid to see a dead body, I was nervous about approaching it. But the elderly, frail woman inside, her hands clasped around a rough-hewn wooden cross, seemed so peaceful. I knew she wasn't just asleep; none of the too-handy funeral phrases applied to her. This was only her body. The real Dorothy wasn't there at all. She had been home with her Lord, her Friend, since she had died five days earlier.

While Dorothy lay dying in a nursing home, my minister husband sat with her. When he returned home, I searched his face, concerned for his weariness and sapped strength during the eleven-hour vigil. But instead of exhaustion I saw a strange light in his eyes. He was slightly exhilarated. *How can he be like this?* I wondered. And asked.

"It wasn't sad at all. It was rather peaceful," he said. "One of the aides came into the room and rededicated her life to Christ this afternoon. She had seen and heard Dorothy these past months and had been impressed by her." Dorothy's open, loving life was effective even as she lay dying, her blood pressure so low it couldn't be measured.

When Jesus rules our lives, we demonstrate God's love in ordinary, daily living. The continuous presence and influence of God's love in our lives makes possible what happened in Dorothy's last hours. Even in her dying, God's caring love touched someone.

Knowing and sharing the love of God doesn't give any guarantes of a peaceful, unruffled existence with no pain. In Psalm 23:4, we read that David went through his valley. Sometimes it seems that not only are Christians not exempt from pain, but they experience more pain.

When a missionary couple returned to Africa from furlough, they left a teenaged son at boarding school in England. A few days after their arrival back in Africa, the son was killed

Betty Douglas Street is a homemaker and a free-lance writer. She and her pastor-husband, Gary, are parents of two children and live in Culbertson, Montana.

in an accident on the soccer field. The parents could not attend the funeral; there was no way for them to make the long trip from their station to England so soon after furlough. They simply had to rest in the knowledge that their son was now alive with God.

As we are called by God to endure trials, we are offered strength to hold on and to go on. Christ, "for the joy set before him endured the cross" (Hebrews 12:2). The roll call of tested and victorious saints in Hebrews 11 makes one thing clear; these people strove and suffered, and then experienced victory. Sometimes in life they overcame hurdles; sometimes death ended their trials. But they did win. God has assured us of final and lasting victory.

As faith is encouraged and grows in love, it reaches out to embrace others. Life can be a series of events in which faith may be encouraged or forced to grow as disappointments, misfortunes, and sorrows come along. This mature kind of faith will then reach out in love beyond self to help others bear their burdens. It is a kind of circle: the love received from God eventually finds its end in praise and thanksgiving back to the Maker and Sustainer of all things. Along the journey, love touches and affects family, friends, co-workers, and casual acquaintances.

The love we receive and return to God needs to be guarded zealously and nurtured. We need strong, steady encouragement from the Word and from fellow believers to continue in his love. Time spent alone in prayer helps build strong ties to the Father's heart. This kind of communion restores what was depleted, uplifts, and arms us for the future.

We must also exercise great care to guard against love's enemies: bitterness and resentment. These emotions brings forth actions that cause love to flee. When bitterness takes root, it causes trouble and may hurt many (Hebrews 12:15). Bitterness in one area of our life invariably colors all areas; then it reaches out to hurt other people. Bitterness can be passed from one generation to the next. The only solvent for bitterness is God's cleansing love, which is available for the asking.

Resentment is one of the most subtle enemies of love. It is our natural reaction when our feelings are trampled upon or when someone goes over our head. When things go wrong that aren't our fault, but we are blamed, resentment may come. When our spouse or children are unjustly (or even justly) criticized, resentment rears its head. Resentment may seem small and harmless, but it is like bitterness—it festers and grows, and mars relationships. Only the Spirit of God can lance and clean pockets of resentment. Forgiveness received from God and extended to others completes the healing.

Everything that happens to us influences us in one way or another. But only God's great, unchanging love can take each experience and use it for his glory and shape us into what he intends us to become.

David
Insights for Discovery
■ ● ■

1. Read 1 Samuel 17. How do you feel when you suggest a plan or share a conviction of yours and someone "shoots it down" or belittles you? How do you handle rejection? How can you become less defensive when someone criticizes something you've done or judges your character and motives?

2. From 1 Samuel 16; 24:10–13; and 26:22–25, what can you conclude from David's willingness to trust God's sovereign plan for him to become king over Israel? What similarities or differences are there in the lessons David learned in 2 Samuel 7?

3. Study 2 Samuel 11–12 and Psalm 51. Then meditate on 2 Corinthians 5:17. Is it difficult for you to say, "I'm sorry"? How has Christ given you a new heart? Does he satisfy your heart? How does he sustain your heart? What do you appreciate about the privilege that God grants to live in his presence?

4. Reflect on Psalm 78:72 and 1 Kings 9:4. What is integrity of heart and why was David able to walk and to lead with integrity? How does this relate to the teaching in 1 Samuel 13:14; 2 Chronicles 16:9; and Acts 13:22?

5. David's integrity can be compared to Paul's authenticity. See 1 Corinthians 4:17 and 2 Corinthians 10:11. In what ways can you grow in being more genuine and honest, motivated to please God and not men?

6. Locate one of your favorite psalms and spend time thanking God for his protection, guidance, and strength.

Part II
Our Sorrow, God's Joy
■●■

Many centuries ago some philosophers taught that the highest good was to avoid pain and embrace pleasure. There is obviously something very appealing about this idea. Normal people much prefer pleasure to pain and will expend much time, energy, and money in pursuit of the former and escape from the latter. One of the initial concepts on which the United States of America was founded was that God has given man some inalienable rights including "the pursuit of happiness." So it is not at all surprising that pleasure and pain are paramount in our society's thinking. In fact, many people now operate on the principle that if something brings pleasure it is therefore right, and conversely, if it brings pain it must be wrong.

However, this approach is also raising questions. One astute observer of our society has written a book entitled *Amusing Ourselves to Death!* He makes several powerful points, but they are not altogether new. In the 1830s a French sociologist named Alexis de Tocqueville toured the United States and wrote a most insightful book called *Democracy In America*. He wrote, "In America I have seen the freest and best educated of men in circumstances the happiest to be found in the world, yet it seemed to me that a cloud habitually hung on their brow and they seemed serious and almost sad even in their pleasures." He added, "They never stop thinking of the good things they have not got." To embrace pleasure can leave arms full of nothing much.

Avoiding pain has its problems too. Incredible amounts of money are spent in an effort to banish sickness, disease, and everything else that elicits pain. Expectations of painless, problem-less life run to unrealistic heights. When tragedy comes, as it not infrequently does, the response is so often either an incredulous "Why me?" or a vehement rage-filled reaction. Despite all efforts, pain refuses to go away. Hospitals are in great demand, funeral homes stay in business, divorce courts continue to operate, prisons are overcrowded. If pleasure, *when embraced*, disappoints you, and if pain, *when avoided*, still comes calling, is there another way to live life?

The answer is an emphatic *yes*, and it is found in the Scriptures in the lives of people like Joseph, Hosea, Elizabeth, and Stephen. Murphy's law, "If something can go wrong, it will," could have been written about Joseph. Hosea had a dreadful marriage but behaved in an exemplary manner. Elizabeth was infertile for most of her long life (in her culture that was a social stigma), but she came through it well. And Stephen was mercilessly martyred in his prime, but he died as winsomely as he had lived effectively.

These people show us how a believer can find fullness of life, not by endeavoring to manipulate circumstances to his or her liking, but by acknowledging the grace and wisdom of God at all times. We thereby discover what Paul experienced at his point of extremity: "I delight in weaknesses, in insults, in hardships, in persecutions, in difficulties. For when I am weak, then I am strong" (2 Corinthians 12:10).

Joseph:
He Believed in His Dreams

— ■●■ —

Glenn E. Schaefer

A True Servant Attitude
──────── ■ ● ■ ────────

The Lord was with Joseph and he prospered, and he lived in the house of his Egyptian master (Genesis 39:2).

Success conjures up in our minds the images of an influential businessman, a person moving rapidly up the corporate ladder, or a family with many expensive possessions. Because of these images, we do not immediately think of Joseph as successful. He was a slave in a foreign country. The phrase "successful slave" sounds contradictory to us.

However, Joseph was a success because whatever he did, he did to please the Lord. When he worked for Potiphar, his master immediately saw his faithfulness over small matters and made him overseer of his household (Genesis 39:4). In prison, his faithfulness in seemingly insignificant ways was seen and appreciated by others; he was rewarded by receiving greater responsibility (Genesis 39:20–33). Pharaoh rewarded him by making him overseer of Egypt (Genesis 41:41). Each step of the way Joseph reflected a servant attitude, and it became his stepping-stone to greater responsibility.

Jesus told a parable about a master who distributed talents to his servants. When two of the servants increased the worth of what had been given them, the master exclaimed, "Well done, good and faithful slave. You were faithful with a few things; I will put you in charge of many things, enter into the joy of your master" (Matthew 25:21, NASB).

Jesus' disciples found the concept of servanthood difficult to grasp. Jesus sought to teach them how to succeed as his disciples by contrasting it with pagan success. He said, "Whoever wants to be first must be slave of all. For even the Son of Man did not come to be served, but to serve, and to give his life as a ransom for many" (Mark 10:44–45).

In order for servanthood to become a reality in our lives, we need to be like Christ, who "made of himself nothing, taking the very nature of a servant." (Philippians 2:7–8). Then we will be successful.

Glenn E. Schaefer is Chairman, Division of World Ministries, and Professor of Bible at Simpson College in Redding, California.

Joseph—II
The Lord Was With Him
■ ● ■

His master saw that the Lord was with him and that the Lord
gave him success in everything he did (Genesis 39:3).

A common theme in the narration of the life of Joseph is that
"the Lord [Yahweh] was with him." This phrase was used of
him in Potiphar's house and in prison. It was intimated in
Joseph's rise to power. That presence was acknowledged by his
acquaintances wherever he was.

Surprisingly, there is no evidence that Jacob or Joseph's
brothers ever perceived that God was with Joseph. Nonbelievers saw that "the Lord was with him" far more clearly than did
anyone in his own family.

How did these unbelievers know that "the Lord was with
him"? What evidence was there that God was enabling him in
his tasks? With so many gods in Egypt, how were Joseph's
Egyptian acquaintances able to discern that it was the Lord, the
God of Israel?

Joseph openly recognized the Lord in his life (Genesis
41:16). He verbally confessed that if he was able to accomplish
what others could not do, he did it through the Lord's enabling.
In addition, his words and his life were one; there was no
duplicity. He witnessed with his life as well as with his words.

Do we see the Lord's presence among our family members,
or are we as blind to it as were Joseph's brothers? Can we see
the Lord's presence among the family of God, the church?
Affirmation of God's presence in believers brings with it love,
unity, and a power seen by unbelievers.

Joseph—III
Always Sees God's Hand
■ ● ■

God sent me ahead of you to preserve for you a remnant on earth and to save your lives by a great deliverance. So then, it was not you who sent me here, but God" (Genesis 45:7–8).

Joseph's brothers had done a terrible thing to him. They conspired to sell him into slavery in a foreign country. In addition, they agreed to trick their father into believing that Joseph had been attacked by a wild animal and killed. However, they were never able to get those acts of cruelty out of their minds. They were afraid that once their father died, Joseph would show his true colors and punish them (Genesis 50:15).

Joseph, however, saw the hand of God in these events. That perspective gave him the ability to review his life without bitterness. He could forgive his brothers for what they had done to him, for he was confident that God had used their evil deeds to work out deliverance for his family. After his father died, he repeated this belief to his suspicious brothers: "Ye thought evil against me; but God meant it unto good" (Genesis 50:20, KJV). It was he who sought to comfort them.

On several occasions in the book of Acts, the apostle Peter declared that God was pleased to work out his will for mankind through the evil deeds of the religious leaders in Jerusalem. The apostle Paul affirms a similar idea when he wrote to the church at Rome, "We know that all things work together for good to them that love God, to them who are the called according to his purpose" (Romans 8:28, KJV). To those who learn the secret of this truth there is a deep sense of security and trust: the Lord knows what he is doing.

Joseph—IV
Enabled by God
—————— ■●■ ——————

*"It is not in me: God shall give Pharaoh an answer of peace."
... Pharaoh said unto his servants, "Can we find such a one as
this is, a man in whom the spirit of God is?" (Genesis 41:16, 38,
KJV)*

Joseph spent several years in prison after he was charged with
the attack on Potiphar's wife. The only notable event that
happened during his prison experience involved the dreams of
two other inmates, former members of the pharaoh's select
group of employees. The two men were sad, for no one was
there to interpret their dreams for them. Joseph's response to
them is enlightening: "Do not interpretations belong to God?
tell me them" (Genesis 40:8, KJV). Here he acknowledged that
he had the ability to interpret the dreams, but the ability was
God-given.

Later, the pharaoh recounted his dreams to Joseph, noting
that no one in Egypt among the wise men could determine the
significance of the dreams. Joseph acknowledged that he too
could not give the pharaoh a correct interpretation of the
dream. However, the Lord through Joseph could give an
interpretation of the dream to the pharaoh. Again, Joseph
credited the Lord with the interpretation; God enabled Joseph
to predict accurately what would happen.

After Joseph explained to the pharaoh what would happen
during the next fourteen years, the pharaoh inquired of his men
if they could find a person who could administer such an
assignment. The pharaoh noted that the person would have to
be endowed with "the spirit of God" (Genesis 41:38). In his next
breath, the pharaoh gave that assignment to Joseph, for he
discerned "the spirit of God" in Joseph.

Often we differentiate between "native abilities" and "God-
given abilities." This does not appear to be the case in the life
of Joseph. When Joseph was asked to interpret the dreams, he
confessed that they were beyond his ability to do so. The Spirit
of God had given him certain abilities at birth, while other
abilities came to him as an adult. All of them, however, were
from the Lord. He acknowledged that and gave God the glory.

Joseph: How Does This Apply to Me?
When the Dream Seems Blocked
■ ● ■
Rebecca Price Janney

"I just don't get it," I told a group of friends. "God has given me a marvelous vision for my life, so much encouragement and training. But now it's as if he has put me on a shelf. My talents are being wasted, and I'm facing opposition."

My confusion was understandable. God had blessed me with many gifts and a deep love for Christ. But circumstances suddenly turned against me. At what should have been just the beginning of my career, my search for a position went unrewarded. I asked the Lord to intervene. He was silent.

"What happened?" I painfully questioned. "Did God forget me? Why doesn't he use me as he promised? Have my dreams been only 'my dreams'?"

The biblical experience of Joseph seemed starkly reminiscent of my own. Everything about young Joseph spelled success. He was clearly a rare and outstanding individual and the favorite son of his adoring father. He was strong and capable. One day he received a vision that he would be such a great man that his older brothers would bow down to him. They became filled with a jealous rage. In a fit of anger they sold Joseph into slavery. His time of exile had begun—a period of painful, restless soul-searching.

The son of Jacob was reduced to being the chattel of some Ishmaelites. Then he was purchased by Potiphar, the pharaoh's captain of the guard. Joseph was degraded, shamed. Yet, he persevered.

God blessed Joseph with a strong sense of the Lord's guiding presence. Soon he became one of Potiphar's favorites. Joseph was promoted and placed in charge of his master's entire household. But just as things began to look up, another strong wind blew against him.

Potiphar's wife had a roving eye, and Joseph became her object of desire. But the young man respected God's commandments, and he wanted to remain loyal to his generous master.

Rebecca Price Janney, a free-lance writer, is an adjunct history professor at Cabrini College, Radnor, Pennsylvania and is currently studying for a Ph.D. in history at Temple University. She and her husband, Scott, also do interim pastoral work.

Joseph refused her designs, and he was thrown into a dungeon.

The world seemed to close in on Joseph. He was hungry and homesick, seemingly forsaken by God. Perhaps he considered that his wonderful dream about the future had been a cruel joke, made at his expense. Many questions about God and his existence must have played over and over in his restless mind. Maybe he had been all wrong.

"If God truly loved me," Joseph may have reasoned, "surely I wouldn't have to endure such torment." The teachings of his day suggested that God rewarded those he loved with good fortune. Perhaps God didn't love Joseph. Nevertheless, he refused to quit believing.

No doubt Joseph thought long and hard about the contradictions in life. Why do people with noble dreams have to suffer so much opposition along the way? When God reveals his plans for us, aren't the paths we take supposed to be smooth and sure? Shouldn't we go from Point A to Point B without a hassle?

Apparently not.

Paul said, "The foolishness of God is wiser than man's wisdom" (1 Corinthians 1:25). Therefore, when we encounter seemingly insurmountable difficulties in striving to do his will, we may be certain that it is all part of a greater plan. Paul also declared, "We know that all things work together for good to them that love God, to them who are the called according to his purpose" (Romans 8:28, KJV).

I began to understand this as I plowed my way through my roadblocks with God's strength and guidance. I made several important observations. First, after an intense inner battle, I confessed that my dreams had become more significant to me than my rightness with the Lord. My life was out of focus.

I realized that my first priority in all things had to be my relationship with the Lord. Am I right with him? Do I desire him more than anyone or anything else?

Second, I also discovered that my inclination was to try to place the blame for my predicament on people or circumstances. I wanted to lash out in anger at every obstacle that stood in my way. I was playing on the edges of bitterness. Then something toward the end of the story of Joseph caught my attention.

When Joseph had finally been vindicated, when his dream

had come true, making him second in rank in Egypt only to the pharaoh himself, his brothers were grief-stricken over the pain they had caused him. They wondered how he could ever forgive their cruelty and the "lost" years he had spent in servitude and in prison. Yet Joseph's words ring out his supreme trust in God's plan, "You intended to harm me, but God intended it for good" (Genesis 50:20). Joseph believed that God had been supporting him every step of the way. No one but God had been in control during Joseph's long ordeal. There was no need to fix blame, only to offer forgiveness.

Bitterness is not an acceptable option when we understand that God is Lord and is in control. Feelings, people, and circumstances aren't in control. God knows the way when we suffer: "For now we see in a mirror dimly, but then face to face. Now I know in part; then I shall understand fully, even as I have been fully understood" (1 Corinthians 13:12, RSV).

Another thing I learned from my period of testing was the importance of redeeming the "meantime"—the time between the giving of a dream or goal and its fulfillment.

The meantime was a testing ground for me and revealed what was truly inside me. I asked God whether I was in accord with his will. Was the opposition a sign to try another route, or a test to promote my endurance and the building of my character? Were there sins in my life that needed to be confessed? Did I need to forgive anyone for wrongs committed against me?

In addition, I considered what my behavior was communicating about my faith to others. Did it illustrate supreme trust in God's purpose and timing, or did it smack of fearfulness? Did it say, "Though he slay me, yet will I hope in him"? (Job 13:15) Was my attitude a witness to the awesome power of Christ to save us?

The story of Joseph illustrates the importance of putting our total trust in the Lord at all times and leaving it there, especially when the path ahead is covered by fog. We can emerge from the meantime as deeper, more mature believers, and the fulfillment of our dream can become a reality. At times, we may be confused by delays and detours. We may think God seems remote. Yet, the more intimate our relationship with the Master becomes, the more we will trust him for the business of our lives.

Joseph
Insights for Discovery
─────── ■●■ ───────

1. From Genesis 37:3, what parenting mistake did Jacob make? If Jacob had demonstrated his love equally, how differently do you think Joseph's brothers would have treated their younger sibling?

2. How do you react when you see the blessings of God being showered upon another Christian brother or sister you know?

3. Study Genesis 39:1–20; Proverbs 7. Contrast Joseph's victory over temptation and the fall of the youth to the adulteress. From Philippians 4:8 and 1 Peter 2:11, what is the connection between pure thinking and pure living?

4. Study Genesis 50:15–21 and Proverbs 19:11. What can you apply to your life to demonstrate the beauty of forgiveness?

5. Reflect on Genesis 45:1–8. Daniel's trial in the lion's den (Daniel 6) parallels the plight of Joseph. What about God's sovereign control over the events of one's life encourages you as you try to please him? What can you do to strengthen your personal devotion to God?

6. When do you see the presence of God in your life? Read Nahum 1:7, then write a psalm of praise to the Lord for his faithfulness to you.

Hosea:
He Understood God's
Suffering
■●■
Michael Griffiths

The One He Loved Was Unfaithful

———— ■ ● ■ ————

"Go, take to yourself an adulterous wife and children of un-
faithfulness, because the land is guilty of the vilest adultery in
departing from the Lord" (Hosea 1:2).

Hosea's broken marriage becomes a dramatized parable of
God's grief over the unfaithfulness of Israel. It isn't clear if
Hosea knew that Gomer was a prostitute, or if the text leaps
ahead to tell us what became clear later: that she was a shallow,
mercenary woman.

Since her children were not born yet, it's possible that her
adultery and "children of unfaithfulness" were still future. The
first child was named *Jezreel* after a notorious massacre. Gomer's
unfaithfulness is indicated by the names of the second child,
"unloved," and the third child, "none of mine" (Hosea 1:6–8).
Later, she ran off with another man, leaving Hosea and the
children.

The agony for the sensitive prophet of being married to a
person who did not return his love is something we can only
imagine. God used Hosea to portray something much deeper.
Hosea must have suffered greatly, but the Lord said to him,
"This is how I suffer because Israel, my people, my bride, is
spiritually unfaithful to me. Now, Hosea, you know how I feel
about those who are unfaithful to me" (cf. Hosea 2:13).

Hosea's broken heart is a model of how the Lord feels when
we have covenanted with him, and then deliberately turn our
backs and disobey him. We may not always think of our own
failure and disobedience this way, but we need to recognize the
pain and grief we cause the Lord. Here, we penetrate the
mystery of the cross and the suffering of God because of the sins
of the whole world.

We should marvel at the Lord's deep care and concern for
us. His attitude can lead us to repentance, reconciliation, and
a much deeper relationship with him: "All day long I have held
out my hands to an obstinate people" (Isaiah 65:2).

Michael Griffiths, formerly a missionary to East Asia, served as Principal of London
Bible College until 1989. He and his wife, Valerie, have four grown children.

Hosea—II
He Accepted His Unfaithful Wife
─────── ■ ● ■ ───────

"I will betroth you to me forever; I will betroth you in righteousness and justice, in love and compassion" (Hosea 2:19).

Hosea's name means *salvation.* It comes from the same root as the names *Joshua* and *Jesus.* God commanded Hosea to live up to his name: "Go, show your love to your wife again, though she is loved by another and is an adulteress. Love her as the Lord loves the Israelites, though they turn to other gods" (Hosea 3:1).

Gomer apparently didn't last long with her lover, and she ended up in the slave market for sale to the highest bidder. Would any man, with any self-respect, bother to redeem such a woman in these circumstances? Hosea ran down to the market to buy her. From his meager resources he scraped together half the value set on a slave (Exodus 21:32). He had to make up the rest from his grainstore, and he paid the balance with barley (Hosea 3:2).

By commanding Hosea to do this, God allows Hosea's agonized love to portray a further aspect of God's own gracious character. In spite of Israel's spiritual adultery, he didn't write her off, but redeemed his people again.

As in the parable of the Prodigal Son, God seems to have no reserve or self-respect. But the Prodigal Son had repented and come a long way toward home when his father ran to meet him. Gomer was incapable of redeeming herself out of the slave market, and Hosea went all the way there to buy her back.

In the same way, God himself, while we were still hostile and estranged sinners, came in Christ all the way down to us in order to redeem us. Isaiah gave us a vivid picture of the Lord, using his Servant Messiah "to free captives from prison and to release from the dungeon those who sit in darkness" (Isaiah 42:7).

Hosea provides a remarkable picture of the depths of the Lord's love for us as sinful failures. We need to identify ourselves as captives in prison or the slave market. The Lord has liberated us, bringing us out into his light to lead a new life.

Hosea—III
He Adopted Her Children
————— ■●■ —————

"I will show my love to the one I called 'Not my loved one.' I will say to those called 'Not my people,' 'You are my people'; and they will say, 'You are my God'" (Hosea 2:23).

Two of Hosea's "children of unfaithfulness" are given names, "unloved" and "none of mine," which suggest that Hosea knew he was not their genetic father. Yet the children could not be blamed for the sins of their mother. So Hosea welcomed them as his own, changed their names to "loved" and "mine," and took Gomer back.

Paul and Peter used Hosea's words to illustrate God's mercy to the Gentiles (Romans 9:23–26; 1 Peter 2:10). We had no claim to be children of the covenant. We were strangers to the covenants of promise (Ephesians 2:12). We had no right to call on God. Yet he took the initiative to find us and adopt us as his own children.

Hosea's experience—the realization that Gomer was making a fool of him—must have been intensely painful. It was costly to accept her children as his own. This selfless act by Hosea was prophetic, but several centuries passed before the reason for it became clear. A broken, alienated family was reconciled to one another. What a vivid image for the church, built of people from different ethnic families, all adopted together as "one in Christ Jesus" (Galatians 3:28).

We also are called to be merciful. Babies of all races and colors cannot speak any language. They cannot be held responsible for the sins of their parents, just as Gomer's children could not be held responsible for their illegitimacy or the pain that their coming caused Hosea.

We read in Jesus' parable that the unmerciful servant was condemned because he didn't extend to others the mercy he himself had received for a much greater debt (Matthew 18:21–35). We need to show others the same forgiveness we have received as forgiven sinners.

Hosea—IV
He Hated Religious Superficiality

——— ■ ● ■ ———

"What can I do with you, Ephraim? What can I do with you, Judah? Your love is like the morning mist, like the early dew that disappears" (Hosea 6:4).

The Lord expressed his own pain and suffering through Hosea. Both the northern and southern kingdoms of Israel expressed love to the Lord, but it was temporary and unsubstantial. They drew near to God with their mouths and used religious cliches, but their hearts were far from him (Isaiah 29:13).

Hosea amusingly described them as being like a half-baked cake. The round, flat scones baked on hot stones had to be turned at the precise moment or one side would burn (Hosea 7:8). In *The Book of the Twelve Prophets*, G. A. Smith asks of today's church, "Of how many Christians is it true that they are but half-baked—living a life one side of which reeks with the smoke of sacrifice, while the other is never warmed by one religious thought?"

Many of us keep our lives in compartments and use pious language in church on Sundays. But the rest of the week we live like pagans. We've never allowed the warmth of God to penetrate through to our business dealings. Our spouses and children fail to find God's warmth in us.

Let's pray for the reality of God to penetrate every part of our lives and for genuineness and integrity. Let's avoid being half-baked!

Hosea: How Does This Apply to Me?
Learning Through Suffering

■●■

Nanette DeLaittre

The frozen lake resembled a sheet of glass. My girlfriend and I were on the ice, volleying tennis balls back and forth. Suddenly, the ball curved sharply to the right. My friend lunged to catch it but missed. As she approached the ball and was about to grasp it, the ice cracked beneath her.

Immediately she was engulfed in darkness. I raced to help, feeling sure that I could save her.

As I jumped into the swirling darkness, I called to her. In her desperation, she struggled and beat against the waves, but she wouldn't look toward me. I drew nearer and reached out, yelling at her as loud as I could. I was the only one who could save her, yet she wouldn't acknowledge me or allow me to assist her. She was losing strength.

I opened my eyes and lay very still. What a vivid dream! I began to think of my recent struggles with various people who had needed my help. I tried to help them as I felt the Lord was leading me, but they turned away from me, misunderstanding my motives. I recalled the pain of not being believed, or not being heard, of being rejected.

Then I recalled how many times I, in the midst of difficult circumstances, have turned to everything and everyone but God. Could it be that the heart of God is grieved when, in my desperation, I choose to struggle, when he wants me to turn to him, acknowledge him, and cling to him?

Hosea, one of the prophets of the Old Testament, came to understand and experience a little of the broken heart of God for the rebellious nation of Israel. Through Hosea's own heartbreak over an unfaithful wife, he became acquainted with God's heart and his suffering over his faithless bride.

"How can I give you up, O Ephraim? How can I surrender you, O Israel? How can I make you like Admah? How can I treat you like Zeboiim? My heart is turned over within Me, All my compassions are kindled" (Hosea 11:8, NASB).

Nanette DeLaittre is a free-lance writer living in Atlanta, Georgia. She attends Mt. Paran Church of God.

God laments for his people. He cared for them in the wilderness and in the land of drought, but they became proud, and satisfied, and forgot him. God, however, does not forget them. He continues to grieve for them as he seeks to bring them to himself.

God, being holy, does not simply overlook or excuse sin. Through the prophet Hosea, God reveals his judgment concerning Israel's idolatry: "They will not return to the land of Egypt; But Assyria—he will be their king, Because they refused to return to Me" (Hosea 11:5, NASB). God allows Israel to suffer at the hands of Assyria, yet this very suffering is the means through which God intends to draw his people back to himself.

God's final words through his prophet are a plea for Israel to repent, and his promise to heal and restore them if they are repentant: "I will heal their apostasy, I will love them freely, For My anger has turned away from them. I will be like the dew to Israel; He will blossom like the lily, And he will take root like the cedars of Lebanon" (Hosea 14:4–5, NASB).

God does not leave his people, but rather suffers with them. Out of a heart of compassion and love, he points them to himself: "It is I who answer and look after you. I am like a luxuriant cypress; From Me comes your fruit" (Hosea 14:8, NASB).

It is this steadfast love of God who suffers for and with his people that draws us into intimacy with him. As we begin to know in our heart God's unconditional love, and see in our experiences his concern and suffering with us, we want to run to him with open arms. The vision of God's love drives us to love him more.

A few months ago my life was in a tailspin. Besides working long hours for an advertising agency, I had become caught up in too many church functions and activities. My phone seemed to ring endlessly with various friends desiring to share problems with me, friends who needed prayer or encouragement. Night after night, my time was wrapped up in other people's lives, their joys and sorrows. For a time, life seemed exciting and full.

But one afternoon, I had lunch with my Bible study leader. In the course of our conversation, I pointed out areas in her life in which I thought she was slipping. She received what I said with love and patience. As I talked, however, my spirit was grieved. What could be wrong? Wasn't everything I was telling her scriptural? Wasn't I looking out for her best interests?

After the luncheon I knew in my heart that something was amiss, but didn't take the time to seek God about it. Instead, I called friends to ask for counsel.

One Sunday, a young man sitting next to me in church gently asked me if I needed prayer. Tearfully, I nodded my head. After praying, he looked at me and asked, "Have you gone before the Lord yourself and asked him about this?"

I thought, *Of course, I have—or have I?* Amid all my spiritual activities and hectic schedule of "doing good," had I pushed God out of the picture?

After church that day I sought the Lord for answers. I began to see that my Christianity had become merely religious activity. I had been running on a treadmill of performance out of pride and a need for others' approval. Looking to myself and others for answers, I had stopped seeking God with my whole heart.

In my pain I began to see the various ways God had tried to refocus my attention on him. My lack of peace had been his way of letting me know I was off course. In the same way that he had dealt with Israel, God allowed the process of suffering to draw me back to his side, to the rest that is in him.

We serve a loving and faithful God who suffers for his people and with his people. Hosea, through his own suffering, came to know God and his suffering for his people. He gained an understanding of God's heart.

Our relationship with God is deepened when we allow our suffering to lead us into fuller communion with him. Through our sorrows we can come to know the "Man of Sorrows" and gain heart knowledge of his faithfulness to us and unending love for us.

Hosea
Insights for Discovery
— ■ ● ■ —

1. Study some of the serious charges leveled against Israel (Hosea 2:5, 8, 13; 4:1, 10–12; 7:10–16; 13:6).

2. In Hosea 8:2–3, observe how Israel acknowledges God, but then rejects what is good. Compare this with the similar behavior of the Pharisees in Matthew 15:1–9. Focus on verse 8.

3. Notice both the consequences of Israel's sinful action and God's promised punishment (Hosea 2:3–4; 5:6, 14–15; 8:13–14; 9:15–17).

4. In Hosea 9:7, God warns Israel about imminent judgment. In light of this thought, consider the Second Coming of Jesus Christ; in particular, note 1 John 2:28; 3:2–3.

5. Meditate on the depth of God's love and forgiveness of his people in spite of Israel's blatant sin (Hosea 2:14–23; 3:1; 11:8–11). Find parallel passages in Judges 6 and 10.

6. Notice the specific exhortations in Hosea 10:12; 12:6; 14:1–2. Study the similarity between Hosea 6:6 and 1 Samuel 15:22–23.

7. Compare Hosea 13:4 with Exodus 20:3–4. Note the related thought in Acts 4:12.

8. Meditate on Psalm 25 and consider how these verses apply to you.

Elizabeth:
A Noble Woman
■●■
Aida Besancon Spencer

Elizabeth—I
A Righteous Woman
■●■

They were both righteous before God, walking in all the commandments and ordinances of the Lord blameless (Luke 1:6, RSV).

Luke, the historian and physician, makes it clear that both Zechariah and Elizabeth were righteous. Sometimes in today's society, women are tempted to allow the spirituality of their husbands to represent them before God. However, Luke observes that Elizabeth was as righteous as Zechariah.

This couple would have had many friends and neighbors who traveled with them to Jerusalem (Luke 1:10). As Zechariah did, other priests would come twice each year from Judea and Galilee for a week to perform priestly duties. An average of three hundred priests, four hundred Levites, and lay representatives would make the trip together from a village to the temple at Jerusalem. Sometimes all the residents of a village would also come to encourage the priests.

But Zechariah and Elizabeth had more than approval from their peers. They were "righteous before God." Elizabeth and Zechariah were righteous because they walked blamelessly in all the commandments and regulations of the Lord.

Elizabeth had an elite background. She was a descendant of Aaron, the first high priest of Israel. Jewish women, as well as men, kept careful accounts of their ancestry. To ensure that husband and sons would qualify for priestly office, both husband and wife had to come from priestly backgrounds. Neither could be divorced or have had any adulterous affairs (Leviticus 21:7). In accordance with God's regulations, both Elizabeth and Zechariah were righteous because of their priestly backgrounds.

Because of their righteousness in his presence, God chose Elizabeth and Zechariah, obedient believers, to "make ready for the Lord a people prepared" for the full force of God's Spirit (Luke 1:17, RSV).

Aida Besancon Spencer is Associate Professor of New Testament at Gordon-Conwell Theological Seminary in South Hamilton, Massachusetts. She and her husband, William, have one son.

Elizabeth—II
A Believing Woman
■ ● ■

"Blessed is she who believed that there would be a fulfillment of what was spoken to her from the Lord" (Luke 1:45, RSV).

The angel Gabriel told Zechariah that his son would be filled with the Holy Spirit even while still in Elizabeth's womb. The angel said that the son would turn many of the children of Israel to the Lord their God (Luke 1:15–16).

Apparently, both son and mother were filled with the Holy Spirit at Mary's arrival. Filled with extreme joy, the child could not speak, so he leaped. But Elizabeth could express her joy by speaking. She didn't whisper, or speak softly, or even speak in a conversational tone. She "exclaimed with a loud cry, 'Blessed are you among women, and blessed is the fruit of your womb!'" (Luke 1:42, RSV)

Elizabeth was content to bear a forerunner. She could have been jealous that Mary's baby would be more important than her own child. Instead, she was able to praise the younger Mary as "the mother of my Lord" (Luke 1:43). Elizabeth praised Mary as blessed because of whom she was bearing.

Moreover, as a prophet, Elizabeth perceived Mary's faith and affirmed her: "Blessed is she who believed" (Luke 1:45, RSV). Elizabeth encouraged Mary as a person whose happiness came because she believed that God would fulfill his promises.

Elizabeth also believed that Mary bore the "Son of the Most High" (Luke 1:32). And Elizabeth believed—despite her age and years of not having children—that she too would bear a child as God had promised. Because of her belief in God's sure Word, Elizabeth served as a friend of encouragement to Mary.

Elizabeth—III
A Proclaiming Woman
──────── ■●■ ────────

They would have named him Zechariah after his father, but his mother said, "Not so; he shall be called John" (Luke 1:59–60, RSV).

Even as Elizabeth had congratulated Mary, Elizabeth's neighbors and friends all came to congratulate Elizabeth. They wanted to be present at the circumcision of her son, a sign of his being part of God's holy people. Circumcision was so important that it was one of few actions not forbidden on the Sabbath. The child had to be circumcised even if the eighth day following his birth was the Sabbath.

Those who had come for the circumcision were already beginning to call the child by the name of his father, Zechariah, in accordance with traditional practice (Luke 1:59). Had they already performed the rite and named the baby Zechariah? Or were they simply informally calling him that as they prepared for the circumcision?

Elizabeth, the upright women who could shout her faith, was left by herself to stop the group's momentum. Traditional practices were shutting out God's wishes. But Elizabeth put a stop to the group's questions and assumptions with an emphatic, "Absolutely not. He will not be called even by my husband's name" (cf. Luke 1:60).

Elizabeth didn't hesitate. She didn't say, "He should be called John," or, "Let's explore the possibility of naming him John." She declared, "He shall be called John."

Because God had commanded a certain action, Elizabeth, as an obedient believer, could take no other action. And she demonstrated that her obedience to God was greater than submission to the pressures of her family and friends.

Elizabeth—IV
A Team Minister
————— ■●■ —————

All who heard them laid them up in their hearts, saying, "What then will this child be?" For the hand of the Lord was with him (Luke 1:66, RSV).

When Zechariah entered the holy place of the temple to bring the incense offering, he was terrified by the presence of Gabriel. But in spite of his fear, he also expressed doubt. When told that he and Elizabeth would have a child in their old age, Zechariah demanded evidence of God's promise. As God's messenger, Gabriel left Zechariah with that proof: Zechariah would not be able to speak until the child was born (Luke 1:9–20).

Throughout Elizabeth's pregnancy and up until the child was eight days old, Zechariah could not speak. At the baby's circumcision Zechariah heard people calling his child by his own name. What could be more proper or appropriate? But then Elizabeth insisted that the child be called by the name of John. And the group turned toward Zechariah, making signs in his direction to inquire what he would have the child called. Zechariah wrote, "His name is John" (Luke 1:63).

By his action Zechariah finally showed his own faith in God. He gave the child the name that God had given, John, "The Lord has been gracious." Zechariah no longer needed evidence of God's power, so his tongue could move and he spoke. His first words were to bless God.

At first, the friends and relatives were filled with wonder. Then they left to spread the news of what they had seen throughout the mountainous region of Judea. All who heard concluded that only God could have caused all these unusual happenings, and wondered what special appointment God might have for this unusual child.

Elizabeth and Zechariah each had trusted in and acted on God's promises. But when they acted as a team, their exemplary faith had ever-enlarging circles of influence. This couple affected not only their province, but their son who became a righteous person—the one who prepared and praised the Messiah's way (Luke 1:75–77).

Elizabeth: How Does This Apply to Me?
God Gave Me Other Children

—————— ■●■ ——————

Bette Sobel Vidrine

"Special service honoring mothers."

When I saw this announcement in the church bulletin about the next week's service, I knew what would be coming: a sermon on how wonderful it is to be a mother; flowers for the oldest mother; flowers for the youngest mother; flowers for the mother with the most children. The hurt of not having children would be brought to the forefront of my heart again. I couldn't face it. I didn't go to church that Sunday.

As I sat at home feeling sorry for myself, I picked up my Bible. I thought that reading it might help me forget the empty womb and the empty room—originally built to be a child's room, but now a guest room.

I believed that something must have been wrong with me because I didn't have children, but the medical tests showed nothing. Was it a moral failing? A spiritual failing?

Opening to the Gospel of Luke, I began to read: "But they had no children, because Elizabeth was barren; and they were both well along in years" (Luke 1:7). Suddenly my attention was riveted to the story. Here were people like me.

In the previous verse I read, "Both of them were upright in the sight of God, observing all the Lord's commandments and regulations blamelessly." I knew I didn't come up to that standard, but I wondered, *Do you mean, God, that maybe my not having children is not a punishment? Perhaps it's not because you have put a curse on me, as some people have said.*

I kept reading. The angel Gabriel came to Zechariah and told him that Elizabeth would bear him a son to be named John. Zechariah was skeptical; Elizabeth joyfully and thankfully believed: "This is the Lord's doing; now at last he has deigned to take away my reproach among men" (Luke 1:25, NEB).

Elizabeth was highly esteemed by God, yet held in little repute by the world. A message started to come through to me. Other women in the Scriptures who once had been childless

Bette Sobel Vidrine is a free-lance writer, harpist, and lab technician. She and her husband, Emile, live in Lafayette, Louisiana.

and felt reproached (Sarah, Rebekah, Rachel, Hannah) had been instrumental in the history of God's people, prior to the coming of the promised Messiah. I began to believe that God could use my childlessness for his purposes and glory.

Six months after Gabriel's proclamation to Zechariah, the angel announced the coming birth of Jesus to Mary, Elizabeth's cousin. Mary wondered how such a thing could happen, since she was a virgin. Gabriel told her of Elizabeth's pregnancy as evidence that "nothing is impossible with God" (Luke 1:37).

Mary hastened to visit her cousin. When Elizabeth heard Mary's greeting, John leaped in her womb. Elizabeth was filled with the Holy Spirit and was the first to call Jesus "Lord."

Mary spent the next three months with Elizabeth. The one who would bear Christ's herald was tended by the one who would bear the Christ. I could see that I, too, should be thinking of others instead of only myself.

Then one day a classified ad caught my eye: "Wanted: loving homes for boys of all ages. Contact Smithdale School for Boys." I discussed it with my husband, Emile. He was also interested, so we answered the ad. I thought perhaps we could help children in need and could satisfy my desire to be a mother at the same time. We applied and were accepted. We became parents to thirteen foster children—not all at one time!

Foster children satisfied my need to be a mother. Changing diapers and discipling teenagers became part of my life. I could now share these things with other women, rather than just sitting on the sidelines of their conversations. With all the love we had, my husband and I loved the children who came into our home.

But foster mothering is beset with frustration and anguish. Often I questioned if the pain for the children and me was worth the doing. Perhaps Elizabeth sometimes went through agonies while raising John.

I decided that, whether or not I could help the children in any other way, I could teach them about Jesus. They could learn nothing more important.

Whether a boy stayed with us for two days or five years, he heard about the Lord Jesus. We gave him his own Bible and read it with him. In this way, we were truly able to show our love for the children and help them.

We helped the boys in other ways too. We often had to teach them basics like cleanliness, table manners, and eye contact while talking to someone. Schoolwork was usually a problem. Often emotional disturbances had caused the boys to miss being educated even if they were physically in school.

Glenn, a fourteen-year-old who had never made any grade higher than a C, became an honor roll student his last two years in high school. He had found a family who cared about how he did and was willing to help.

Glenn had been moved from foster home to foster home for years, then was institutionalized for two years before coming to us. He'd had some religious training when younger, but his family's overwhelming problems prevented him from understanding. As was our custom, we gave Glenn a Bible, and we read it together.

In the morning before he went to school we had a short lesson from Proverbs on how he should behave during the day, and in the evening we went through the New Testament a chapter at a time. He had to come to church with us, an activity he soon came to love.

When Glenn was sixteen, we attended a week-long summer Bible conference in Minneapolis, Minnesota. The second day day he made a decision for Christ and was baptized. Now twenty-nine years old, he has never reneged on his decision. Although his life has been far from easy, he has always known that he is loved by the Lord and by us.

In my journey toward becoming the woman God wants, I look to the Bible for guidance. Elizabeth stands as a model of a Christlike woman. She was righteous; she and Zechariah were "careful to obey all of God's laws in spirit as well as in letter" (Luke 1:6, TLB).

As I opened my life to serve needy children and to bring them to Jesus, I could see God being glorified in their belief and love. We probably would not have had foster children if God had given us the natural family we had originally wanted. God used my childlessness to lead others—our foster children—to salvation. Through our children, as through Elizabeth's child, Jesus is glorified and his kingdom is increased.

Elizabeth
Insights for Discovery
■ ● ■

1. Compare and contrast the experiences of Zechariah and Elizabeth in Luke 1:5–25 with those of Abraham and Sarah (Genesis 17:1–18:15) and of Elkanah and Hannah (1 Samuel 1:1–2:11).

2. From Luke 1:5–7, observe how Zechariah and Elizabeth walked with God, yet had not been blessed with children. What purpose could God have had for leaving this desire in their lives for so long?

3. Notice, in Luke 1:18, Zechariah's response to the declaration that he and Elizabeth would bear a son. (Study 2 Corinthians 5:7 and Hebrews 11:1, 6.)

4. Reflect on Elizabeth's conclusion in Luke 1:25; then examine Psalm 40:5. Praise God for occurrences in your life that only he could have initiated.

5 Meditate on how Elizabeth must have bolstered Mary's faith as seen in Luke 1:42–45. (See the related thought in Ephesians 4:29.)

6. How can David's prayer in Psalm 36:10 apply to you? (Study similar prayers by Paul in Ephesians 1:15–21; 3:14–19 and Colossians 1:9–14.)

7. Elizabeth and Zechariah did not hide their righteousness; they proclaimed it. From Psalm 40:9–10, how does God want you to communicate your faith?

Stephen:
From Death to Victory
■●■
Roy R. Matheson

Stephen—I
A Man Full of Grace and Power
■ ● ■

Now Stephen, a man full of God's grace and power, did great wonders and miraculous signs among the people (Acts 6:8).

The drama of Stephen's life begins with that significant description. "A man full of . . . grace and power" provides a fitting caption for Stephen's entire career and would have furnished a worthy epitaph for his tombstone.

The power evident in Stephen's life is documented in subsequent passages. His "great wonders and miraculous signs" were mighty acts and prove to be a catalyst for the strong opposition that follows. Stephen's life was so controlled by the Spirit that the deeds he accomplished can be attributed only to God's Spirit working through him.

Stephen's life was a channel for the extraordinary. His career forces us to ask, "What is evident in my life that cannot be explained in human terms alone? What happens that can only be attributed to God's power within?"

The power in Stephen's life was revealed in his actions and words: "These men began to argue with Stephen, but they could not stand up against his wisdom or the Spirit by whom he spoke" (Acts 6:9–10). Stephen knew the Scriptures thoroughly, and he responded effectively to his opponents' objections.

The balancing feature in Stephen's life was that he was also a man full of God's grace. The word *grace* carries a broad spectrum of meaning, but in this chapter it is similar to our English word *gracious*. It was said of Jesus: "All spoke well of him and were amazed at the gracious words that came from his lips" (Luke 4:22).

It is possible to be a powerful person, but to exercise that power insensitively. The claims of Christ should be presented in an attractive manner, with grace and power, compassion and courage. An irenic spirit is needed when we face opposition. This is not possible with our meager resources, but God's grace is sufficient for such challenges (2 Corinthians 12:9).

Roy R. Matheson is the Dean and Professor of New Testament at Ontario Theological Seminary in Willowdale, Ontario. He has written numerous articles and a book titled *Loving God's Family*.

Stephen—II
A Man Who Digs for Truth
——— ■ ● ■ ———

"You stiffnecked people, with uncircumcised hearts and ears!
You are just like your fathers: You always resist the Holy
Spirit! Was there ever a prophet your fathers did not persecute?
They even killed those who predicted the coming of the Righ-
teous One. And now you have betrayed and murdered him—
you who have received the law that was put into effect through
angels but have not obeyed it" (Acts 7:51–53).

Before the Sanhedrin, Stephen traced the history of Israel from
the time of Abraham until the construction of the temple by
Solomon. He pointed out that Israel had always shut out the
voice of God as given by his chosen messengers, and had been
stubborn and unresponsive.

It was more than Stephen's clear unmasking of their unbe-
lief that produced their anger. It was the fact that he found new
truths in Old Testament texts which they had completely
overlooked. He explained they needed to abandon structures
like the temple that were important for that time but that had
outlived their usefulness. Israel still clung tenaciously to old
rituals, but now it was necessary to leave those ceremonies
behind.

We too may cling to old "structures" and not surrender
programs and methods that were effective fifty years ago but
now are no longer relevant to reach today's generation.

He sounded another note. They were encouraged, like
Israel of old, to move out instead of settling in. Some of God's
greatest acts for Israel transpired when they were outside
Palestine. God was not tied down to one geographical location
like the temple in Jerusalem. God's people in the Old Testament were a group of pilgrims with no fixed address.

God's call to pilgrim-living echoes down the centuries and
challenges twentieth-century Christians. Stephen used familiar Old Testament texts to make fresh applications and give
reminders the church had forgotten. Today we're just as
challenged to search our Bibles to see what we have missed
(Hebrews 4:12). Have we lost truths the Scriptures teach about
discipleship, material possessions, or repentance?

Stephen—III
A Man Who Radiates Confidence
——— ■●■ ———

All who were sitting in the Sanhedrin looked intently at Stephen, and they saw that his face was like the face of an angel (Acts 6:15).

I once talked with a Christian leader who had returned from Africa where he had ministered to a host of missionaries in several countries. "What is the greatest problem on the mission field today?" I asked, expecting him to discuss the difficulty of ministering in an alien culture.

He replied, "It's the fact that missionaries often do not know how to handle conflict. As a result, their ministry may be considerably weakened."

Stephen was no stranger to conflict and was able to confront it boldly, yet lovingly. For a number of reasons, he radiated confidence in crisis and in hostile settings, even though it ultimately cost him his life.

Stephen had learned the secret of the transformed life. The Sanhedrin, when gazing upon Stephen, saw the face of an angel, because his transformed face was the outward evidence of an inner change. They could *read* the presence of God. Paul described it when he said, "We, who with unveiled faces all reflect the Lord's glory, are being transformed into his likeness with ever-increasing glory" (2 Corinthians 3:18).

The expression on the faces of many Christians today is all too similar to the average passport photo—sad, sullen, and with little evidence of God's life within.

Stephen was able to demonstrate confidence for another reason. He had caught a glimpse of glory. He looked up to heaven just before his martyrdom and saw Jesus standing at the right hand of God, as a witness for Stephen in heaven (Acts 7:55–56).

Stephen also displayed confidence in that he was able to forgive his enemies. What seemed easy and gracious for Stephen may be incredibly difficult for us. The words, "I forgive you," stick in our throats, and we're unable to utter them. Forgiveness is not something we can always offer immediately. It often takes time.

Stephen—IV
A Man Who Witnesses Triumph
■ ● ■

While they were stoning him, Stephen prayed, "Lord Jesus, receive my spirit" (Acts 7:59).

David Watson, a dynamic British clergyman, carefully chronicled the last year of his life in a personal diary. It revealed his constant prayer for healing from cancer. God worked differently, however, and David did not recover. His death turned out to be even more of a testimony than his life, and his diary has ministered to those traveling through the valley of death.

Stephen's death was another situation where a tragedy is turned into a triumph. He became the first martyr of the church; and while God did not condone this act of violence, he used it to further his purposes.

Stephen lived by the truth conveyed in Philippians 1:21: "For to me, to live is Christ and to die is gain." He experienced death as a decided gain.

Most people today fear discussing death because it reminds us of our personal mortality. Death in any circumstance is difficult, but it seems especially tragic when a person's life is snuffed out in midstream through seemingly meaningless circumstances.

But God turned the tragedy and wickedness of Stephen's death into a mighty victory. It became a factor in the conversion of Saul of Tarsus. Paul credited Stephen with being a faithful witness in his death. The fact that Paul mentioned it years later shows the profound impact Stephen's death made on him (Acts 22:20).

Stephen's death was also a triumph because it forced the church out into unevangelized territory. The persecution caused by his martyrdom nudged the church to take the gospel to unreached people (Acts 8:1–4).

Death is always a great victory for the believer. We can face it with expectancy and courage and, when it comes time, pray, "Lord Jesus, receive my spirit" (Acts 7:50).

Stephen: How Does This Apply to Me?
Right Where I Am
──────── ■ ● ■ ────────
Louise M. Craig

"Your son is dead."

"No!" my heart screamed silently as I sat in the hospital emergency waiting room waiting for my husband, Richard. Our son, David, had been struck as he tried to remove a stalled truck from the train tracks.

In a world that is constantly on the move, our national statistics state that approximately forty-five thousand people die every year and one person dies every twelve minutes in some type of traffic accident.

Reading the statistics, or even specific cases, may bring compassion to our hearts and sorrow for those concerned, but what a numbing, heart-crushing emotional difference when those words are about your only son.

After Richard arrived and the initial shock of David's death subsided, we fell to our knees, pouring out our anguish to God and asking for his strength and guidance. We wanted David's death to be a witness.

During the months following our son's fatal accident, I attempted to sort out my emotions and find meaning in the tragedy. I thought about Stephen, the young Christian disciple who was stoned to death in the first century for his belief in a risen Lord.

Stephen was unknown, yet chosen to serve on the "social committee" (Acts 6:1–8). When the apostles needed time for preaching and teaching, they searched for young disciples who could minister to the widows of both native Jews and Hellenistic Jews, so that none of the widows would be left out. Stephen was selected because he was of good reputation and full of the Holy Spirit and faith.

As Stephen ministered in obscurity to those in need, he also publicly performed wonders and spoke with great fervor and wisdom. Although other disciples lived and served longer, only Stephen's death is recorded in detail by Luke. Two

Louise M. Craig is a retired elementary public school teacher and the music director for Mowatt Memorial United Methodist Church in Greenbelt, Maryland. She and her husband, Richard, are the parents of four children.

chapters in the book of Acts highlight Stephen's witness—so inspiring and so brief. The power of his faith as he defended himself incited the mob to violence, resulting in his death by stoning. Even in death, Stephen was the victor, because through Christ he was able to forgive.

My witness must carry me through joyful and sorrowful experiences. My death may not be a violent one, as in the stoning of Stephen or the train crash of our David. Perhaps my persistent witness to the Lord and my obedience to him might lead me into poverty, isolation, separation, self-denial, or some injustice that an uncaring world or community may inflect. However, as with young Stephen, God calls me to stand firm, my eyes fixed on him; he will provide the power to overcome even while I endure the test.

Reflecting on my son's death, I wondered about Stephen's mother. Was she proud of her son as he demonstrated love, compassion, and service? Had she caught the vision of Stephen's magnificent witness through martyrdom? Had she moved closer to the risen Lord into greater service because of her grief?

Such is my prayer for my family and me. David did not die as a great martyr of the church, but he did lose his life while attempting to save someone else's property. Am I willing to catch the vision of selflessness and total surrender to the Lord's will for my life and let his Holy Spirit flow through me to minister to those around me?

The apostle Paul tells us, "No temptation has overtaken you but such as is common to man; and God is faithful, who will not allow you to be tempted beyond what you are able, but with the temptation will provide the way of escape also, that you may be able to endure it" (1 Corinthians 10:13, NASB). The way of escape is the power to be able to bear the testing or temptation.

Life, death, adversity, and triumph, although experienced differently and uniquely by each of us, are yet common to all of us. Enduring and overcoming adversity through our Lord's magnificent grace, sharing our love for the risen Lord with others are our ways of witnessing to the incredible power of the Holy Spirit today, just as Stephen displayed his ultimate witness in his martyrdom.

Even while I experienced the pain of David's death, God protected and surrounded me with his power. The pain didn't go away. The protective power of the Holy Spirit provided the ability to bear the pain and the loss without bitterness, knowing that the Lord would work the pain for good and would make something worthwhile of the loss. The experience became a testimony to Romans 8:28 (NASB): "And we know that God causes all things to work together for good to those who love God, to those who are called according to His purpose."

We never know how even the smallest act can influence others. Some months after David's death, we planned a cookout for his friends. Between fifty and sixty young people came to the cookout. We had a great time reminiscing about our experiences and talking about future camping trips. As each young person was ready to leave, I was able to have a few private minutes with him. At that time I gave each one a verse of Scripture, David's recent college graduation picture, some printed highlights of their lives together, and a small New Testament.

They left with a good feeling in their hearts, a bit of Scripture tucked away in their minds, and the Word of God to read as the Holy Spirit prepares their hearts. The lines of communication remain open even today after more than three years, providing the avenue for further witness and service.

God calls us to be witnesses, as he called Stephen. Like Stephen, we are to be full of faith, grace, power, light, wisdom, courage, love, and God's precious Word. Such a witness cannot be achieved in our own power. But we can continually call upon the power of the Holy Spirit as we daily place our will in his control through obedience and commitment.

Through the tragedy of losing David, I have found there is no greater power available on earth. Suffering is not something I choose to do, but I thank God that I have been given the way of escape so that I am able to bear it.

"Go into all the world" (Mark 16:15, NASB) does not necessarily mean for us to travel the continents like Paul. Like Stephen, we are to demonstrate God's great power flowing through us right where we are, in our homes, in our communities, and in our weakness.

Stephen
Insights for Discovery
■ ● ■

1. Read Acts 6–7, paying close attention to 6:3, 8–10. Identify specific character traits that attracted the early church leaders to select Stephen as among the seven men chosen for special service. In what ways can you grow in these attributes? (See also Romans 12:9–12.)

2. As Stephen made his defense before the Sanhedrin, notice how well versed he was in the history of the people of Israel. Now read Psalm 78 and Psalm 105. Why is it critical for Christians to be knowledgeable in biblical history and in the history of the Christian church? How can you become more proficient in Christian doctrine?

3. From Matthew 10:1–31, what role does the Holy Spirit play in helping believers to give witness to Christ? Study also: John 16:7–11; 2 Corinthians 2:14–3:6; 2 Corinthians 3:17–18; 2 Corinthians 4:1–15; 1 Thessalonians 1:5–10; and 1 Thessalonians 2:1–2, 7–13.

4. Meditate on 1 Peter 3:14; 4:12–19. How do you feel when non-Christians misunderstand you while talking to them about Christ? What is the difference between being persecuted for your faith for righteousness' sake and being poorly treated because of a shoddy testimony presentation or because of exhibiting impatience or arrogance toward the non-Christian?

5. Becoming a martyr for the cause of Jesus Christ just doesn't happen. To be "prepared" to give your life for the Savior requires making daily sacrifices in your life and learning how to first die to self. Reflect on Romans 12:1–2. Ask God for his wisdom, guidance, and power to submit—or recommit—areas of your life to the Lordship of Christ.

Part III
Growing Stronger

———— ■●■ ————

Self-improvement is a hot topic. We have all kinds of evening classes to help us improve our education; color coordination classes to improve our appearance; health spas to improve our health; therapists to improve our self-image; and countless other things, all designed to help us feel better and look better. Listen to any conversation and you'll probably hear, "You look good!" And the response, "Gee, thanks, I feel good!" But we rarely hear conversations about "being good" and "doing good." Please don't misunderstand me, I do appreciate how wonderful it is to feel and look good, but I must insist that true self-improvement should include being and doing good, too.

The problem is, that kind of improvement or growth can be, and often is, difficult, arduous, and slow. For instance, personal growth means a personal relationship with the living God. This includes coming to grips with his will or purpose for our lives. An example is Abram (Abraham). Abram's divine encounter led him from his homeland, which was remarkably congenial, to an underdeveloped piece of real estate populated by not very friendly people. I doubt that Abram felt good about that at times, but he certainly did good by obeying God's command. Mary's encounter with God must have been devastating, particularly when she walked around her village, visibly pregnant. I doubt that her suspicious neighbors stopped her to say, "Wow, Mary, you sure look good today!" Nevertheless, she accepted the Father's will for her life. Noah's dreamboat was the laughing stock of his home folks because he had nowhere to sail it, and his explanations about why he was building it only added to their amusement. And what can we say about Jeremiah whose very name meant: "A Tale of Woe"? Who would want to be around him as he pronounced his doom and gloom messages? He didn't feel too good about the way the people were upset with him. But what he said was right, just as what Noah did was right. In this knowledge they persevered.

Perseverance in doing God's will despite discouragement and delay is one of the greatest of all personal growth factors. "Give me patience and give it to me now!" does not work in the divine growth plan. Waiting many years for a son like Isaac, building and preaching for years like Noah, prophesying and explaining for years like Jeremiah, and suffering the sword in heart during her Son's life and death, as Mary did, are the growth factors of which Scripture speaks.

It should also be noted that patient hope and trust are the growth qualities which so often produce lasting results. Take a minute to think about where the human race would be without Noah; where the covenant people would be without Abraham; where the exiles would have been without Jeremiah; and where we would all be without Mary's Son, Jesus Christ. Their growth was clear and inescapable. These people have much to teach us about *true* self-improvement—growing "in the grace and knowledge of our Lord and Savior Jesus Christ" (2 Peter 3:18).

Abraham:
Friend of God and
Father of the Faithful
■●■
Ronald B. Allen

Abraham—I
The Man God Blessed
■ ● ■

"I will bless those who bless you, and whoever curses you I will curse; and all the peoples on earth will be blessed through you" (Genesis 12:3).

Abraham (Abram) was a man born of pagan parents who lived in a land distant from the place to which God was calling him. Yahweh selected this one man, along with his wife, Sarah (Sarai), to be the progenitors of the people through whom he was determined to bring blessing to all the peoples of the world.

God's words to Abram in Genesis 12:1–3 are the foundation words of his promise, his covenant, upon which the rest of the story of the Bible unfolds. These words present God's commands to Abram to leave everything, and all his extended relationships and responsibilities, to gain the abundant blessing of God in his life, in his prosperity, and in his destiny.

Yahweh's provisions for Abraham had seven elements. The first three presented personal blessings to Abraham: he would father a great nation; he would enjoy God's blessing in his own life; and he would realize great renown (Genesis 12:2). The covenant that God established with Abraham was ultimately dependent upon the faithfulness of Yahweh to his own promise (Genesis 22:17). Generally, when one takes an oath, it is in terms of one who is greater than oneself. There is none greater than the Lord, so he took an oath grounded in his very being. This oath is therefore immutable, for God may not lie, nor may God deny himself (Hebrews 6:13–18).

Genesis 12:2 was a command to Abram: "You will be a blessing." We may understand this command to be God's directive to Abraham to bring blessing to others in his walk.

The most significant aspect of the blessing of Yahweh on Abraham is: "All the peoples on earth will be blessed through you." Ultimately, these words are realized in the Lord Jesus Christ, the son of Abraham who is God's means of bringing blessing to all peoples.

Ronald B. Allen is Chairman, Division of Biblical Studies and Professor of Hebrew Scripture at Western Conservative Bible Seminary in Portland, Oregon. He has written numerous articles and books, including *Worship: Rediscovering the Missing Jewel.*

Abraham—II
The Expectant Man
■ ● ■

When Abram was ninety-nine years old, the Lord appeared to him and said, "I am God Almighty; walk before me and be blameless" (Genesis 17:1).

Even though Abram had followed the commands of God in his life, he did not achieve very quickly the birth of the son whom God had promised. In fact, Abram and Sarai had participated in expected practices of their own day in order to achieve the heir that God had promised them. At one point Abram appointed one of his slaves as his heir. Later Sarai encouraged Abram to turn to her slave Hagar as a surrogate mother (Genesis 16:2). God blessed and protected Hagar and her son, Ishmael, but it was not through this son that the promise was to be realized.

Twenty-four years had passed waiting for God's promise. Abram was now ninety-nine; Sarai was ten years younger. They still did not have their child. Then God came to the old man and told him his name: "I am God Almighty." Before he reiterated his promise, God revealed himself to be the God who is Shaddai. This word speaks of God pictorially as an exalted, magnificent mountain in which there is a hiding place, a shelter from the assaults of life. In the seemingly interminable years of awaiting God's promise to be fulfilled, the Lord presented himself to Abram as a great reward, a protective shield (Genesis 15:1).

The revelation of the name Shaddai had bound with it an ethical demand of God on Abram's life: "Walk before me and be blameless." In our age where nearly everything is instant, we have lost not only a patient trust before the Lord, but also a sense of integrity in our walk before him. God's call to us, as to Abram, is to wait confidently in hope and to live in integrity before the Lord who is Shaddai, a protector and provider during all times of stress.

Abraham—III
The Obedient Man
■ ● ■

"Do not lay a hand on the boy," he said. "Do not do anything to him. Now I know that you fear God, because you have not withheld from me your son, your only son" (Genesis 22:12).

At last the child was born, just as Yahweh had promised (Genesis 21:1–3). The child of the aged Abraham and Sarah, a boy, was named Isaac, the name that God had selected. Then, years later, God comes to Abraham again. He directs Abraham to put Isaac to death, to sacrifice him as a devoted offering to the Lord—an awful test of his faith in God (Genesis 22:1–18). We are not told Abraham's thoughts, or Sarah's. All we observe in Genesis 22 are Abraham's actions.

At the point of intolerable tension, God intervenes. Isaac is atop the wood that would be his pyre, his limbs bound, his father grasping in his hand the sacrificial knife pressed against Isaac's neck where the carotid artery throbs.

Abraham's faith in God was so intense, so full, so unconquerable, that he believed in some way God would raise his son from the ashes of the altar. In fact, Abraham had told his servants, whom he had left behind with the donkey that had carried the wood, "And then we will come back to you" (Genesis 22:5). The writer to the Hebrews so understood Abraham's faith: "By faith Abraham, when God tested him, offered Isaac as a sacrifice. . . . Abraham reasoned that God could raise the dead, and figuratively speaking, he did receive Isaac back from death" (Hebrews 11:17, 19).

Then came the voice of God telling Abraham to withdraw his hand, to spare his son. Yahweh did not wish the child to die, but desired that Abraham might demonstrate for all time the nature of his faith in God. Never again would man be presented with such a command.

When Abraham was willing even to offer his uniquely born son to God in trust, even when all the promises of God rested in the life of that son, the depth of his faith was demonstrated in an unforgettable manner.

Abraham—IV
The Faithful Man
■ ● ■

Abram believed the Lord, and he credited it to him as righteousness (Genesis 15:6).

Abraham's faith in Yahweh was the superlative mark of his life. Think of the demands that came on him. When God came to Abram and told him to leave his land, his kindred, and his father's house, Abram obeyed God without hesitation: "Abram left, as the Lord had told him" (Genesis 12:4). When God came with the intolerable demand in Genesis 22:2, there was again the action of obedience: "Early the next morning Abraham got up and saddled his donkey" (Genesis 22:3).

God determined that the faith of Abraham was saving faith. Moreover, Abraham's faith is the prototype for our own faith in Christ. The apostle Paul argues, "We have been saying that Abraham's faith was credited to him as righteousness" (Romans 4:9). Again Paul reasons that God's reckoning of faith for righteousness was not just for Abraham, but for us as well: "But also for us, to whom God will credit righteousness—for us who believe in him who raised Jesus our Lord from the dead (Romans 4:24). It is for these reasons that Paul argues that Abraham's justification by faith is the model for our own justification: "Understand, then, that those who believe are children of Abraham" (Galatians 3:7).

Further, in some way Abraham's faith in God included an expectation of the coming of the deliverer, the Lord Jesus Christ. This is the teaching of the shocking words of Jesus to his opponents. John 8:56 records Jesus' stunning statement: "Your father Abraham rejoiced at the thought of seeing my day; he saw it and was glad." This precedes his even more remarkable words in verse 58: "'I tell you the truth,' Jesus answered, 'before Abraham was born, I am!'"

When we think of Abraham, friend of God and father of the faithful, we are inevitably drawn to thoughts of Abraham's God. A hymn of the church begins with these words: "The God of Abraham praise." This was Abraham's desire—our praise of his God.

Abraham: How Does This Apply to Me?
A Listening Heart
■ ● ■
Anna Amster Douglas

Is life an obstacle course where God abandons us blindfolded? Facing the unknown is usually accompanied by fear. But we are not called to peruse life's brochure in advance or read the map which bears our name. The Canaan to which God calls us may, like Abraham's Canaan, be unfamiliar territory. More likely it will be to love the children in the nursery, or to visit the unlovely in a nursing home, a lost co-worker, or a hurting neighbor across the street.

There is, of course, an alternative to obedience. Had Abraham chosen to remain in familiar surroundings, he would have removed himself from God's plan. Certainly Abraham's choice was a step toward the unknown. His step was a step of faith, of trusting God. It is always so.

Joneta is recently widowed, and she told me, "God had been nudging me gently about transferring to the singles class, but this morning I felt an urgent NOW!" Leaving one class and entering the other, she said, "I noticed a woman sobbing. I approached her and was able to minister to this one who had also just lost her husband."

Hearing and listening are similar in meaning but poles apart in actuality. It is conceivable that God may have called many "Abrams" before one responded. But like Joneta, Abraham did more than just listen with his ears. He heard with a listening heart. It was as if God were saying, "Life is in session. This opportunity is coming only once. Trust me. Obey."

What caused Abraham to be willing to take the risk, to abandon security, and accept the challenge required by God? Who cannot recall some fearful firsts of their own—of trusting, of faith—the first day of school, the first job with its requirements, expectations, and relationships? We are all vulnerable to financial collapse, to debilitating disease, to the crushing loss of a spouse, or the devastating rebellion of a child. Can God be trusted through all of these sessions of life?

Anna Amster Douglas is a teacher and a homemaker. She and her husband, Gene, are the parents of five children and live in Tuttle, Oklahoma.

God's design includes situations where he can demonstrate his faithfulness, though the working out of that intention requires more than the blind faith most of us use when turning on the porch light on a dark night. It goes beyond defensive faith while driving, the intelligent purchase of groceries, or the educated faith exercised when taking medications. It is simply taking God at his word. When necessary, it is saying, "I don't understand it all, but I'll stand on God's promises anyway!"

The dictionary refers to *standing* as being permanent or established, suggesting the necessity of a foundation. Is our desire for a heavenly Father not for a Lord, but for a benevolent grandfather with no obligations? We are so anxious to see results, but are we willing to apply the things we know from God's Word that produce the results we desire?

While the necessities of life demand our attention, the only way to avoid life's pitfalls is to obey God's specific direction at each juncture of life. We are free to choose partial obedience, but we are choosing to lose the freedom to be in his perfect will. In so doing, we also forfeit the freedom to be all that he wants us to be.

And what happens to our vision of obedience when we are sidetracked? Did Abraham's detour into Egypt put his call momentarily on hold? Our obvious and deliberate detours down into "Egypt" are not all that distract us. More often we are detoured by little annoyances and ordinary events which have the potential for great spiritual harm.

I am grateful that God's purposes are not stymied by our occasional distractions. In spite of his faithlessness, Abraham was not rendered useless. As I taste the bitter fruit of selfish attitudes and wrong choices, God promises forgiveness and healing when I acknowledge my sins. Then, restored, I am able to comfort others.

There are no shortcuts to God's best. We may cloak our sins in words like inconsistency, indiscretion, and impropriety. We may rationalize about the embarrassment, shame, and guilt when we reap the harvest of our own sowing. As Abraham waited, sometimes we too must wait longer than the next mail or the next week before we are willing to acknowledge God's sovereignty.

Often it is in our weakness that we are able to recognize the Abraham in ourselves. It is here that we suffer the pain we might not have had if we had followed what we already knew to be God's will.

It encourages me to know that even Abraham experienced some stumbling before he was ready to climb the mountain with Isaac. Though this trial of his faith was the most significant, it surely was not his last one. Neither have I met my final test. But I can be certain that God will provide for me as well.

A listening heart must be willing to obey. The command that God issued to Abraham was unique, but it was given so that Abraham might know who held his highest allegiance. He not only had to die to self, but to his aspirations for Isaac. God called for the death of one, but in Abraham's heart two died before the sacrificial trip was even begun.

I have had to make few real sacrifices in my life, especially compared with those required of Abraham. The few chocolates deferred in favor of losing a few pounds isn't in the same category.

In searching for current examples of Abraham's kind of sacrifice, I am caught short, but grateful. I'm grateful that, though I am willing, I have not had to lay all before God. Rather, my response to God's call necessitates as much a death to selfish attitudes, desires, and ambitions as it does to action.

God is still calling for Abrahams. And though my journey is different from his, Abraham is an example to me. God is still speaking to those who hear with a listening heart.

Abraham
Insights for Discovery

■●■

1. God is more interested in our character than our comfort. Read Hebrews 11:8–19. Is God asking you to take steps of obedience that you're finding difficult? Talk to God about your fears and ask him for his peace as you obey him.

2. Now read Genesis 12:16–20 and Genesis 20:1–13. Why do you think Abraham had a harder time trusting God in these circumstances than when God tested him to sacrifice Isaac? Was he trying to take the reins of control into his own hands?

3. Make a list of promises from God's Word that you have seen God fulfill in your life? How have these stimulated you in your walk of daily discipleship? You may want to start a prayer journal. Keep a running account of your prayers and how God answers them. Abraham didn't see all of God's promises fulfilled in his life. How do you feel about possibly not seeing all of your dreams, goals, or prayers answered before being called home?

4. Meditate on Genesis 17:1–2. What do you think "walking with God" and "being blameless" mean? How do these relate to the admonitions to excel still more in pleasing God (1 Thessalonians 4:1) and to be holy (1 Peter 1:13–16)?

5. Genesis 18:16–33 describes Abraham pleading for the salvation of Lot and his family. For whose salvation are you pleading before God?

6. What is the message of Colossians 2:9–12 and Galatians 3:6–14, 26–29? How can you help someone trust in Christ and not in works of righteousness?

7. Study Genesis 13–14; 1 John 2:15–16; and James 1:27. What scriptural principles can help you to live as a pilgrim in a foreign land on the way to God's promised land? Now read Genesis 12:1–3. Is there any reason why you can't follow Christ to a new home on the mission field?

Jeremiah:
Strength From God
■ ● ■

Milton C. Fisher

Jeremiah—I
The Promise of God's Strength
─────── ■●■ ───────

"Do not be afraid of them, for I am with you and will rescue you," declares the LORD (Jeremiah 1:8).

Fear of rejection, even some form of retaliation, often stands in the way of our witnessing for Christ. We manufacture respectable excuses. "Don't send me," was Jeremiah's, "I am only a child" (Jeremiah 1:6). What an inappropriate response that was! Jehovah God had just informed Jeremiah, "Before you were born I knew [chose] you, sanctified [prepared] you, and ordained [authorized and commissioned] you to be my prophet" (cf. Jeremiah 1:5).

God never calls, never sends, without enabling. We have his promise that his strength will be our portion. His reply to "young" Jeremiah is direct: "Do not say, 'I am only a child.'" Then he reinforces the original order: "You must go to everyone I send you to and say whatever I command you" (Jeremiah 1:7). Note the emphatic tone. These are not just imperatives to be obeyed, but statements of fact: "You must . . . ." Just so, Jesus directs his apostles, "You will be my witnesses in Jerusalem, . . . and to the ends of the earth" (Acts 1:8).

Graciously God adds to Jeremiah's command his promise: "Do not be afraid . . . , for I am with you and will rescue you." When God places his servant in a threatening situation, he also assures him of strength to meet it. Jeremiah knew the stubborn and rebellious mind of his people. They felt proud and secure, and no preacher was going to tell them something else. A century and a quarter after Isaiah warned of captivity in Babylon as punishment for their injustices, idolatry, and immorality, they were less willing than ever to listen. Their defenses were up; they were in a mood to fight back. Jeremiah knew this and was afraid. But the Lord promised, "They . . . will not overcome you, for I am with you and will rescue you" (Jeremiah 1:19).

Milton C. Fisher, a former missionary to Ethiopia, is Professor of Old Testament at Reformed Episcopal Seminary in Philadelphia, Pennsylvania. He and his wife, Merilyn, have three children and live in Upper Darby.

Jeremiah—II
The Assurance of God's Strength
———— ■ ● ■ ————

"I will save you from the hands of the wicked and redeem you from the grasp of the cruel" (Jeremiah 15:21).

Jeremiah's fellow citizens counted him a traitor for predicting Jerusalem's fall to the Babylonians. So vicious was their hatred that God calls it "the hands of the wicked . . . the grasp of the cruel." Yet Jeremiah's utterances were not of his own making or opinion. Jehovah God had said to him at the outset, "Now, I have put my words in your mouth" (Jeremiah 1:9). These people were fighting God and they could never win. The Lord assured supernatural strength for his vulnerable messenger, "I will deliver you, I will redeem you."

The assurance God gave Jeremiah is extended to the age of Christ's church. Some of us may never face physical violence for our faith, but in many places our brothers and sisters in Christ are suffering violence, insult, and deprivation for following the Lord. We must uphold them in prayer, for God is pleased to show his strength in their weakness and suffering. Jesus told his disciples, "In this world you will have trouble. But take heart! I have overcome the world" (John 16:33).

If we don't suffer, does that mean we are in no need of strength from God? Are we on our own unless persecuted in some severe way? Not at all. Although the assurance Jehovah gave his prophet, and our Lord Jesus gave his disciples, related especially to suffering for the faith, God's grace and provision is for all our struggles in this life. "Humble yourselves, therefore, under God's mighty hand," admonishes the apostle Peter. "Cast all your anxiety on him because he cares for you" (1 Peter 5:6–7).

"The grasp of the cruel" sounds extreme for routine earthly cares. Yet for some of us the cares of this world can become a frightful load. It is not uncommon for a dreadful spiral to set in: from disappointment, grief, or pain to discouragement, then into depression and despair. But God's strength in love is sufficient for these times.

Jeremiah—III
The Awareness of God's Strength
■ ● ■

"Is not my word like fire," declares the LORD, "and like a hammer that breaks a rock in pieces?" (Jeremiah 23:29)

Jeremiah smashed a potter's flask as a sign of Jerusalem's doom. Then Jeremiah is struck a fierce blow by one of the priests and secured in the stocks overnight. In spite of these impertinences, Jeremiah continues to pronounce the judgments of the Lord.

But these attacks do seem to get to him. He cries out in desperation, "Cursed be the day I was born! . . . Why did I ever come out of the womb to see trouble and sorrow and to end my days in shame?" (Jeremiah 20:14, 18)

In verses 11 and 13 of the same chapter, Jeremiah shows that he knows better: "The Lord is with me like a mighty warrior." He can actually praise the Lord in spite of the oppression he feels. "Sing to the Lord! Give praise to the Lord! He rescues the life of the needy from the hands of the wicked." It is his awareness of God's strength that enables Jeremiah to praise him for deliverance.

The secret of this awareness is unfolded more fully in Jeremiah 23, "'Am I only a God nearby,' declares the Lord, 'and not a God far away?'" Jeremiah needed this reminder, and so do we. God is present everywhere, far and near, not far removed and unconcerned with our circumstances and our problems. He is a God near at hand, a Father close by. With this awareness as we daily commune with God in his Word and by prayer, we have his strength for our every need for the asking.

Jeremiah—IV
Confidence Through God's Strength
■ ● ■

"I am the LORD, the God of all mankind. Is anything too hard for me?" (Jeremiah 32:27)

Jehovah asks Jeremiah, "Is anything too wonderful, too difficult, too amazing, for me?" The implication is that our God can do anything, and the believer can have total confidence in the strength and goodness of God. We can count on every promise in God's Word. We can rest assured that God will never let us down, that nothing can enter our life, or touch us that is outside God's purposeful control.

In chapter 32, Jeremiah is called upon to hope against hope—to trust God when all seems lost. The Lord himself has delivered the city up to a far more powerful nation, the Babylonians. Yet Jeremiah is ordered to invest in a piece of property, a vivid object lesson that the God of Israel can be trusted to restore that land to the people of Judah. After the period of punitive captivity (seventy years) is up, inheritors will repossess the family holdings (Jeremiah 29:10). Says Jehovah of hosts, "houses, fields and vineyards will again be bought in this land" (Jeremiah 32:15).

Jeremiah expressed his faith in God's power even while praying for understanding of such an order at such a time as this—with the enemy at the gates! God's reassurance comes in the form of a rhetorical question in words similar to Jeremiah's own confession (Jeremiah 32:17, 27).

Sometimes the Lord has to remind us of the truth of what we have professed to believe. At times we sing, pray, or speak "over our heads," beyond our active reach. Then God may take us at our word and cause us to stretch to the limit of what we know in our hearts to be true. This too is by his gracious supply of strength.

And we can take comfort knowing that because he is "the God of all mankind," that is, the Creator of all, he is now and is always in complete control. He is our sovereign Lord.

Jeremiah: How Does This Apply to Me?
Silent Strength
■ ● ■

S. June Presnell

I had always thought of Jeremiah, the Weeping Prophet, as a weak man. However, after getting to know him through Scripture, I see his tough inner strength. Like "a tree planted by the water," his roots go out into the water and he is not defeated by the droughts (Jeremiah 17:8).

This inner strength came from his conversations with God. Not only did Jeremiah talk with God, but he also took time to listen to what God said to him.

We need to follow Jeremiah's example, yet it is hard to hear the voice of God above the other sounds in our noise-polluted world. We have traffic noise, business noise, recreational noise, and even nature's noise. For instance, my husband and I were guests on some friends' houseboat. We were afloat on a lake surrounded by a wall of hills and trees. I was unable to sleep, so I lay and listened to the sounds of the night—the croaking of frogs, the grinding of katydids, and the hooting of the owls. Then at daybreak the night music was replaced with chirping and other sounds of day animals.

When we are surrounded by sounds, we have to concentrate to hear God's voice as he speaks his love, his promises, and his instructions to us.

To listen means to make a conscious effort to hear. We can learn a valuable lesson from the ways deaf people learn to "hear." For example, we have a young deaf friend, Sandy, who said, "Owen never talks softly." Because of the nature of my husband's work, he has formed the habit of talking loudly so that he can be heard above the noise of construction equipment. This habit carries over into his social conversations as well. Sandy listens closely in order to "hear" what others say and how they say it.

As with the deaf, we need to listen with our whole being. We need silent times with God to hear what he is saying to us, and to be able to hear him in the midst of ministry.

S. June Presnell, a free-lance writer, is working on a master's degree in Counseling. She works at Greenwood Counseling Associates and for five years has counseled unwed mothers.

It is in these silent times that we can hear God's love. In the book *Morning by Morning*, C. H. Spurgeon expresses God's love when he writes, "As he [God] looked upon the world he had made, he said, 'It is very good'; but when he beheld those who are the purchase of Jesus' blood, his own chosen ones, it seemed as if the great heart of the Infinite could restrain itself no longer, but overflowed in divine exclamations of joy."

Knowing God loves us above all creation gives us security to believe his promises. This believing means having faith when all circumstances are against us. A few years ago I went through a time of depression. At the time, I didn't realize that my depression was because of a chemical imbalance; all I knew was that I was depressed and I didn't know why. In my times of searching the Scriptures, praying, and crying out to God, my only shred of faith was that God loved me.

Jeremiah also had times of depression and doubts, and he poured out his fears and complaints to God. Then he listened for God's voice of love above the voices of fear and doubt (Jeremiah 15:10–21).

These times of faith often come because of others who spend their silent times interceding with God. My friend Lura was an intercessor. I met her when I began teaching a women's Bible study. This woman had radiated God's presence. She was also an encourager, and I knew instinctively she was praying for me. She was my mentor and prayer partner for many years. She had a heart condition, and her sleepless nights were spent in prayer. I and many others drew strength from her silent times with God.

Whether it is during sleepless nights or busy days, we too can hear God's voice if we will listen. God brings to our mind those for whom he wants us to pray. One morning during my quiet time, God brought to my mind a particular family. I did not know why, but I prayed for them occasionally throughout my day. The next evening at prayer meeting a prayer request was given for a member of that family; he had undergone emergency surgery the day before.

Not only is learning to listen to God a valuable exercise, but right listening will lead to one's calling and commission, as Jeremiah found out. When God told Jeremiah to "Gird up thy loins, and arise, and speak" (Jeremiah 1:17, KJV), God was saying, "Get prepared, Jeremiah. I have a ministry for you." God has a ministry for each of us in which we can use our spiritual gifts for his glory.

The first time I was asked to teach a Bible study, I, like Jeremiah, gave God excuses. First, I had no experience: "I've never done this before, God, and someone else can do it much better. How about the pastor's wife? She's experienced in teaching."

Second, I had no eloquence: "You know, God, no one wants to listen to my Indiana accent."

And third, I quoted Scripture to him: "God, I have family members who will be in this class, and you know that 'a prophet has no honor in his own country'" (John 4:4, RSV). But when I stopped talking and listened to God speak, I gave God my weaknesses in exchange for his strength. It seemed that I could hear God say, "And they [these weaknesses] shall fight against thee; but they shall not prevail against thee; for I am with thee, saith the Lord, to deliver thee" (Jeremiah 1:19, KJV). In her book *What the Bible Is All About*, Henrietta C. Mears wrote, "What God asks us to do, he fits us for; and what he fits us for, he asks us to do."

As with Jeremiah, many of us are called to the battle of confrontation. In counseling with young women in crisis pregnancies I face this challenge, but confrontation doesn't come easy for me. What if they reject what I say? What if they reject me? As parents, we are faced with this same threat of rejection. We must spend much time alone with God and listen to him so that we give his guidelines, not our own. In this we can know his acceptance even if others reject what we say.

Not only courage but a quality of calmness is the result of listening to God. My friend Lyn is the model of calmness. If I didn't know her, I would think she had no problems. Not so!

Lyn is a busy woman. She has three daughters, and her middle daughter has brain damage and requires hours of therapy. Not only that, Lyn is also a teaching leader for Bible Study Fellowship. This requires at least twenty hours of study each week, besides all the the interpersonal problems of leading four hundred women. Because she listens to God as she studies his Word, Lyn is able to stay calm in her busy world.

It is by listening to God in the silent times that we can hear his voice and draw strength in the midst of ministry and in the battles of life. As he said to his disciples, so he is saying to you and me: "Come ye yourselves apart into a desert place, and rest a while" (Mark 6:31, KJV).

Jeremiah
Insights for Discovery
■ ● ■

1. Read Jeremiah 1. What is the significance of verses 7–8? Now read Joshua 1. Find other verses that discuss God's presence in the life of his people, and ask God to make them evident in your own life.

2. Meditate on Jeremiah 9:23–24. Why is God worthy of our worship? What do you know and understand about God? Why would God delight in kindness, justice, and righteousness? What can you apply from Micah 6:8?

3. Study Jeremiah 17:5–10 and Psalm 1. What warning does God give? To whom does God promise special blessing? Why is the status of our heart so important to God? (Take additional notes from Matthew 15:1–16.)

4. What principles of business can you derive from Jeremiah 22:13? See also Romans 13:7.

5. What lessons can you learn from the lying prophets in Jeremiah 23:9–40?

6. Reflect on Jeremiah 26:4–6. How do you feel when you continue to witness to a friend, but he or she won't listen? Make a list of five to ten non-Christians you know. Pray that the Lord will open their eyes to his truth and to your testimony. Now study Jeremiah 29:7 and pray for the salvation of the city in which you live.

7. No one deserves God's love and mercy. We all deserve God's eternal punishment. What speaks to you from Jeremiah 33:1–11?

Noah:
The Man Who Built
While Others Mocked
■●■
Leslie C. Allen

Noah—I
A Model of Faith
———— ■●■ ————

By faith Noah, being warned by God concerning events as yet unseen, took heed and constructed an ark for the saving of his household; by this he condemned the world and became an heir of the righteousness which comes by faith (Hebrews 11:7, RSV).

Hebrews 11 supplies its readers with a series of role models from the Old Testament, and Noah is one of them. It would be good to read Genesis 6 and familiarize yourself with the first part of the narrative of Noah and the Flood.

Early Jewish expositors spoke of Noah being mocked. In so doing, they wanted a Jewish minority, despised and ridiculed in a Gentile world, to identify with Noah and to hear a pastoral reassurance that God was with them, as he was with Noah.

The writer to the Hebrews wanted his readers to identify with Noah. He saw in Noah a prototype of Christian faith, which he defined as "the conviction of things not seen" (Hebrews 11:1, RSV). The Christian has made a heavy investment in a spiritual future, without immediate tangible returns in many respects. "We walk by faith" (2 Corinthians 5:7, RSV), bearers of an open secret that by no means all want to know.

Was not Noah in this situation in the days before the Flood? Noah lived in God's world with ears and eyes open to God—as we do—while men and women around him were deaf to God's call and blind to the signs of his presence.

In Hebrews, we read that faith is a spiritual quality of imaginative courage. It is a resolute readiness to walk in step with God's drumbeat, even while others are blatantly out of step. Experiments in social psychology have shown how group pressure can turn conviction into doubt, and even into denial.

The writer of Hebrews wants us to learn from Noah's resolute stand. He calls us to "run with perseverance the race that is set before us" (Hebrews 12:1, RSV), reinforcing his call with the example of that supreme role model, Jesus himself.

Leslie C. Allen is Professor of Old Testament at Fuller Theological Seminary in Pasadena, California. He is the author of several books and commentaries, including *Word Biblical Themes: Psalms.*

Noah—II
A Model of Right Living
——— ■●■ ———

Noah was a righteous man, blameless in his generation; Noah
walked with God (Genesis 6:9, RSV).

At times the Bible teaches moral standards by means of contrast. Noah's goodness stands out against the vignettes of an
evil world presented in Genesis 6:5–12. Here in Genesis 6 we
read that God's exasperation with a wicked world is contrasted
with his approval of Noah, who "found favor in the eyes of the
Lord" (Genesis 6:8, RSV).

Noah's moral and spiritual qualities are contrasted with
minds and wills given over totally to evil (Genesis 6:5, 9). God
is represented not just as the stern judge of wrongdoing. He
also is a disappointed patron who suffers over the degenerate
behavior of his proteges, just as a parent grieves over wayward
children. However, he finds a ray of joy and hope in contem-
plating Noah.

Noah is presented first as "righteous." In the Old Testament it is a positive word that connotes fair play and doing the
right thing by other people. It means living up to one's
relationships with others and acting honorably in light of them.

Second, Noah is characterized as "blameless" (Genesis 6:9,
RSV). The term speaks of wholeness. It is used in sacrificial
passages of an animal "without blemish" (Exodus 12:5, RSV).
In human terms it means moral integrity. It is an ethical quality
marked by sincerity and devoid of hypocrisy or divided loyalties.

Third, Noah receives a spiritual accolade: he "walked with
God." It is a tribute that he shared with his great-grandfather
Enoch. It speaks of a life lived in the light of God's moral will.
Noah was one who identified himself with that will and la-
bored for it to come true in the practical matters of his daily life.

Noah—III
A Model of Obedience
—————— ■●■ ——————

They that entered, male and female of all flesh, went in as God had commanded him; and the Lord shut him in (Genesis 7:16, RSV).

Noah's obedience is the theme of Genesis 6:22–7:16. It runs through it like a refrain, marking the ends of four paragraphs in turn. In each case some aspect of entering the ark is broached: God commands and Noah complies.

Obedience is on the way to becoming a lost art in modern Western culture. To do one's own thing is regarded as an inalienable right in a free society. There is good in these tendencies, provided that they are not pushed too far. Unfortunately, God is sometimes the loser in the pursuit of individualism.

Not that we can isolate the modern world for blame. Disobeying God is as old as Adam and Eve. Noah's obedience is a fitting counter response to God. He heads up a new humanity, in a fresh start for himself and his fellow creatures.

In the New Testament we read of the contrast between Adam and Jesus: "As by one man's disobedience many were made sinners, so by one man's obedience many will be made righteous" (Romans 5:19, RSV). If obedience marked the Master, it must also mark us who serve him. It is no accident that the letter to the Romans begins and ends on the note of "obedience to the faith" (Romans 1:5; 16:26, RSV). From faith is to flow obedience, so that in response to God's revelation we first trust and then obey.

Throughout the Flood narrative, God takes the initiative. The obedience of Noah fits this overall theme. So does the next clause, "and the Lord shut him in" (Genesis 7:16, RSV). Was Noah a prisoner? No, the ark was the means of his preservation. It was like stepping into an elevator, to be whisked to where one needs to go. Paradoxically, Noah's confinement in the ark won him his freedom and self-fulfillment.

Noah—IV
A Model of Worship
————— ■ ● ■ —————

Then Noah built an altar to the Lord, and took of every clean animal and of every clean bird, and offered burnt offerings on the altar (Genesis 8:20, RSV).

It was an act of thanksgiving. Noah gave thanks to God for survival and a safe landing on firm ground. In the later ritual of the Old Testament the burnt offering, which was a complete sacrifice with nothing back for a sacred meal, was to be a lavish way of expressing gratitude to God (2 Chronicles 29:31–33).

One might have envisaged Noah stepping out of the ark and striding away, with his eye on new worlds to explore and conquer. Instead, he paused to give thanks.

What Noah did was also an act of dedication. Later in Genesis Abraham, traveling through the promised land, was to build altars as he went, consecrating himself and the territory to God. He was flying God's flag over it, as it were. If you are involved in some new enterprise in life, let God hear your dedicatory prayers.

It was an act of worship. Noah took samples "of every clean animal and of every clean bird" (Genesis 8:20, RSV) to offer as burnt offerings. It was a token that everything belonged to God. Similarly, in the Old Testament, Sabbath worship was an indication that every day in the week was God's, and the giving of tithes was an admission that all the increase belonged to him. It was this type of burnt offering that Paul used as a metaphor for Christian commitment: "I appeal to you therefore, brethren, by the mercies of God, to present your bodies as a living sacrifice, holy and acceptable to God, which is your spiritual worship" (Romans 12:1, RSV).

Batteries need to be recharged and resources have to be claimed for the next stage of the journey. In Noah's case, as so often in the Old Testament and in the Christian life, worship was the prelude to blessing (Genesis 9:1–7).

Noah: How Does This Apply to Me?
Building for Life
■ ● ■
Rebecca Olson

Many people watched curiously as we tore the roof off our house. When they discovered we were adding a second story, they offered unsolicited advice, telling us we were doing it wrong. Everyone knew a better way.

That isn't unusual. Almost every building project has at least one sidewalk superintendent. I had a hard time dealing with the pressure that their advice generated. If that many people thought we were doing it wrong, maybe we were. Only when I recalled the reasons behind our plans did I feel confident again. Five winters have passed since then and have proved the wisdom of our decision. The crowds were wrong.

The crowd is often wrong. That is as true today as it was in the days of Noah. Following the crowd would certainly have been the path of least resistance. But Noah stood unyielding for one hundred and twenty years against a tide of public opinion. The result was life.

In Genesis 6:9 Noah is identified as a righteous man even before the subject of ark-building surfaced. But Noah's righteousness was not self-made. It was a result of his decision to have a personal relationship with God. Then he continued to make choices that would help him follow the right way. When the crowds began to mock, he was undeterred because his heart and mind were settled on a predetermined course.

Our decision to receive Christ as Savior is the most crucial decision we will ever make. But how well do we make the continuing choices to stay on the right path?

Often we let a crisis or temptation force us to make a hasty choice. Then there usually isn't enough time to weigh carefully all the options. This is why we encourage our teenagers to take a stand before temptation comes along. Young people who decide beforehand not to take drugs or to enter into a sexual relationship will have the added strength of that decision when under pressure.

Rebecca Olson is a homemaker and part-time music teacher. She and her husband, Jon, are the parents of two sons and live near Union Grove, Wisconsin.

Noah had another quality that helped him withstand crowd pressure. He was "blameless among the people of his time" (Genesis 6:9). Noah's outward life matched his inner convictions; his actions were consistent with his words.

With my children, I sometimes fall into the "do what I say, not what I do" trap. It's easier to tell them what I want than to show them. Recently I talked with my sons about not calling people names like "dummy." But how I react the next time a careless driver pulls out in front of me will be a much more powerful lesson than anything I may have said.

Making a decision to follow Christ, and translating that decision into observable action are necessary first steps, but sooner or later we face the crowds. What did Noah do once he had decided to be God's man? In Genesis 6:22 we observe his obedience. God supplied Noah the measurements and a materials list for the ark. By knowing and following the plan, Noah was sure that the finished product would be correct.

Our master plan, the Bible, gives us the general dimensions of how we should live. It provides instructions on how to handle the details.

My husband, an electrician, once came across an interesting blueprint. The plan required a series of light fixtures to be spaced evenly across the ceiling in a large factory. On the blueprint were three different measurements for the spacing—twenty-four feet; twenty-four feet six inches; and twenty-five feet. The architect couldn't decide which of the measurements would space the fixtures evenly, so he wrote them all down. The electricians would have to calculate which was correct.

God is not that kind of architect. He doesn't give us three options and then tell us to figure out the right one on our own. Scripture is rich with God's specific directions. The key is in knowing what they are.

Spending time in God's Word is essential if we want to know his plans. Some days a passage that I have already read time and again seems to leap off the page. This is one way God directs me. I write those verses on cards, and keep them above the kitchen sink. As I do the dishes, I think about the verses.

Recently, I felt left out when a group of women discussed a television series. From what they said I knew that the show was devoid of moral principles, and yet I was tempted to watch it just once in order to feel like part of the group.

Philippians 4:8 went on my card that week. The Lord

directed me to this verse to remind me that I am to think of pure, honest, praise-worthy things. Knowing what God wanted helped me to overcome the temptation to watch a program lacking in these qualities.

Noah's example challenges us in a third way. In 2 Peter 2:5 we read that Noah not only decided to obey God's commands but he also preached righteousness. Noah realized he was the one to influence the crowd, rather than the one who was influenced by it. He established a priority, and then for one hundred and twenty years, day after day, his hands built the ark while his mouth proclaimed salvation.

We have distractions that keep us from focusing on the task of reaching people for Christ. Phones, television, newspapers, and busy schedules can keep our minds and hands so occupied that we lose sight of the real goal—effectively winning the lost.

I learned this lesson from an eight-year-old boy. It was the first hectic morning of Vacation Bible School, and as director I was caught up in ensuring that everything ran smoothly. As I was rushing down the hallway, intent on solving a problem, I felt a tug on my skirt. I kept walking, but the tug came again. I stopped and turned impatiently. There stood Robert, beaming a radiant smile.

"I remember you," he said. "Last year you told me how I could know Jesus as my Savior." Just two sentences, and he dashed off. I stood for a while in that hallway, thinking about priorities.

The crowds of Noah's day were caught up in activity. They were so busy eating, drinking, and marrying that they failed to heed Noah's warnings, and they perished. Noah knew they would. But knowing the outcome didn't stop him from seeing their need and telling them about God's plan.

It takes courage to stand against the crowd. It also takes action. A stand for Christ, a consistent life, and obedience to God's clear instructions will lessen the crowd's influence on us. A heart that longs to see people touched with the saving message of the gospel will strengthen our influence on them.

Few of us can expect to have one hundred and twenty years to accomplish the task of helping to fulfill Christ's Great Commission. Like the ark, it is a monumental building project. But the things we learn from Noah's example can help us in the time we have. Our perseverance is critical, because for us and for those who listen and respond, the result is eternal life.

Noah
Insights for Discovery
■ ● ■

1. Study Genesis 6. With so much evil and corruption abounding around him, why do you think Noah was able to maintain a vital relationship with God?

2. How do you feel when people mock you for following God? How can Romans 6:1–14 encourage you to remain faithful in the face of peer pressure to conform to worldly standards?

3. Read Genesis 6:22; 7:5, 9. Then reflect on John 14:21. What is the relationship between obedience to God and knowing God? How can you show your love for God?

4. Meditate on Genesis 7:24–8:1. Have you ever felt as if God had abandoned you? How do you respond when God remembers you and acts favorably toward you for your faithful service? From Genesis 8:20, what altars of praise have you built to remember what God has done in or through your life?

5. After Noah and his family left the ark, God commanded them to be fruitful and multiply on earth—the same commandment he gave to Adam and Eve. Once God saves us from the penalty of our sin, he desires for us to reproduce ourselves spiritually. Begin praying for a person whom you can nurture in the Christian faith, so he or she can reach others for Christ. (See 2 Timothy 2:2.)

6. What do Genesis 8:20–21 and 1 Timothy 2:1–4 teach you about God's patience? Take time to thank God for his loving-kindness and long-suffering and that he was willing to wait for you to come to him in repentance.

Mary:
Blessed by God

■●■

Marianne Meye Thompson

Mary—I
Servant of the Lord
———— ■●■ ————

"I am the Lord's servant," Mary answered. "May it be to me as you have said" (Luke 1:38).

These familiar words are Mary's response to the angel Gabriel's announcement that she is to bear a son. Gabriel's message was surely unsettling. Mary expressed her puzzlement with the question, "How can this be, . . . since I am a virgin?" (Luke 1:34)

Gabriel replied that the birth of Mary's child would be brought about by God's own Spirit. With God "nothing is impossible," not even that a virgin could have a child. In affirmation of God's power Mary responded, "I am the Lord's servant. . . . May it be to me as you have said" (Luke 1:37–38).

Mary found herself in the company of other men and women who were part of God's ongoing plan. Isaac was born to Sarah and Abraham uncommonly late in their lives (Genesis 21). Samuel's birth to Hannah and Elkanah was an extraordinary gift (1 Samuel 1). John the Baptist was born when Zechariah and Elizabeth were elderly (Luke 1).

In each of these accounts an extraordinary birth became the means by which God continued his plan of salvation. This reminds us of God's power to work through the unpromising circumstances of our lives for his glory and our salvation.

The second part of Mary's reply deserves attention as well. Her statement means, "May it be to me according to your word." God had chosen Mary to bear the Messiah, but Mary had a choice too. When she heard the word of God, she obeyed.

Jesus said, "My mother and brothers are those who hear God's word and put it into practice" (Luke 8:21). In Mary's response to Gabriel we have a model of one who hears the word of God and does it.

Marianne Meye Thompson is Assistant Professor of New Testament at Fuller Theological Seminary in Pasadena, California. She is the author of *The Humanity of Jesus in the Fourth Gospel*. She and her husband, John, have one daughter.

Mary—II
Model of Discipleship
■ ● ■

"Why were you searching for me?" he asked. "Didn't you know I had to be in my Father's house?" But they did not understand what he [meant] (Luke 2:49–50).

Jesus' family came from among the Jews who were poor yet faithful in their observance of Jewish customs. Male Jews were expected to journey to Jerusalem to keep the Passover, and as Joseph fulfilled that obligation, his family accompanied him.

On the trip back to Galilee, Mary and Joseph were unable to find Jesus. When they returned to Jerusalem and found him in the temple, they asked him why he had caused them needless worry. Neither Mary nor Joseph understood his reply.

This story is primarily about Jesus, and secondarily about Mary. Jesus' first words in the gospel of Luke showed that his obedience to God took precedence over his obedience to his earthly parents. In fact, Jesus seemed to have distanced himself from Joseph and Mary.

This story is similar to the account in John 2 where Jesus changed water into wine at the wedding at Cana. When the wine ran out and Mary implored Jesus to help, his reply seemed almost gruff: "Why do you involve me, woman?" (John 2:4). But this was no an impolite form of address, and no lack of love was demonstrated here. Jesus' statement informed Mary that she needed to surrender her maternal claims on him.

Both accounts show Mary as a model disciple who was growing in her understanding of Jesus, although her maternal relationship seemed to impede rather than aid her. This struggle to understand and then to relinquish claims on Jesus is part of the meaning of Simeon's statement: "A sword will pierce your own soul too" (Luke 2:35).

Mary's growth was not without personal pain. Ultimately it culminated in the grief caused by Jesus' death. Yet Mary was not rebuked for her pain or her struggle, because growing to full knowledge of the Son of God constitutes the path of true discipleship.

Mary—III
Part of a New Family
—————— ■●■ ——————

When Jesus saw his mother there, and the disciple whom he loved standing nearby, he said to his mother, "Here is your son," and to the disciple, "Here is your mother" (John 19:26–27).

Of all the stories in the Gospels involving Mary, this is perhaps the most poignant. She stood at the foot of the cross awaiting the death of her Son. Surely this was not the way she had expected it to end.

Again, Jesus rather than Mary was the main character. Even at the moment of death he remained sovereign and in charge. He took the initiative, giving his mother into the charge of "the disciple whom he loved," traditionally identified as John the son of Zebedee. In turn, this disciple was to be as a son to Mary.

This story can be taken simply as an instance of Jesus' love and concern for his mother. Yet perhaps a deeper meaning is here as well. Throughout the Gospels Jesus used the human family as a metaphor for the family of God. He said that those who left their homes and families would receive one hundred times as much in the present age: "homes, brothers, sisters, mothers, children and fields." Those who follow Jesus are welcomed into a new family, the family of "the age to come" (Mark 10:30).

When Jesus said, "My mother and brothers are those who hear God's word and put it into practice" (Luke 8:21), he did not disparage our earthly family ties. Jesus was using the most intimate and common of human relationships to image the heavenly family into which his followers are adopted.

At the foot of the cross Mary and John were given into each other's care. Their new relationship was a participation in and a foretaste of God's new family, made possible by Jesus' death.

Today we can experience that same kind of relationship in the fellowship of the church.

Mary—IV
Early Believer
■●■

They all joined together constantly in prayer, along with the women and Mary the mother of Jesus, and his brothers (Acts 1:14).

Luke mentions Mary as being among the company of early believers. This means that she must have confessed the resurrection of Jesus. The community of faith gathered not because they awaited his resurrection, but because Jesus had already been raised.

Also, Mary was among those who were "constantly in prayer." Throughout the book of Acts Luke drew attention to the devotion of the early Christians, characterizing them as a community which prayed together; Mary was among them.

Mary had not suddenly become a believer in God. In the opening chapter of Luke's Gospel Mary had confessed her willing obedience to God with her words of praise known as the "Magnificat" (Luke 1:46–55). She and Joseph were observant and faithful worshipers, taking Jesus to the temple when he was eight days old and journeying regularly to Jerusalem to celebrate Passover. But among the company of believers after Christ's resurrection, Mary began to understand the fullness of God's plan of salvation as she participated in the community formed by and around the risen Lord.

Mary was a disciple of the Lord, though she had to grow in her knowledge and insight to understand his identity. Mary seems to have come to that fullness of knowledge. From her obedient response following the angel's announcement of Jesus' forthcoming birth to the confession of his resurrection, Mary portrayed for us the path of growing understanding and obedience along which a disciple is to walk.

Mary: How Does This Apply to Me?
Saying "Yes" to God

———— ■ ● ■ ————

Lucinda Secrest McDowell

Hanging up the telephone, I looked at the tiny frame in my hand. One word had been carefully cross-stitched into the fabric: "Yes." Why had my friend Sally chosen that day to give me such a gift? How could she have known that I was struggling with an important decision?

A call had come from three thousand miles away, from a church near San Francisco, California. This church of four thousand had offered me the position of missions director. The job would entail organizing one hundred lay people into task forces, administering a $1 million missions budget, and training church members to go to the mission field.

The task to me seemed a mammoth one. How could they possibly have chosen me for it? Perhaps I had adequate credentials with regard to seminary training and international exposure, but I was still quite young and had never served on a church staff. Was God asking me to leave the security of friends and family for this unknown challenge?

Sunny California seemed like another world as I prayed that cold December day nine years ago. In my Bible study I was reminded of another young woman who had been chosen for something which had seemed far beyond her own abilities. I looked at the tiny frame again. Hadn't Mary said *yes* to God?

Because of her willing response to God, Mary, the mother of Jesus, has become known as the most blessed of all women. Her cousin Elizabeth was one of the first to recognize this when Mary visited her. Elizabeth's baby leaped in her womb, and she exclaimed, "Blessed is she who has believed that what the Lord has said to her will be accomplished!" (Luke 1:45)

We are introduced to Mary when the angel declared that she was chosen by God: "You have found favor with God. You will be with child and give birth to a son, and you are to give him the name Jesus" (Luke 1:30–31). Through the years many people have wondered at God's seemingly unlikely choice for

Lucinda Secrest McDowell is a writer and a broadcaster for Blue Ridge Broadcasting in Black Mountain, North Carolina. She also produces a daily radio news program called "Christians Around the World."

the mother of the Messiah. But how consistent of God to choose "the weak things of the world to shame the strong" (1 Corinthians 1:27).

As I began my new ministry in California, I believed that God had chosen the weakest of his servants to carry out this particular task. I had said "yes," and I believed that I was in the will of God. But in the early months I had difficulty establishing my niche and advocating more mission exposure in the full-orbed ministry of the church. Sometimes the one promise that kept me going was that I had been chosen by God, and I believed that "the one who calls you is faithful and he will do it" (1 Thessalonians 5:24).

Mary was not only chosen but willing to accept God's will for her life. Finding out that she was to be pregnant before the wedding, Mary asked, "How will this be?" (Luke 1:34)

In other kinds of situations I have often asked the Lord, "How will this be?" Just when my own life seems to be ordered and well-planned, God changes my direction. After four years as missions director, with our outreach and training programs established, I was able to have more international contact myself. Life was full. To know what was down the road, all I had to do was to consult my trusty datebook.

Then God asked me to change my plans and marry a widower with three small children. I was filled with both joy and fear at this marvelous gift. My questions to God were answered in much the same way that the angel had responded to Mary: "Nothing is impossible with God" (Luke 1:37).

Through this experience I learned from Mary the most important lesson of all—pure and simple obedience to God. Mary answered, "I am the Lord's servant. . . . May it be to me as you have said" (Luke 1:38). She didn't ask the angel to discuss various options or to debate the practicalities, the timing, or the sense of it all. She merely said, "Yes, I'll do it."

Obeying God usually means turning our backs on the popular or expedient way. We are often vulnerable to being misunderstood or rejected. When we say "yes" to God, of necessity we may need to say "no" to something else.

Saying "yes" to a godly man whom I loved was wonderful. But marriage meant a complete change in my life as I moved to the unfamiliar Pacific Northwest, traded my career for the full-time job of homemaker, and took on the responsibility of adopting and rearing three young children. There were a few people who asked, "Are you crazy?" But, like Mary, I knew in my heart that this "yes" was my own act of obedience to God and that I would be blessed because of it.

It also became important to me to recognize that praise and joy are an integral part of a life committed to Christ. Mary knew this, and her "Magnificat" (Luke 1:46–55) has become one of the most well-loved songs of praise poetry in the Bible.

Today one of the greatest needs in my life is to worship and praise God for his faithfulness to me. Sometimes I become lazy in this spiritual discipline, but increasingly God has opened doors for me to recount, as Mary did, all he has done for me.

Another aspect of Mary's life that has become an example to me is her lifelong commitment to be both lifegiver and nurturer. Mary never stopped being Jesus' mother, even when his ministry took on dramatic or radical proportions. She was not only the mother who gave her body to carry the Baby Jesus, but she spent her whole life nurturing and letting go.

I can imagine a panicky Mary thinking that Jesus was lost in the big city of Jerusalem, only to discover a newly independent son on the verge of manhood (Luke 2:41–52). With two sons in their early teens, I am learning to let go of them and to let them make choices, even mistakes. It is one of the hardest parts of being a nurturer.

When our children are grown, I want to be able to support them as adults, as Mary supported Jesus during the marriage feast. She opened the door for Jesus to turn the water into wine by telling the servants, "Do whatever he tells you" (John 2:5). Our children may never be great or famous in the eyes of the world, but I hope I can encourage them to be all that God created them to be. For me this could include suffering as it did for Mary. It was prophesied of Mary: "A sword will pierce your own soul too" (Luke 2:35). She felt the deep pain of watching her son ridiculed, rejected, and then crucified.

As I reread the story of Mary, I am touched in an even deeper way, for in 1989 God has once again brought blessing to my life. I have had the privilege of being a lifegiver for the first time. Holding our new baby in my arms, I am speechless with awe and wonder. Now I can truly understand why "Mary treasured up all these things and pondered them in her heart" (Luke 2:19).

Mary
Insights for Discovery
—— ■ ● ■ ——

1. Carefully examine Mary's encounter with the angel Gabriel in Luke 1:26–38. Why do you think Gabriel's comment, "You have found favor with God," would have calmed Mary's fears? Does God's Word, especially Ephesians 1:1–14, help to calm your fears?

2. What does Mary's answer (Luke 1:38) tell you about her relationship with the Lord? (See also 2 Samuel 22:31.)

3. Consider the impact on Mary of the baby leaping in Elizabeth's womb when Mary entered the home of Zechariah and Elizabeth (Luke 1:39–45).

4. Note the similarities and differences between Mary's song (Luke 1:46–55) and Hannah's prayer (1 Samuel 2:1–10). Think about what each has to say concerning God's interaction with us.

5. Meditate on Acts 1:1–14, focusing on verse 14. How do you think Christ's crucifixion, resurrection, and ascension affected the prayer life of Mary?

6. Reflect on your relationship with the Lord. (See Psalm 126:3 and Isaiah 63:7.) Write your own song of praise to God, remembering the different ways in which he is involved in your life.

Part IV
Learning to Serve

———— ■●■ ————

Most people speak warmly of mothers, and not just on Mother's Day when we give them a corsage and take them out for brunch. When asked, "Who made the greatest impact on your life?" an amazing number of people choose their mothers. No doubt you've also noticed that professional athletes, when placed in front of a TV camera, immediately shout, "Hi, mom!" Why is this so? I think the answer lies in the fact that mothers are, by definition, givers. They give of their bodies to bring us to birth and to nourish our earliest days. They give of their time and energy to help in our formative years. They do without food if there is not enough to go around, without sleep if someone is sick, and often without recognition for their worrying, caring, and praying. They are servants, and we respect and love them.

Strangely enough, we admire such devotion and sacrifice but find it difficult to emulate. There is nothing new about this. The ancient Greeks despised service. Jesus' disciples were not too enthusiastic about serving, either. You remember when they all arrived at a house and the customary washing of feet ritual was not made available to them. The disciples sat uncomfortably waiting to see what would happen, knowing only that they, personally, had no intention of making anything happen. Then Jesus shamed and startled them all by washing their feet. When Peter objected to having his feet washed, Jesus told him that although he didn't understand what was happening, he soon would. Jesus, in remarkable humility, was preparing people to understand his cross as the means of washing away sin with blood. In both instances, he demonstrated a servant spirit and told his disciples he expected to see the same spirit in them.

While we all revere Christ as our example in such things, there is a tendency for us to excuse ourselves by saying, "Well, of course, he was unique." But Scripture, which we have already seen gives illustrations of human failure, also gives striking examples of humble and effective service. The delightful story of Ruth and Boaz shows two people who knew how to serve. Ruth committed herself to the well-being of her widowed mother-in-law despite her own very real problems, and Boaz served Ruth when other people refused to fulfill their obligations. Incidentally, notice a principle here. Those who are willing to serve in the hour of someone else's need usually find someone to serve them when their crisis time comes.

Another example is Barnabas, surely one of the most delightful of all New Testament characters. He was prepared to encourage people even when it meant going out on a limb for them. It was he who persuaded the Jerusalem church to accept the new convert called Saul of Tarsus, whom they did not trust. He also rescued John Mark from the "spiritual casualty ward" when Paul refused to have him on the team. Try to imagine what the New Testament would be like if Barnabas hadn't rescued Paul and Mark! Lydia, a new convert, needed no prompting to start opening her home and sharing her resources. Aquila and Priscilla were wonderfully supportive of Paul in his arduous lifestyle. What these people teach us is that there is a lot of serving to be done and it can be done by anyone, anytime, anywhere—provided they believe the Master's example is worth reproducing and his expectations are worth fulfilling.

Ruth:
She Takes Refuge in God and Finds Favor
∎●∎
Paul S. Haik

Ruth—I
Her Resolve: Return With Naomi

———— ■●■ ————

"Don't urge me to leave you or to turn back from you. Where you go I will go, and where you stay I will stay. Your people will be my people and your God my God" (Ruth 1:16).

During a time in Israel "when the judges ruled" (Ruth 1:1) and when "everyone did as he saw fit" (Judges 21:25), we see, portrayed in the book of Ruth, a godly family who, despite personal troubles, had faith in the providence of God. The drama unfolds in four acts—one in each chapter of the book.

In act 1, a famine in Israel forces the family to go from Bethlehem in Judah to the land of Moab to search for food. The severity of the famine forces them to stay in Moab at least ten years.

The man, Elimelech ("my God is King"), and his wife, Naomi ("pleasant one"), have two sons. After Elimelech's death, the sons marry Moabite women named Orpah and Ruth. But it isn't long before Naomi's misfortune in losing her husband is compounded by the deaths of both sons, without their leaving sons to carry on the family name.

When Naomi hears that the Lord is providing food for his people in her homeland, she sets out from Moab with her two daughters-in-law to make her way back to Judah. Realizing that she has nothing left for Orpah and Ruth, Naomi suggests that they return to their mothers' homes. Her parting concern for them reveals her faith in the God of Israel. She prays that Jehovah will show them his covenant-keeping love and grace and that the Lord will enable them to find rest in the home of another husband.

Orpah kisses her mother-in-law good-bye, but Ruth clings to Naomi. Then from Ruth's lips comes a beautiful resolve. Ruth adopts Naomi's people and Naomi's God. As the two return to Bethlehem at the beginning of the barley harvest, Naomi experiences the changes from famine to harvest—and her feelings ascend from depression to hope.

Paul S. Haik is a Professor of Bible and Chairman of the Department of Bible at Moody Bible Institute in Chicago, Illinois. He and his wife, Mary, have four grown children.

Her Refuge: Wings of the Almighty
■●■

"May the Lord repay you for what you have done. May you be richly rewarded by the Lord, the God of Israel, under whose wings you have come to take refuge" (Ruth 2:12).

The personal tragedies in act 1 give way in act 2 to God's sovereign provision for Naomi and Ruth as they arrive in Bethlehem. Since Moabites were excluded from the congregation of Israel, Ruth was there by grace. By faith she had adopted the covenant-keeping God of Israel as her God.

We are now introduced to Boaz, a person with great abilities and wealth. He is a close relative of Elimelech, the deceased husband of Naomi. Boaz becomes the instrument of God's blessing in the lives of the two widows.

Ruth takes the initiative and asks Naomi for permission to go into the fields to pick up the grain which is left behind by the reapers. This was God's provision in the Mosaic Law for orphans, widows, and foreigners (Leviticus 19:9–10; 23:22; Deuteronomy 24:19). Ruth finds herself working in a field belonging to Boaz, not by chance, but by divine appointment.

Boaz responds graciously to Ruth. He urges her, "Don't go and glean in another field and don't go away from here. Stay here with my servant girls" (Ruth 2:8). He also commands the men not to touch Ruth, and she is to be given special privileges during working hours.

Overwhelmed by this kindness, Ruth bows down with her face to the ground. She is amazed that she, a foreigner, has found such favor in the eyes of this landowner. But Boaz knows all about Ruth's devotion to her mother-in-law. Ruth's sacrifice, courage, and faithfulness have not gone unnoticed.

The prayer of Boaz, in Ruth 2:12, shows us that he was impressed by her decision to take refuge under the wings of the God of Israel.

This figure of speech denotes God's care for his people. Just as a mother bird protects her young by spreading her wings over them, so the Lord protects his children by providing shelter and security for them.

Ruth—III
Her Request: Marriage to Boaz
———— ■●■ ————

"Who are you?" he asked. "I am your servant Ruth," she said.
"Spread the corner of your garment over me, since you are a
kinsman-redeemer" (Ruth 3:9).

In act 3 of this drama Naomi plays the role of matchmaker as she
suggests a plan for Ruth to cultivate the love of Boaz. If Boaz
had been a brother of Elimelech, the law of levirate marriage (In
a levirate marriage the brother of a husband who dies childless
would marry his widow so that his deceased brother would
have an heir; Deuteronomy 25:5–10) would have obligated him
to marry Ruth. Even though he is not a brother, Boaz as a close
relative can still act as kinsman-redeemer. He can purchase the
property Naomi is forced to sell because of poverty and thus
restore it to the family (Leviticus 25:23–28). Furthermore, the
name of Elimelech can be carried on by an heir through the
marriage of Boaz and Ruth.

Ruth is instructed by Naomi to wash and perfume herself,
put on her best clothes, and go down to the threshing floor of
Boaz. There the landowner stays with his men near the grain,
guarding it so that it is not stolen. Ruth is to uncover his feet,
and lie down.

In the middle of the night Boaz is startled and awakes to see
a woman lying at his feet. Identifying herself as his servant,
Ruth says, "Spread the corner of your garment over me, since
you are a kinsman-redeemer" (Ruth 3:9). There is nothing
improper in their actions. Ruth is requesting a pledge that he
will marry her.

Boaz recognizes the sincerity of Ruth and prays God's
blessing upon her for her kindness not only to Naomi but also
to him. He agrees to her proposal, adding that she is "a woman
of noble character" (Ruth 3:11).

But a legal problem has to be solved before they can be
married. There is a nearer kinsman-redeemer who has the
claim to the property of Elimelech before Boaz. Boaz would
wait until morning and present the proposal to him. If he rejects
it, Boaz vows that he will take care of Noami's property and also
marry Ruth.

Ruth—IV
Her Reward: Redemption by Faith
— ■ ● ■ —

The women said to Naomi: "Praise be to the Lord, who this day
has not left you without a kinsman-redeemer. May he become
famous throughout Israel!" (Ruth 4:14)

The drama in the book of Ruth comes to its climax in act 4. Boaz
enters the gate of the city where business matters were conducted. There he encounters the relative who is first in line as
kinsman-redeemer. Ten men of the elders of the city are called
to witness the transaction.

Boaz informs this closer relative of his rights, reminding
him that he—Boaz—is next in line if the closer relative declines
the option. The relative agrees to the proposal.

It is evident that Boaz wants to marry Ruth because he
mentions the redemption of the property first. Then he reminds his lawful competitor that a kinsman-redeemer has
another obligation in fulfilling that role—he also would have to
marry Ruth to maintain the name of the deceased.

With this turn of events the closer relative declines. The
financial burden of buying the property and also supporting
Ruth and her family would jeopardize his own inheritance.

Boaz is now free to acquire the land and marry Ruth. All the
people in the gate join the elders in pronouncing a prayer of
blessing upon Boaz and Ruth and their offspring. Later the
village women bless the Lord for not leaving Naomi without a
kinsman-redeemer.

The child who is born to Boaz and Ruth is named Obed, and
he becomes the father of Jesse, the father of David. In the
fullness of time a royal Son is born in Bethlehem—Jesus Christ,
the Son of David.

God's providential purpose in the book of Ruth has become
clear. The faith of Ruth was rewarded. She took refuge in God
and found his favor. Through her child Obed and his seed,
Christ would ultimately come into the world. Christ Jesus,
God's Son, was God's provision for the redemption of the
world. The greater Son of David is our Kinsman-Redeemer.

Ruth: How Does This Apply to Me?
Looking for a Kind Word
and a Warm Smile

■●■

Mary Wilken

I'd like some of that meat, please," I said, pointing to what looked like ground beef. Smiling uneasily and hoping this young clerk would help me, I felt conspicuous holding up the line of people behind me.

I couldn't speak much of the language in the European country where my husband and I now lived, but I knew some residents were familiar with English. The clerk apparently understood me, but she looked at me disdainfully and muttered something to her co-worker, making me the brunt of a joke that I couldn't understand. Everyone laughed as I fumbled for the package. The humiliation I felt brought tears of anger and frustration as I fled the store to find refuge in our row house.

As a foreigner, I was painfully aware of my alienation whenever I made a simple trip to the marketplace. During the early weeks of my adjustment, I was often overwhelmed with feelings of rejection and loneliness.

In light of this experience I studied the story of Ruth in the Scriptures. I gained respect for her decision to leave her homeland and to follow Naomi to Israel. Because of my husband's job, I had left the comforts of my homeland to become an alien too. Many people are forced into this status by political upheavals and wars. But Ruth had determinedly clung to Naomi: "Don't urge me to leave you or to turn back from you. Where you go I will go, and where you stay I will stay. Your people will be my people and your God my God" (Ruth 1:16). Ruth was willing to abandon her home, parents, and all that was familiar to become an alien for love's sake.

As a Moabite living in Bethlehem, Ruth faced certain rejection because the Moabites were despised by Israel. But Ruth's reputation quickly spread throughout the countryside, and she

Mary Wilken is a homemaker and a free-lance writer. She and her husband, Terry, have three children. They live in Asheville, North Carolina, where they attend Bent Creek Baptist Church.

became known as a woman of noble character because of her faithfulness and loyalty to Naomi. When Ruth went to work in the fields of Boaz, a close relative of Naomi, her high regard won Boaz's unexpected kindness: "You have given me comfort and spoken kindly to your servant—though I do not have the standing of one of your servant girls" (Ruth 2:13). Boaz made provision for Ruth with food and protection. His kindness was a wonderful encouragement.

Each time I ventured from my new home, I eagerly looked for a kind word or a warm smile. I was surprised at how much these small acts of acceptance meant to me. Very few of the citizens of my new country were as antagonistic as the young grocery clerk. More often I found strangers who were willing to reach out to me with actions of benevolence. I took great comfort in these actions. They eased my feelings of estrangement. I resolved then to remember the potency of such kindnesses, especially when I returned to the United States, where I could reciprocate to internationals struggling to make their home in a new country.

Ruth was also an example to me in her humility and thankfulness. Because she was a foreigner, she was particularly vulnerable as she gleaned the fields. When Boaz told her to stay with his servant girls and commanded his men not to touch her, Ruth bowed down with her face to the ground and exclaimed, "Why have I found such favor in your eyes that you notice me—a foreigner?" (Ruth 2:10) Ruth showed respect to Boaz by calling him lord, and she expressed heartfelt gratitude by acknowledging his generosity to her.

In my outings to the market and nearby stores I soon discovered that many people were willing to help if I approached them with a respectful attitude for their culture. My efforts to speak their language were usually disastrous, and we laughed over my mistakes. But often the attempt won their approval. It wasn't always easy to be so open, and I naturally felt defensive and frustrated. But a sincere desire to learn a new culture opened doors for rewarding friendships. My thankfulness deepened toward the strangers who were willing to reach out to me.

Ruth depended on Boaz to make intercession for her. He stood before the elders and spoke on her behalf, seeking after her welfare. As my husband worked with a Christian organization to prepare for an international conference, we faced problems. We depended on the concern and support of friends at home to pray persistently for us, and their prayers helped us through many difficult times.

One of Ruth's most fortunate days in her new land must have been the day of her marriage to Boaz—her kinsman-redeemer. She became united to his family and was no longer an outsider.

I can imagine the comfort she must have felt, finally having acceptance and fellowship. Families from twenty-eight countries were represented at my husband's office in Europe. Yet, in spite of our cultural differences, and perhaps because of them, we realized a deep sense of kinship in our love for the Lord Jesus: "Consequently, you are no longer foreigners and aliens, but fellow citizens with God's people and members of God's household" (Ephesians 2:19). These Christian friendships became a wonderful place of security for me—a place where I was understood and accepted. Together we shared the pain and joy of being strangers in another land. Membership in God's household while living in a foreign land proved to be a blessed haven.

Ruth became more than a mere member of Boaz's family. His words to her were marvelously fulfilled: "May you be richly rewarded by the Lord, the God of Israel, under whose wings you have come to take refuge" (Ruth 2:12). Ruth, an outcast, became the great-grandmother of David, the great king of Israel. Ruth had been redeemed—into the very lineage of the Messiah—worthy to receive the inheritance reserved for his people.

I too have a Kinsman-Redeemer—Jesus Christ. In my times of painful loneliness as a foreigner I knew I could seek solace from the heavenly Father because of my redemption through Christ. I learned to turn to the sanctuary and stronghold of the Father's love, where I am accepted unconditionally. There I am safe: "My salvation and my honor depend on God; he is my mighty rock, my refuge" (Psalm 62:7).

The humiliation and rejection I experienced in that grocery store in Europe cannot reach me in my hiding place. What a liberating lesson of love! Though my family is often uprooted to live in unfamiliar states and countries, the eternal refuge I find in God is constant.

Ruth
Insights for Discovery
■ ● ■

1. Read the four chapters of the book of Ruth and pick out the details that shed light on Ruth's personality.

2. Given Ruth's background as a Moabitess, reflect on the significance of her decision described in Ruth 1:8–18. In Matthew 1:1–6 notice how God honored Ruth's choice to devote herself to Naomi and to follow him—the God of Israel. What truth does this blessing reveal?

3. Ruth 2:12 reveals a glimpse of Ruth's relationship with the Lord. Meditate on Psalm 91 and on what it means to take refuge in the Lord.

4. Review Ruth 2:1–23 and 3:1–4; take note of the qualities in Boaz that made him an appropriate kinsman-redeemer for Ruth. How do these qualities contrast with the unnamed kinsman-redeemer in Ruth 4:1–8? How do they compare with the qualities that Jesus possesses as our Kinsman-Redeemer?

5. Study Ruth 1:19–22 and Ruth 4:13–22. What effect did Ruth's life have on Naomi?

6. How do you think Ruth fits into the promise given to Abraham in Genesis 12:1–3?

7. Just as Ruth was a blessing to Naomi, we can be a blessing to those around us. Examine 1 John 3:11–18 and 1 John 4:7–21. From what source does love come? How can you live out the command given in John 13:34?

Barnabas:
He Believed God Could Transform Losers Into Winners

■●■

Darrell L. Bock

Barnabas—I
The Giver
■ ● ■

Barnabas (which means Son of Encouragement), sold a field he owned and brought the money and put it at the apostles' feet (Acts 4:36–37).

Among the major figures in the book of Acts are a host of minor characters. Unlike Peter, Stephen, and Paul, these people made brief appearances here and there, not occupying positions of prominence. Yet their labors for the church and God were significant enough to be memorialized in Scripture. Joseph, better known as Barnabas, was one of those figures.

In Acts 4:36 we are introduced to him and learn that he was a Levite. That meant he had been reared in a Jewish home with priestly roots even though he lived in Cyprus far away from Israel. He was so well known to the apostles that they called him Barnabas, which means "Son of Encouragement."

Barnabas gained a reputation for encouraging in many ways. He gave of himself in resources, in friendship, in sharing, and in restoration. In the book of Acts Luke has revealed enough of Barnabas's character for us to understand that he received his name because he encouraged so many.

By providing his resources to the church, Barnabas encouraged the body. The church engaged in sacred work and its members had personal needs which the community as a whole felt responsible to meet. So Barnabas sold a field he owned and, with no strings attached, gave the proceeds to the apostles. The leadership of the church chose how the money would be used.

Barnabas's action stands in sharp contrast to that of Ananias and Sapphira, in Acts 5. They also brought money to the apostles, claiming to have given all their money to the church, when they actually had kept some for themselves. Their deaths are a reminder that God knows when we lie to him.

Barnabas knew the church needed the aid his gift could provide. We can only imagine the encouragement felt by those whose needs were met by Barnabas and his generosity.

Darrell L. Bock is Associate Professor of New Testament Studies at Dallas Theological Seminary in Dallas, Texas. He also serves as minister of the Word at Trinity Fellowship in Richardson, Texas.

Barnabas—II
The Personal Supporter
■ ● ■

Barnabas took him and brought him to the apostles. He told them how Saul on his journey had seen the Lord and that the Lord had spoken to him, and how in Damascus he had preached fearlessly in the name of Jesus (Acts 9:27).

The gospel is designed to call sinners to God. But sometimes when a sinner responds, others are slow to accept his claim of faith. Rather than joy, skepticism often greets conversion.

What an encouragement to Saul to have a greatly respected believer such as Barnabas say, "I saw his conversion and I saw him stand up and proclaim his faith in Jesus." The church knew that Saul had approved Stephen's stoning (Acts 7:56–8:1). He had arrested and imprisoned Christians. Surely he was beyond the reach of the gospel. Heads shook in disbelief when the news arrived that Saul had been converted. Many may have thought he was part of some undercover plot to infiltrate the Christian movement.

Only a respected man could reverse the doubt. Without worrying about his own reputation, Barnabas spoke up for the newly converted former persecutor. He recalled the events of Saul's conversion. He told of Saul's vigorous defense of Jesus in the synagogues of Damascus (Acts 9:19–22).

After Barnabas spoke, Saul was accepted. Imagine the encouragement Saul must have felt when Barnabas personally supported him in the midst of skepticism.

Barnabas—III
The Evangelist-Teacher

■●■

They sent Barnabas to Antioch. When he arrived and saw the evidence of the grace of God, he was glad and encouraged them all to remain true to the Lord with all their hearts. He was a good man, full of the Holy Spirit and faith, and a great number of people were brought to the Lord (Acts 11:22–24).

These verses contain one of the longest descriptions we have of Barnabas. The church at Antioch began to share the gospel with the Greeks, an unprecedented move. The church in Jerusalem sent one of its most respected members, Barnabas, to examine this innovative expansion of the gospel's audience and to provide guidance to the new churches.

Barnabas led the church to reach out to others as many more came to the Lord. His concern was not simply that people were saved. Evangelism did not stop with conversion—evangelism was the start of a relationship with the living God, a relationship which needed to be encouraged.

These new relationships required time and attention. They flourished when those involved were faithful. When Barnabas arrived at a church filled with new believers, he rejoiced at what God had done. He encouraged the new Christians to remain true to God with all their heart—to be dedicated totally in their walk with God.

They heard his message, and the church continued to draw others to the Lord as they demonstrated their commitment to God in their lives. Barnabas encouraged others both through declaring the gospel and by calling on others to walk hand in hand with their gracious God.

Barnabas—IV
The Restorer
—— ■ ● ■ ——

They had such a sharp disagreement that they parted company. Barnabas took Mark and sailed for Cyprus (Acts 15:39).

Sometimes we think that spiritual people don't become angry at each other, but Scripture is more realistic than that.

Paul, whom Barnabas had endorsed, had a strong difference of opinion with Barnabas about Mark. Mark, Barnabas's cousin, had journeyed with Paul and Barnabas before but had returned to Jerusalem (Acts 12:25; 13:13). Paul did not want to risk another failure by taking Mark along again. A sharp disagreement resulted.

Despite their differences, Paul and Barnabas worked out a solution that was a compromise. Barnabas and Mark undertook their mission, while Paul went his own way. Later in life Paul echoed Barnabas's faith in Mark when he urged the Colossians to receive Mark if he came to them (Colossians 4:10).

Mark must have been greatly encouraged when Barnabas defended him before the apostle. Years later Mark was still ministering, and he wrote the Gospel that bears his name.

Barnabas certainly was an encourager. He encouraged by helping those who once had failed. Whether giving his own resources, providing personal support, spreading the gospel and encouraging a believer's walk, or restoring someone who had failed by showing confidence in him, Barnabas touched the people to whom he ministered. His ministry of encouragement often transported them from the depths of rejection or despair to the heights associated with knowing and serving God. Many experienced victory in their walk with God because of the ministry of Barnabas.

Barnabas, the Son of Encouragement, is an example of what we can accomplish when we encourage others by serving them and pointing them toward the living God.

Right Shoes, Wrong Attitude
■ ● ■
Christine Wood

"With such incompetent salesclerks, it's a wonder this store isn't bankrupt," I snapped. The flush on her face deepened as I handed back the excess change she had given me.

I grabbed my parcel from her trembling hand and swung away.

My husband awaited me outside, and I expected a rebuke for lateness. Instead Douglas asked, "What's wrong? You look all frayed at the edges."

So I told him about the irritating salesclerk. "First, she brought me the wrong shoes, although I had clearly indicated which style I wanted," I said. "Then, when she got the style right, she brought me black shoes instead of blue. In the end she produced the right style and color, but they were the wrong size."

Douglas laughed, but I felt too harassed to see the humor. "That's what comes of leaving things to the last minute," he commented.

He was right, of course, but the wisdom of his remark was lost on me, brimming over as I was with blame for that salesclerk. Home at last, I took my new outfit from the closet and dressed for the party to which we were invited.

The shoes I had bought looked exactly right, yet I felt oddly deflated as I looked at my reflection in the bedroom mirror.

All evening the shoes mocked me, making it hard to join in the festivities. Each time I looked at them they confronted me with my shortcomings: You were rude to that salesclerk. You could see how anxious she was to rectify her mistakes!

With relief I at last said good-night to our hostess. My feet ached, and I could not get the new shoes off fast enough. As I shut them behind the closet door, I also shut the salesclerk out of my mind and went to bed. But it proved a restless night with only fitful sleep.

Sunday morning our minister was away at a youth camp,

Christine Wood was the British Editorial Associate for *Decision* magazine. She is a free-lance writer and has published seventeen children's books. She and her husband, Douglas, make their home in Surbiton, Surrey, England.

and I looked forward to hearing insights from a student preacher. I wasn't disappointed.

The young visitor announced his text from Acts 4:36 (NASB): "Joseph, a Levite of Cyprian birth, who was also called Barnabas by the apostles (which translated means, Son of Encouragement)."

"The Bible tells us that Barnabas 'was a good man, and full of the Holy Spirit and of faith,'" (Acts 11:24, NASB), the student preacher began, "and I want us to notice how that goodness and faith worked out in his life."

He explained that Barnabas was generous, courageous, humble, and painstaking, yet his greatest gift was encouragement. He was a man with a kind word for all, especially to the slow, the disillusioned, the downhearted, and the failures.

The preacher's words began to flow over my head. Instead of his face, I saw the face of yesterday's flustered salesclerk. Who was I to call her incompetent? How dared I judge her harshly and speak in that rude, ill-tempered way? Had I forgotten that I once was slow and awkward and considered the dullest pupil in the class?

At ten years old I was often in trouble for laziness and lack of attention. Lessons bored me—until the day that Sister Monique came to the convent school I attended. This young nun was French. She knew little English, but taught us to sew by sitting beside us and demonstrating what to do. Maybe she sensed my feelings of awkwardness and rejection; she often devoted extra time to teaching me new embroidery stitches.

One day Sister Monique smiled at my handiwork and said, "It is well, Christine, it is very well." Those few words in broken English lifted me as if on eagle's wings.

Because Sister Monique encouraged me instead of belittling my grubby, clumsy needlework, I began to work harder in her class and in others. And my school grades improved considerably.

"Yes, Mark was a failure, but Barnabas encouraged him and gave him a second chance." The young preacher raised his voice and jolted me back to the present. "Had it not been for that Son of Encouragement, the apostle Paul could never have later said, 'Mark is useful to me in my missionary work.' And who knows, but for the encouragement that Barnabas gave him, Mark may never have written the Gospel that bears his name."

"You're very quiet," my husband said when we emerged into the sunshine.

"I'm thinking hard," I replied. "I'd never realized that encouragement is one of God's gifts. It costs so little, yet it can lift someone from the depths of despair and defeat and give him the courage to press on and try again."

"Yes, Barnabas did a lot for Mark," my husband replied, but I was not thinking about Mark.

I was remembering Sister Monique and how my talents had blossomed in the warm climate of her encouragement. I was also getting my attitude straightened out. I knew that I owed that salesclerk an apology.

"Encouragement costs so little," I had said, but in practice that was not entirely true. It had cost Barnabas a dissention with Paul, his friend and co-worker. I also needed to heal a breach and apologize before I could offer encouragement to the girl on my heart and conscience.

The next morning pride got in the way. I had a string of excuses why I could not return to the shoe store: Monday was wash day, wasn't it? The kitchen floor needed cleaning; the refrigerator required defrosting.

All the excuses added up to the one fact that I was reluctant to face that salesclerk. The inner tussle continued and eventually drove me to my knees in prayer—a prayer that God answered by giving me the the strength and ability I lacked.

In all the hassle of buying the shoes, I had forgotten to ask for a tube of blue shoe cream. My forgetfulness proved a blessing in disguise, for when I returned to the store, the same clerk served me.

"Can I help you, madam?" she asked eagerly.

"Yes, but first I want to apologize for being so angry and impatient with you last Saturday," I replied.

"You . . . you don't have to apologize to me, ma'am," the surprised clerk said. "Why should you when I got everything wrong?"

"It wasn't deliberate. You served me so willingly that I know you really wanted to please," I explained. "Keep trying and you'll become an excellent salesclerk. Experience teaches us all."

Stars seemed to shine in the clerk's eyes, and her smile set my heart aglow. Did those few words of encouragement, sincerely spoken, make her day? I like to think so. It certainly made mine to pass along encouragement such as I had once received as an awkward schoolgirl.

Barnabas
Insights for Discovery
─────── ■●■ ───────

1. From Acts 9:26–27, contrast the reaction of the disciples with the behavior of Barnabas after Saul's conversion. (The proof of Barnabas's belief in Saul came not when he spoke highly of him, but when he went and brought him to the apostles.)

2. Study Barnabas's spiritual and ministry credentials in Acts 11:22–24.

3. Examine how the commitment of Barnabas and Paul to proclaim the gospel and to minister to believers didn't diminish in the heat of spiritual warfare (Acts 13:49–14:28).

4. Reflect on how Barnabas may have felt leaving his good friend and co-laborer, Paul, in Acts 15:36–41, to go instead with Mark. Think about that parting from Mark's perspective.

5. Jesus apprenticed his disciples by having them with him (Mark 3:14). In light of that, consider what Mark must have learned by being with Barnabas (Acts 12:25; 15:39).

6. To appreciate the ministry of encouragement more, study these verses in Proverbs: 12:25; 15:23; 17:17; 18:24, and 27:17. (Also look at Galatians 6:10 and Hebrews 10:24–25.)

7. From 1 Samuel 18:1–4 and John 15:13, meditate on the sacrifice of a friend.

Lydia:
The Career Woman With a Heart Open to God

─── ■●■ ───

Manfred T. Brauch

Lydia—I
Active in the Marketplace
———— ■●■ ————

We went outside the city gate to the river, where we expected to find a place of prayer. We sat down and began to speak to the women who had gathered there. One of those listening was a woman named Lydia, a dealer in purple cloth from the city of Thyatira, who was a worshiper of God (Acts 16:13–14).

Who was Lydia? First, she was part of a group of women who had gathered in "a place of prayer." We do not know precisely what her religious background was. But she was a person who recognized that human ability is insufficient for facing life's tasks. The act of praying is a recognition of dependence upon our Creator. Prayer opens us to God's will and purposes.

Second, she was a dealer in the purple dye and cloth for which the town of Thyatira in western Asia Minor was famous. She had apparently established residence in Philippi.

A common misconception among Christians is that God's exclusive purpose for women is that they be nurturers and caregivers in the home. The example of Lydia, and of numerous other women throughout the Bible, demonstrates that God has gifted both women and men for involvement in the broad range of human activities.

God's purpose, however, is that involvement in the marketplace of life does not crowd out the critical need for the parents' nurture of their children, as well as attention to the spiritual aspects of life, namely our relationship with God. Though a career woman, Lydia did not allow her career to consume her.

Third, Lydia was a "worshiper of God," a term referring to devout Gentiles whom the Jews called "God-fearers" (Acts 10:2). These were Gentiles who left behind their polytheistic practices and accepted the ethical monotheism of the faith of Israel. When the gospel was largely rejected in the synagogues, it was among the God-fearing Gentiles where the Word of the Lord took hold. Lydia was a result of God's promise that light should come to the Gentiles (Isaiah 42:6).

Manfred T. Brauch is Professor of Biblical Theology at Eastern Baptist Theological Seminary in Philadelphia, Pennsylvania. He has written numerous articles and four books, including *Hard Sayings of Paul*, published by InterVarsity Press, 1989.

Lydia—II
Active in Seeking God
───── ■●■ ─────

The Lord opened her heart to respond to Paul's message (Acts 16:14).

Lydia had already emerged from heathenism and become a worshiper of the God of Israel. But her journey toward the abundant life was still in its infancy.

In the midst of a busy life as a career woman, Lydia took time to grow. She invested the time to listen to Paul and Silas. She could have been satisfied with the faith she already possessed. She could have concluded that what she knew and understood about the sovereign Lord and his will was sufficient. But Lydia was a seeker. Her limited knowledge of truth about God and herself challenged her to pursue deeper truth. Listening is always the first step toward greater understanding. It was Lydia's seeking heart and listening ear which made her receptive to the message about Jesus.

The statement in the text which speaks of the Lord opening Lydia's heart does not mean that the door of her heart was forced open by God. God does not coerce us to know and worship him. What this language about "opening hearts" does affirm is that, in the final analysis, salvation is God's action from start to finish. It cannot be secured by good behavior or religious ceremonies or pious achievements. Nor can God finally be found by the exercise of our rational faculties.

God cultivates the soil of our hearts and drops in the seeds. It is God who reaches toward us and calls us into relationship with himself. And it is that relentless quest to bring a lost humanity home to himself which confronted Lydia and called her to decide.

Her heart was touched by the Good News of Jesus. The divine initiative had come to its conclusion. Now it was Lydia's turn. The seed had been planted. Into what kind of soil had it fallen? That was the decision which Lydia was to make. She responded with her life, and thus took a giant step toward the abundant life which Jesus promised (John 10:10).

Lydia—III
Active in Obedience
————— ■ ● ■ —————

She and members of her household were baptized (Acts 16:15).

Lydia's openness to the Good News and her positive response to it had numerous consequences. From this passage and many others in the New Testament we see that salvation is deeply personal, but not individualistic. The transformation of one's life has an impact on the totality of that life: values, goals, relationships. Lydia's new faith was contagious. It led to the conversion of her entire household.

Several incidents in the life of the early church show that "household conversions" were not unusual (Acts 11:14; 16:31–33). The gift of new life cannot be bottled up; it must find its way into our relationships. And the most natural and primary arena is that of our families and the people with whom we are in regular contact.

Yet, these also can present the most difficult situations for the sharing of our faith and the living of it, because our flaws and failings are obvious. The people near and dear to us can see quickly the discrepancies between our faith affirmations and our living.

Lydia was apparently the head of her household. We can conclude that she was either unmarried or a widow. Her household, in addition to possible children, would have included servants and other dependents, perhaps even some of her co-workers and the women who were with her at the place of prayer. As a person of authority, her new faith made an impact. She, together with her household, was baptized.

Lydia's household became the first house-church in Greece. According to Acts 16:40, after Paul and Silas were released from prison, they went to Lydia's house to meet with the Christians there. Lydia's status as a leading career woman who had been transformed and energized by the gospel had quickly become the vehicle for the work of God's Spirit in the creation of a community of God's people.

Lydia—IV
Active in Hospitality
———— ■●■ ————

She invited us to her home. "If you consider me a believer in the Lord," she said, "come and stay at my house." And she persuaded us (Acts 16:15).

It is eminently true that we are known by our fruits. Every good work is evidence of the fruit of the Spirit (Matthew 12:33; Colossians 1:10). It is one thing to confess that Jesus Christ is Lord of my life. It is quite another to bring that Lordship to bear on the way in which that life is lived.

These truths are demonstrated in Lydia's response to the gospel. It led her to faith and to action. She gave practical proof of the authenticity of her conversion by inviting relative strangers to her home. This is love in action in a concrete, specific way: she extended hospitality.

Gracious hospitality to strangers and travelers is a distinguishing mark of God's people throughout the Old Testament. In the book of Job we read that one of the evidences of his faithfulness to God was that "no stranger had to spend the night in the street, for my door was always open to the traveler" (Job 31:32).

The New Testament continues to lift up this good work. Being open to strangers, said Jesus, is a sign that one is a member of the kingdom of God (Matthew 25:35). Peter and Paul mentioned hospitality as a manifestation of the Spirit's gifting (1 Peter 4:9–10) and a result of offering one's life to the service of God (Romans 12:13). And in 1 Timothy 3:2 we read that hospitality is especially enjoined upon leaders in the church.

The extension of Lydia's hospitality seemed to have flowed naturally and joyfully from her new and vital faith. Her conversion was real. Her faith bore fruit. The openness of Lydia's heart to the Lord led to the openness of her home and the caring for others. In this she became, as the later converts in Thessalonica, "an example to all the believers" (1 Thessalonians 1:7, NASB).

Lydia: How Does This Apply to Me?
I Didn't Have the Time
■●■
Dorris J. Gillam

My resistance stiffened. From the pulpit our pastor admonished the congregation: "Remember. You have been given an opportunity by God to extend the hospitality of your home to this visiting evangelist. Open your hearts and the doors of your homes to him, just as Lydia did for the apostle Paul in Thyatira." Everything the pastor said collided with what I was thinking—I was just too busy.

To begin with, who was Lydia, where was Thyatira, and what did Lydia have to do with Paul? My thoughts churned, but the answer remained the same: *I still don't have the time!*

I began to mutter to myself: "Teaching is a full-time career, and I always have the housework waiting for me at the end of each day. My two teen-aged sons, one in a wheelchair, require many hours each week. This leaves little time to entertain anyone, much less this visitor."

Throughout Sunday afternoon the pastor's words echoed through my mind. I knew God was speaking to me, yet I resisted. Excuses readily surfaced every time I considered the pastor's appeal. This inner conflict grew until I finally picked up the Bible to search for Scripture concerning Lydia.

Lydia is mentioned briefly in Acts 16:14–15. This short passage contains a wealth of information, yet it does not detail Lydia's profound influence on the Christian faith in Europe.

Lydia sold purple cloth in Thyatira, a small town considered by some historians to be unimportant. Purple-dyed cloth was a rare commodity and became a symbol of nobility in the ancient world.

It is thought that each Sabbath Lydia left the city to worship with the Jewish population along the banks of the Gangites River. It was here that Paul came to preach the salvation message to the small gathering along the river bank. Lydia listened to Paul and, because her heart was open to the call of the gospel, she responded and accepted Christ as her Savior.

Dorris J. Gillam is a special educator. She and her husband, Kermit, are the parents of two children and live in Potosi, Missouri. They attend Potosi Southern Baptist Church.

Lydia extended her hospitality to Paul and his followers while they were in Thyatira. Through this one generous gesture, Lydia became the instrument for the conversion of her entire household to Christianity and the establishment of the first Christian church in Europe.

Lydia was an ordinary woman, yet God used her in an exceptional manner. Ordinary people can be used in the most extraordinary manner by the Lord. God then supplies the power to succeed in the tasks he places before us.

What began with one busy career woman who extended the hospitality of her home to strangers in her land had far-reaching implications for the rest of the world. Our pastor had appealed for hospitality for a visitor. "Lord," I began to pray, "if you are speaking to my heart and desire me to open my home to this evangelist, then help me to heed your call and act accordingly. Help me to find a way to minister to his needs."

After discussing this project from several angles, my family and I agreed to cooperate on our "Lydian Plan." I called our pastor and volunteered our services. We would bathe our efforts with daily prayer. Each family member would be responsible for a particular phase of the project. The chosen tasks would match our talents and skills as individuals within our family.

Phase one included preparing a room for the evangelist which would be ideal for sleep and, after adding a desk, lamp, typewriter, and a few other office supplies, suitable for additional duties and activities.

My sons took on the responsibility of thoroughly cleaning the room and moving in the desk and accessories. Within three days the room sparkled. Each night I could hear them quizzing each other to see if anything had been overlooked and making plans for the next day's chores.

My husband planned the various church-related activities to be conducted during the evangelist's stay. He outlined everything on a large sheet of paper. Then he added the week's agenda which included speaking engagements and several dining invitations. He coordinated the church services with these outside engagements. He included time for daily prayer and meditation.

My tasks encompassed planning the meals—including where, when, and who would attend, serve, and prepare the meals. The schedule that my husband had prepared helped me decide how many meals were required. Then I planned a specific menu for each meal.

Many women in my Sunday school class expressed a willingness to serve. I placed calls asking for food on specific days. Several women would combine their efforts to provide one meal. I repeated the process until each meal had been planned. Other church members would also assume the responsibility of acting as host and hostess for me while I was at work.

As the planning week drew to a close, our family gained a new bond because we had worked as a team. It was satisfying to know that our entire family had taken an active role in every phase from planning to execution, and as a result I did not experience those last-minute jitters which usually accompany the anticipation of guests.

Our family was ready. Our church had been actively praying for the success of the coming week. The way had been prepared for the evangelist.

The next week flew by. We discovered that our planning and organization, coupled with everyone's cooperation which kept the itinerary from becoming a burden to any one person, were the keys to a successful venture.

At the next women's meeting we discussed our cooperative effort. My overall impression was one of satisfaction in knowing that we had completed a job and that we had done it well. Our women's organization wrote the "Lydian Plan" as a work booklet and used it as a guideline for hospitality.

Every month a new hostess assumed the duties for visitors. The outline included a prayer list, a monthly church calendar of events, a list of church groups, a list of volunteers to call upon for food or chauffeur services, an entertainment committee, and a complete church membership roster. The chairwoman is responsible for keeping the hospitality information current before passing it along to the next hostess. It was a learning experience for all of us.

I'm still as busy as ever, but I am acutely aware of the rewards of giving and in carrying out my responsibilities to God. Often I find myself looking for opportunities to serve God and doing things I never thought possible. God's wealth is limitless, just as my willingness to serve him must be limitless.

Lydia
Insights for Discovery
────── ■●■ ──────

1. From Proverbs 31:10–27, what is attractive about the wife (woman) of noble character?

2. Study Acts 16:11–15. What does this passage reveal about the importance and effectiveness of personal evangelism in the marketplace? Get together with a Christian friend or an associate at work and pray faithfully for your colleagues.

3. When you're witnessing to someone who is religious and claims he or she is a Christian, what do you say?

4. How is salvation God's action? How did God open the door of your heart?

5 Is it difficult for you to witness to members of your family? Why, or why not? What steps can you take to help them come to Christ?

6. Compare Acts 16:40 with Acts 2:42–47. Now read Hebrews 10:23–25. What is the value of a small group Bible study or fellowship? If you're not taking part in one, join one—or start one at your church. What have been some of the times you have been encouraged the most by Christian friends?

7. Meditate on Colossians 1:24–25. How can we become servants in our churches? Can you show hospitality to someone by inviting them to your home?

Priscilla and Aquila:
A Couple Who
Ministered Together
— ■●■ —

Murray J. Harris

Priscilla and Aquila—I
Committed to One Another
——— ■ ● ■ ———

There he met a Jew named Aquila, a native of Pontus, who had recently come from Italy with his wife Priscilla, because Claudius had ordered all the Jews to leave Rome. Paul went to see them, and because he was a tentmaker as they were, he stayed and worked with them (Acts 18:2–3).

When Paul arrived in Corinth from Athens in the fall of A.D. 50, he met a Christian couple whose occupation was the same as his—making tents. Aquila was an immigrant Jew from Pontus on the Black Sea. His wife, Priscilla, was not a Jew but was probably a member of an aristocratic Roman family. She may have been a Jewish proselyte before she found Christ.

Aquila and Priscilla are always mentioned together, never separately. This couple seems to have possessed a single mind. When the Roman emperor Claudius issued the edict in A.D. 49 that compelled all Jews to leave Rome, the Roman Priscilla left Italy with her Jewish husband and settled in Corinth. There they established a new branch of their business.

As we trace this couple's later movements from Corinth to Ephesus, back to Rome, and finally to Ephesus again, we see them side by side, toiling at their craft, adjusting to new situations and creating new circles of friends. Always they were involved in Christian service. There was no pulling in opposite directions, no contention over travel plans, no pursuit of separate goals. They were one in marriage and one in Christ. They acted in unison because they were committed to one another in Christian love and marital fidelity.

The apostolic age affords no clearer example of the positive spiritual influence of a Christian marriage and a Christian home. Aquila and Priscilla acted in unison as they served together.

Murray J. Harris is Professor of New Testament Exegesis and Theology at Trinity Evangelical Divinity School, Deerfield, Illinois. He and his wife, Jennifer, have two children. They live in Lake Forest.

Priscilla and Aquila—II
Committed to God's Truth
——— ■●■ ———

He began to speak boldly in the synagogue. When Priscilla and Aquila heard him, they invited him to their home and explained to him the way of God more adequately (Acts 18:26).

In this verse Luke is referring to Apollos, a Jew from Alexandria who was "a learned man, with a thorough knowledge of the Scriptures. He . . . spoke with great fervor and taught about Jesus accurately, though he knew only the baptism of John" (Acts 18:24–25).

When Priscilla and Aquila heard this eloquent and learned professor engage the Jews in public debate in the synagogue at Ephesus, they were deeply impressed by his ability and potential as a Christian communicator. However, they noticed that he lacked any knowledge of baptism in the name of Jesus Christ.

Instead of comparing Apollos unfavorably with Paul or criticizing him for his limited understanding of Christian doctrine, the couple invited him to their home so that the three of them could talk in depth about "the way of God." It is a tribute both to the tactfulness of Priscilla and Aquila and to the humility of Apollos that a distinguished Jewish Christian scholar was willing to learn from a humble Christian couple.

Only because Priscilla and Aquila had advanced beyond the basic elements of Christian truth were they able to explain to Apollos God's way in greater detail. We can share with others only what we already know. The Bible is God's truth. We mature as Christians by reading and obeying the Bible. And like Priscilla and Aquila we can multiply our influence for God's kingdom by identifying those who are open to receive further instruction in Christian truth and then teaching them with graciousness and tact.

Priscilla and Aquila—III
Committed to God's Work
——— ■ ● ■ ———

The churches in the province of Asia send you greetings. Aquila and Priscilla greet you warmly in the Lord, and so does the church that meets at their house (1 Corinthians 16:19).

Paul wrote 1 Corinthians from Ephesus where he ministered for about three years. During this time he probably lived in the home of Aquila and Priscilla and worked with them at tent-making, as he had done earlier in Corinth. So it was natural for him to name them specifically as he related greetings to the Christians in Corinth from the groups in and around Ephesus.

Priscilla and Aquila demonstrated their hospitality by opening their homes in Corinth and Ephesus. The New Testament teaches that showing hospitality is an important contribution Christians can make to God's work. In 1 Peter 4:9, Peter says, "Offer hospitality to one another without grumbling." Paul encourages us to "practice hospitality" (Romans 12:13) as eagerly as a hunter pursues his quarry, not letting it escape. And the author of Hebrews surprises us with the command: "Do not forget to entertain strangers, for by so doing some people have entertained angels without knowing it" (Hebrews 13:2). Hospitality is not only a Christian duty but a privilege that brings unexpected benefits.

But Priscilla and Aquila found another use for their home. Not only was it their place of business, a place where private Christian teaching took place, and a home open to entertain guests, but their home was also a center for worship where one of the household churches in Ephesus met. When this couple later moved to Rome, they again made their home a place for the Lord's people to meet.

In turn, we should make our homes available for God's work—not only for church-related meetings or for visitors, but also as a refuge for those with desperate physical or spiritual needs (Matthew 25:35–36).

Priscilla and Aquila—IV
Committed to God's Servants
■●■

Greet Priscilla and Aquila, my fellow workers in Christ Jesus.
They risked their lives for me. Not only I but all the churches
of the Gentiles are grateful to them (Romans 16:3–4).

From Corinth Paul wrote the epistle to the Romans. By this time
Priscilla and Aquila were back in Rome. Romans 16 contains a
long list of greetings from the apostle, and his stalwart friends
Priscilla and Aquila top the list.

Paul honored this couple by calling them his fellow workers in the service of the Lord. They had worked harmoniously
with one another and with the apostle. Their devotion to one
another did not make them self-centered. Rather, from the firm
base of their mutual loyalty, they were able to reach out to
others in friendship and service. They were able to offer Paul,
a single man, the benefits of a man's comradeship and a
woman's friendship in circumstances that were totally above
suspicion. One of God's choicest gifts to a single Christian
worker is the shelter of a Christian home where there is a ready
and permanent welcome, constant encouragement, and sympathetic listeners.

The friendship of Priscilla and Aquila for Paul was not
merely a "fine-weather" relationship. Paul said that "they
risked their lives" for him. We don't know when this occurred,
but we know that Priscilla and Aquila earned the gratitude of
all the churches of the Gentiles for their willingness to die so
that Paul's life might be spared. Their actions showed they had
learned the lesson that commitment to the Lord involves
commitment to servants of the Lord (2 Corinthians 8:5).

And one of the best gifts we can offer our pastors and their
families is our unfailing and sacrificial friendship. Then we
become worthy successors of Priscilla and Aquila, a couple
who ministered together and who were committed to one
another, to God's truth, to his work, and to his servants.

Priscilla and Aquila: How Does This Apply to Me?
Serving Together
———— ■●■ ————
Mary K. Kasting

My husband, Art, and I had made a purchase last year in a shop in Gatlinburg, Tennessee. While awaiting change, I commented to the clerk, "We're going to use these dishes for our anniversary dinner."

"What anniversary?" he asked.

"Our forty-fifth anniversary, Christmas Day!" Art replied.

Looking at my husband, then pointing at me, the clerk chortled, "You mean you've been married to this same woman for forty-five years?"

"Yes," Art cheerily replied, "and loving every moment of it!"

The clerk threw his hands in the air. "Incredible!" he laughed.

By today's standards it is incredible! We are living in a world of fractured relationships.

God's Word gives us an excellent picture of a successful marriage in the record of Aquila and Priscilla. Laboring together as tentmakers and teachers, theirs was an extraordinary husband-wife ministry. The lives of this devoted couple demonstrate the importance of a firm foundation for a lasting, fruitful relationship. Their foundation was Jesus Christ.

Our own marriage was also built on the foundation of Jesus Christ. I remember when Art brought a handmade engagement ring to me. Neatly engraved triangles encircled the band. "The eternal triangle?" I asked.

"Not the one the dictionary describes," Art answered. "The base line is God who brought us together—our Foundation. You are one side. I am the other. We are connected through faith in Jesus Christ, pointing us to our ultimate goal—heaven. The ring is circular, endless, indicating eternity."

This ring was a symbol of our personal solid foundation. While the devil and the world push and tug at the triangle from all sides, faith is the vehicle that keeps it unbroken. With the

Mary K. Kasting is a homemaker and a free-lance writer. She and her husband, Arthur, have four grown children. They live in Indianapolis, Indiana, and attend Calvary Evangelical Lutheran Church.

solid foundation of Jesus Christ, a husband and wife are able to build a life of ministry together. Priscilla and Aquila reach down through the ages and illustrate how to minister today.

Jesus was first priority in the lives of Priscilla and Aquila, who were well versed in the Scriptures. When our four children were small, I was swamped with household duties and never had enough time to complete any task. It was a time of spiritual dryness in my life. During this situation our pastor came to call.

Our church was beginning a new in-depth Bible study course. The pastor was searching for members to take the two-year teacher training class and later to serve as instructors when all congregational members and friends would be involved. Training would require three hours each week, year round, with many outside reading assignments plus memorization and quizzes. Upon completion of the course, teaching assignments of at least two years would follow, along with additional courses in the future.

"Impossible!" was my initial response.

"Please," the pastor encouraged, "will you and Art pray about it and talk it over together?"

This new opportunity posed as a monumental interruption into my already disorganized day. However, a stirring began in my heart. Later that night I picked up our Bible, something I had not done recently.

While reading the gospel of Mark, a particular verse penetrated my heart: "Jesus said unto him, If thou canst believe, all things are possible to him that believeth" (Mark 9:23, KJV).

Art sat down beside me and asked, "Remember the prayer we wrote in the Bible the night we bought it?"

Turning to the worn page, we read aloud, "Grant us, dear Lord, sufficient wisdom to do thy will, and faithfully follow, word for word, the teachings written here in thy Holy Word."

The next morning we called our pastor and said "yes." The result of this decision meant a change in our lives. Our faith began to grow. Dealing with the complexities of daily living was easier because of prayer. Our self-reliant attitude was given over to trusting God. And God, now able to use us for his purposes, gave us opportunity to minister together.

Like Priscilla and Aquila, we opened our home to those wanting to know more about the Christian faith. As we taught others about the Word, we learned to trust in the Lord for the results of witnessing.

One woman who came to our home Bible study remarked, "I came to listen, not participate or read aloud. I can't do that in front of people so don't call on me to pray."

During the two-year study we saw a remarkable change take place in her. One evening she asked, "May I have the closing prayer?" With that she asked Jesus to come into her heart. Art and I prayed with her. She then closed with a moving prayer. Some time later she called to tell us that she was leading a Bible study group in a nursing home and that one of the residents had accepted Christ as Savior.

One evening Art and I visited the hospital where a seriously ill friend of ours was dying. We sat in silent prayer at his bedside. His fiancee burst into the room and dropped to the floor in front of us. Grasping my hands, she tearfully pleaded, "I've heard you say he's going to heaven and he will live forever with Jesus. Please, tell me how!"

As I tightly held her hands, the Holy Spirit gave me the words to speak. A Bible verse came to my mind and I quoted it to the distraught young woman: "For God so loved the world that he gave his only Son, that whoever believes in him should not perish but have eternal life" (John 3:16, RSV). Art and I prayed with her, and God's peace enveloped us as the young woman asked Jesus into her heart as her Lord and Savior. The young man died that night.

Commitment and a willingness to serve are two more characteristics of Priscilla and Aquila. In Acts 2:18 we read that they are sailing for Syria with Paul on a new mission. Paul later relates, in the book of Romans, that this couple risked their lives for him, so committed were they to spreading the gospel.

In 1975, when Art and I prayed for a new ministry together, we had visions of serving on the foreign mission field. But instead of giving us a sailboat and saying, "Go!" the Lord supplied us with a bolt of cloth and said, "Stay!"

We had visited a church in which worship banners were displayed, and decided that banners were a gift we could give to our own church. With our pastor's approval we had our first banner completed by Easter. Hung at the front of the sanctuary, the banner declared: "Alleluia! Jesus Lives!"

In the past thirteen years Art and I have made thirty-five banners for many occasions. We want every banner to tell of the Lord's goodness. So before beginning a banner, Art and I pray, "How can we glorify you, Lord?"

Priscilla and Aquila
Insights for Discovery
—— ■●■ ——

1. From Romans 16:3–5, note the reputations of Priscilla and Aquila among the Gentiles. Consider the attributes of character necessary to earn such standing.

2. In Acts 18:1–3, Priscilla and Aquila opened their home to Paul to live and work with them. Study about the Shunammite woman in 2 Kings 4:8–10; Dorcas in Acts 9:36–42; and the Philippian jailer in Acts 16:33–34. Reflect on the part that practical service plays in bringing the Good News to others.

3. Read Acts 18:24–28. Think about the value of Priscilla and Aquila's attention to Apollos' preaching. See related thoughts in 1 Peter 4:7–11.

4. By exercising their spiritual strengths Priscilla and Aquila were able to accomplish much to the glory of God. In light of Romans 12:4–16 and 1 Corinthians 12:4–31, what was likely to be their motivation for service?

5. That Priscilla and Aquila are always mentioned together in Scripture says much about their relationship as seen by others. Contrast this relationship with that of Samson and Delilah (Judges 16:4–22). Of what profit is it that Priscilla and Aquila worked as true partners?

6. Allow God to speak to you through the words of Jesus in Matthew 25:31–46. Ask God how he can use you to reach out to others.

Part V
Learning to Lead
■●■

Leadership is determined by "follow-ship." If they aren't following, you aren't leading! In much the same way, teaching is determined by learning. If they aren't learning, you aren't teaching. By this definition Hitler and Marx were great leaders. Thousands of Nazis followed Hitler's orders and marched to his drum beat, and thousands read Marx and subscribed to his philosophy. But both men led the masses into error. So when we talk about leaders, we not only need to examine leadership skills, we must approve the leader's direction.

Charisma is that indefinable quality that a leader possesses which makes people like, admire, or respect him or her enough to want to identify with him. But with charisma there must be character. Jim Jones had charisma to spare when he led his faithful followers to the jungles of South America and the shambles of a death camp. But where was the character? The character question is answered by observing the leader's lifestyle. Is there consistency? Is there maturity? Is there integrity? Is there morality? Is there spirituality?

It is often in the trying times that the leader's qualities are seen to advantage. Winston Churchill had declared himself a failure long before the stresses and strains of World War II revealed his qualities. Followers are well advised to scrutinize their potential leaders. Likewise, leaders are well advised to beware of false steps which could not only jeopardize their own lives, but the lives of many others.

Fortunately, Scripture gives many examples of good leaders who achieved great things in difficult circumstances. Joshua not only had the unenviable task of filling Moses' sandals, but he had to do it while transforming the travel-weary, desert-worn children of Israel into an effective fighting force. They had to be strong enough to overcome a well-entrenched army and humble and brave enough to trust the Lord when the heat was on. Ezra and Nehemiah were responsible for bringing the exiles back from captivity and setting about the task of rebuilding their beloved Jerusalem, despite great and serious opposition. Peter, on the other hand, having failed to distinguish himself in his only recorded attempt at swordsmanship, was given responsibilities quite different from those of the other three men.

Peter was given the task of being a major part of the foundation of a church that would eventually reach the uttermost parts of the earth. The unique character of this church was such that it included racial mixes with which he himself struggled; leadership tensions in which he became embroiled; and matters of great theological and practical significance which would make an impact on the church for centuries.

All of these men tackled their assignments with enthusiasm, lit a fire under their followers, and achieved great success. None of them were perfect; they all confessed to being weak and inadequate. But they were the Lord's men: they loved his Word, his will, his cause, and his people. The people observed these qualities and followed these men. The rest, as they say, is history.

Joshua:
He Resolved to Serve the Lord
■●■
Gerald I. Miller

Joshua—I
A Prepared Leader
■ ● ■

The Lord said to Moses, "Take Joshua the son of Nun, a man in whom is the spirit, and lay your hand on him. Have him stand before Eleazar the priest and the entire assembly and commission him in their presence" (Numbers 27:18–19).

Joshua received his commission not by chance or a stroke of good luck. He had proved himself through several decades of preparation in various leadership roles.

Shortly after the Exodus from Egypt, Joshua commanded a successful military campaign against the Amalekites. By the time Israel gathered at Mount Sinai he had become Moses' attendant and apparently accompanied Moses on his journey up the mountain to receive the Law. Whenever Moses met with God in the Tent of Meeting, Joshua stood as permanent sentry (Exodus 33:11).

In another leadership capacity, representing the tribe of Ephraim, Joshua was one of the twelve spies dispatched from Kadesh-Barnea to explore the land of Canaan. Convinced that, with God's sustaining power, Israel could possess the land, he and Caleb stood alone against the majority who had returned with a report of fear and doubt. The hostile backlash against these two reached the point of threatening their lives. Then, throughout the following wilderness experience, amid seemingly interminable hardships, Joshua witnessed and learned from Moses' steadfast faith.

So when he stood before Eleazar the priest, Joshua was thoroughly prepared for his new responsibilities. He had developed military expertise, leadership capabilities, and spiritual depth. When the day of his installation came, Joshua's qualifications were complete.

God deals with his people today in much the same way. Preparation for a particular vocation or leadership position may seem long and difficult. We may feel insignificant, discouraged, or hopelessly delayed, but God uses our experiences and talents to provide us with unique opportunities for service.

Gerald I. Miller is Professor of Bible and Biblical Languages and Chairman of the Division of Foreign Languages at Asbury College in Wilmore, Kentucky.

Joshua—II
A Spirit-Filled Leader
■ ● ■

Joshua son of Nun was filled with the spirit of wisdom because Moses had laid his hands on him. So the Israelites listened to him and did what the Lord had commanded Moses (Deuteronomy 34:9).

Preparation for leadership and service among the people of God must include more than education and aptitude. From beginning to end, Scripture speaks of the necessity to be filled with God's Spirit.

The spiritual quality of Joshua's leadership was such that the Israelites willingly followed his instructions. Throughout his term of office Joshua continued to give evidence that God's Spirit was upon him. He acknowledged God's sustaining presence with him, taught the people the Law of Moses, and was always careful to give credit to God for all his successes. And God affirmed Joshua's leadership before the people.

The Old Testament pictures the Spirit of God as empowering special individuals: Bezalel the craftsman of the tabernacle, the seventy elders, and judges such as Gideon. But the prophets spoke of a day when God would pour out his Spirit "on all people" (Joel 2:28). That messianic promise was fulfilled in Jesus Christ and the coming of the Holy Spirit on all who believe. The New Testament apostles continually taught the importance of being "filled with the Spirit" (Ephesians 5:18).

Many of us are tempted to rely on our own skills or intelligence. We may even be successful by society's standards. But ultimately God's kingdom is enhanced by committed, Spirit-filled individuals who have put aside self-interest for the cause of Christ.

Others of us remain in the background, convinced that we are not able or worthy to serve. But God's Spirit enables us to become what God intends us to be. If we focus on our own shortcomings or feelings of inadequacy, we limit the power of the Spirit in our lives.

Joshua's Spirit-filled leadership anticipated God's provision for all believers. "Not by might nor by power" (Zechariah 4:6), but by God's Spirit are we able to accomplish his will.

Joshua—III
A Faithful Leader
■ ● ■

Joshua took the entire land, just as the Lord had directed Moses, and he gave it as an inheritance to Israel according to their tribal divisions (Joshua 11:23).

It is one thing to have good intentions; it is quite another to follow through with a solid performance. Joshua was one of those faithful role models whose leadership overcame all obstacles to the end.

Joshua led Israel across the Jordan and captured the city of Jericho, maintaining strict and, what would seem to us, bizarre battle specifications. The emphasis was on the Lord's giving rather than Israel's taking the land. A setback occurred at Ai. But instead of allowing the kind of negative fallout that characterized much of the wilderness period, Joshua dealt with the problem, planned a superb strategy, and led Israel to victory.

Successful campaigns followed against a coalition of southern cities and against an alliance from the north. With Canaan now under Israelite control, Joshua distributed the territories according to the tribal allotments. But the assembly had scarcely dispersed when Joshua had to mediate a misunderstanding between western and eastern tribes. He charged them all to remain committed to the covenant that bound them together and to their God.

Historical memory seems to focus on those who accomplish rather than those who falter. We remember the ones who are faithful, who are steadfast against great odds, who continue when success seems dim. Joshua exemplifies these qualities. If he had lost faith, Israel likely would have been doomed. "Israel served the Lord throughout the lifetime of Joshua" (Joshua 24:31)—no other biblical character could make such a claim.

Joshua's faithful service and humble spirit are appropriate models for Christians, yet often we find ourselves wavering or weak in our faith. We look at the times that we have failed and wonder if God can find us worthy. The promised Good News is that in Jesus we find forgiveness, renewal, and strength.

Joshua—IV
A Resolved Leader
■ ● ■

"If serving the Lord seems undesirable to you, then choose for yourselves this day whom you will serve. . . . But as for me and my household, we will serve the Lord" (Joshua 24:15).

The clan from which Abraham came had worshiped the pagan deities of ancient Mesopotamia. In the following centuries Abraham's descendants were exposed to Canaanite society and religion both while in Canaan and during some four hundred years in northern Egypt. The golden calf episode at the foot of Sinai reflects a fertility worship common in many areas of the ancient Near East. With Moses and Joshua away, many Israelites reverted to their former pagan practices.

Joshua was well aware of the enticements that Israel would encounter in the years to come. There would be a constant source of temptation if the children of Israel wavered in their commitment to the Lord.

Against this kind of background Joshua resolved that he and his own family would maintain a wholehearted commitment to God. In a stirring farewell address at Shechem, Joshua reviewed God's mighty acts on Israel's behalf, emphasizing that "every promise has been fulfilled; not one has failed" (Joshua 23:14). He then led the elders of the tribes in a ceremony renewing the Sinai covenant and updating their relationship with the one true God of their ancestors.

Joshua's intention was to encourage all of Israel to join him in his resolve to serve the Lord. But he would have made the same commitment even if he had stood alone, just as years earlier he and Caleb had remained resolute against majority opinion.

Christians today are called upon to make choices, many of them difficult. Sometimes ambiguity and differences of opinion are a complicating factor. Other times the issues are clear, but what is right and just is unpopular. The believer needs to rely on prayer and mature, level-headed judgment. Joshua's challenge is for a resolve to do what we know is best "without turning aside to the right or to the left" (Joshua 23:6).

Joshua: How Does This Apply to Me?
On Making the Ultimate Choice
——————— ■●■ ———————
Karen Frye

During a week-long family camp, I did not see anyone else displaying the frustration I felt over what the speaker was saying about God. I prayed silently. "Jesus," I said, "I wonder if I am the only one here who believes that you alone are the way to God? How can I be audacious enough to think that I have discovered the exclusive way to you?"

Part of me wants to believe that all people who are sincere and loving will live forever in heaven. Sometimes I even wish that I could agree with those who say that there are many ways to God.

God, however, will not allow himself to be one possible choice among many. Scripture continually points me back to the Cross as the only way of salvation. Acts 4:12 (NASB) declares: "There is salvation in no one else; for there is no other name under heaven that has been given among men, by which we must be saved."

At the family camp God was clearly challenging me with the words of Joshua: "Choose for yourselves today whom you will serve" (Joshua 24:15, NASB).

Having grown up in a Christian home, I had long ago asked Jesus to wash away my sin with the blood he shed for me. When everyone around me believed that Jesus was the only way to salvation, it was easy for me to believe it too.

But choosing God's way is difficult when we are surrounded by people who disagree with us. The decision that the Israelites should obey God's command to conquer Canaan was met by the Israelites' fearful cry: "Let us appoint a leader and return to Egypt" (Numbers 14:4, NASB).

However, Joshua remained firm in his belief that if Israel were obedient, God would be faithful to bring them into the Promised Land. Joshua's courage was built not on self-confidence, but on confidence in God. In Joshua 1:9, God instructed him to "be strong and of good courage; be not frightened,

Karen Frye is a free-lance writer and a homemaker living in Maple Grove, Minnesota. She and her husband, John, have two children. They attend Maple Grove Assembly of God.

neither be dismayed; for the Lord your God is with you wherever you go."

Joshua believed that the Jehovah who had led Abraham, Isaac, Jacob, Moses, and Joseph was the same God who would lead them into the Promised Land. The ark of the covenant was the Israelites' visual reminder of the presence of God. Joshua told them, "By this you shall know that the living God is among you. . . . Behold, the ark of the covenant of the Lord of all the earth is crossing over ahead of you into the Jordan" (Joshua 3:10–11, NASB).

I don't need a physical structure such as the ark to remind me of the presence of God. The Holy Spirit dwells inside me. And yet, because I live in an age of advanced technology, extensive information, and vast material resources, I am sometimes tempted to think that I can fight spiritual battles myself.

But God then reminds me, as he did Joshua, that I can be courageous and victorious because, and only because, he is with me. I can have a steady, realistic sense of confidence in him.

Joshua 1:8 (RSV) says, "This book of the law shall not depart out of your mouth, but you shall meditate on it day and night, that you may be careful to do according to all that is written in it." Meditating on God's Word helps me to stay true to God.

Joshua's imperturbable confidence in God reflected a personal knowledge of his Lord. The groundwork for his faith was no doubt laid throughout his childhood and youth. By the time he was sent into Canaan as a spy, he was already acknowledged as a godly leader.

As I rear my children, I often have thought of Deuteronomy 6:6–7: "These commandments that I give you today are to be upon your hearts. Impress them on your children. Talk about them when you sit at home and when you walk along the road, when you lie down and when you get up."

When my children and I ride in the car, we sing praises to God and thank him for making the world so beautiful. An ambulance darting past provides an opportunity to pray for others and to be grateful for God's protection.

Bedtime is our Bible-reading time. A favorite verse is Psalm 39:7 (NASB): "My hope is in thee." Our children are learning early that they do not have to depend only on themselves or on adults around them. Their hope should be in God. Before they are even aware of the many false gods that will be vying for their allegiance, they already have a deep awareness of God's love and protection.

I want my choosing to serve God to affect not only my children but others with whom I come into contact as well. I am learning how to share "battle stories" with others. I tell them about problems that I am bringing to God and the ways that he is helping me to solve them. Many others have gradually begun to verbalize similar situations to me, allowing me to encourage them and to pray with them.

Perhaps the most glorious result of serving God is that the path of obedience brings us closer to him. A "choosing time" that brought me closer to God came early in our marriage. I had difficulty adjusting to the idea of daily meeting the needs of another person. Although I generally did what was expected of me, I spent months being angry internally and sometimes externally.

One Sunday, as our pastor read a text from Philippians 2:5–7, my heart began to pound harder: "Your attitude should be the same as that of Christ Jesus: Who, being in very nature God, did not consider equality with God something to be grasped, but made himself nothing, taking the very nature of a servant, being made in human likeness." I did not believe that these were words of condemnation, but of hope. God was showing me the way out of my prison of anger.

"OK, God," I prayed. "For one month I will try to be a servant. I will serve because of your example and not because of how I feel or how others act."

During the trial month, God brought new peace and joy into my life and new freedom to serve others with a cheerful heart. That month has now stretched into fourteen years. I have had moments of failure, but God has honored my desire by showing me how to model his servanthood.

The decision to serve God comes not in a moment but in a journey. God knew that Joshua's decision to follow him would be an ongoing, moment-by-moment choice. Joshua's famous declaration, "As for me and my house, we will serve the Lord" is found in the last chapter of Joshua, not the first. The strength of his declaration came from his experiencing all that God had done for him and for the children of Israel.

Joshua
Insights for Discovery
────── ■ ● ■ ──────

1. Look at Joshua 1:1–9. Consider the weight of the responsibility placed on Joshua when the Lord commissioned him to succeed Moses as the leader of the Israelites.

2. Notice Joshua's response to God's command in Joshua 1:10–18. What does this passage reveal about his heart? Read Joshua 11 and observe the depth of obedience that he exhibited.

3. Read Numbers 13:1–14:9. What can you learn from Joshua's faith, determination, and vision? (Take note especially of Numbers 14:6–9.) Meditate on Proverbs 13:17 and 25:13.

4. How does Joshua 24:14–15 shed light on Joshua's final discourse as recorded in Joshua 23 and 24? Compare his statements with the concluding statements of Moses (Deuteronomy 32:44–47), the statements of David (1 Kings 2:1–12), and the statements of Paul (2 Timothy 3:10–4:8).

5. Reflect on the consequences of Achan's disobedience as recorded in Joshua 6:15–7:26. (Compare with Acts 5:1–11.)

6. Consider what Jesus says about being his servant in John 12:26; 13:1–17; and 14:15–21. What are the requirements? What are the rewards?

7. Read Psalm 119:127–128 and James 1:22–25 and think about the importance of the Word of God to a servant. How is God's Word working in your life?

Ezra:
The Man Who Honored God's Word
—— ■●■ ——
Thomas N. Finger

Ezra—I
Studies God's Word
■ ● ■

For Ezra had set his heart to study the law of the Lord, and to practice it, and to teach His statutes and ordinances in Israel (Ezra 7:10, NASB).

The book of Ezra traces the return of the Jews from exile between the years 539 and 457 B.C. Six chapters of the book and eighty-one years of history have elapsed before Ezra appears. Not long after he does, his basic character is briefly but profoundly sketched.

First, Ezra "set his heart to study the law." In the Bible the word *heart* does not simply stand for our emotions. It denotes the deepest center of the entire person—the source of all our thoughts, feelings, and actions.

Ezra turned his innermost being in devotion toward's God's law. This fact is emphasized in the next phrase: Ezra set his heart not only to study the law, but also "to practice it." Ezra could not analyze the biblical text, yet neglect to follow it daily; nor could he lead a good life without seeking to learn what God asked of him. For Ezra, study of God's Word drove him into action, and that life of action continually brought him back to God's Word.

Finally, verse 10 tells us what specific form of action Ezra was called to. He was "to teach [God's] statutes and ordinances in Israel." When we think of Ezra as a teacher, however, we should not picture him simply as a lecturer in a classroom, for Ezra was called, above all, to be a reformer. He informed his kinspeople about God's law and moved them to obey it. This is because Ezra himself honored God's Word not only with his mind, but also in his life.

Ezra reminds us that study of God's Word and action based on it can never be separated. Study without action is fruitless and empty. Yet action divorced from God's Word can be aimless and even damaging. Only by doing both do we truly honor God's Word.

Thomas N. Finger is Visiting Professor of Theology at Eastern Mennonite Seminary in Harrisonburg, Virginia, and author of *Christian Theology: An Eschatological Approach*.

Ezra—II
Trusts God's Word
——— ■ ● ■ ———

For I was ashamed to request from the king troops and horsemen to protect us from the enemy on the way, because we had said to the king, "The hand of our God is favorably disposed to all those who seek Him, but His power and His anger are against all those who forsake Him" (Ezra 8:22, NASB).

Ezra's determination not only to study God's Word but also act on it was soon put to a difficult test. Artaxerxes I, king of Persia, had granted Ezra permission to return to Jerusalem with a company of five thousand people. They would take along much silver and gold which Artaxerxes himself had contributed for the beautification of the temple.

This blessing, however, presented Ezra with a problem. The arduous journey to Jerusalem would take four months. Such a large company laden with so much wealth would be easy prey for highway robbers and for enemies of Israel. Moreover, whole families, including children and the elderly, would be making the trip (Ezra 7:9; 8:21).

It is easy to imagine the anxiety that Ezra probably felt. What if the company would be ambushed on a lonely desert road and suffer many casualties? What if the king's gold and silver were stolen? Yet to ask for soldiers would signal failure to trust God whose Word he studied.

Ezra acted in a way consistent with complete trust in God. Before departing, Ezra proclaimed a fast. The people confessed their inability to protect themselves and their complete dependence on God   Then they set out on the perilous journey. Four months later they reached Jerusalem, testifying that God had "delivered us from the hand of the enemy and the ambushes by the way" (Ezra 8:21, 31, NASB).

This episode reminds us that witnessing to the God whose Word we believe is not just a matter of words. We say that no danger, and not even death, can separate people who trust in Christ from God's love (Romans 8:35–39). Yet if we do not act in a way consistent with this trust, then our words are empty.

Ezra—III
Changed by God's Word
■ ● ■

But at the evening offering I arose from my humiliation, even with my garment and my robe torn, and I fell on my knees and stretched out my hands to the Lord my God (Ezra 9:5, NASB).

Soon after Ezra arrived in Jerusalem, he found that the situation was grave. Not only the people in general, but even the priests and Levites were participating in the perverted religious and social practices of the surrounding nations. Additionally he was told, "In this faithlessness the hand of the officials and chief men has been foremost" (Ezra 9:2, RSV). Ezra sensed that serious work lay ahead.

Ezra could have acted like an angry prophet. But what he did was surprising. Ezra responded with grief. He said, "I tore my garment and my robe, and pulled some of the hair from my head and my beard, and sat down appalled" (Ezra 9:3, NASB). And then, having mourned and fasted all day, he turned to God in prayer.

Ezra's prayer was one of repentance (Ezra 9:6–15). Brokenhearted, Ezra confessed the sins of those living in Judea, and even of Israel through the centuries. When he did so, he always referred to the sinners as "we," which included himself.

This may seem strange indeed. For who could be less guilty of these sins than Ezra? He had not lived in Judea, but had only recently arrived from Babylon. He had not committed the transgressions of his ancestors, but was earnestly trying to help his own generation avoid them.

Nevertheless, God's Word taught Ezra that he too was a sinner. Ezra considered it inappropriate to approach the Judeans as one who put a finger on their sins, appearing "holier than thou." Instead, he approached them as one who shared their sorrow and sin and who needed similar forgiveness.

Ezra's actions remind us that we need to study God's Word and tell others what it says. But before we can speak to others about God, we must let God speak to us. Before we can tell others what changes God requires, we need to be changed ourselves.

Proclaims God's Word
—————— ■●■ ——————

*Now while Ezra was praying and making confession, weeping
and prostrating himself before the house of God, a very large
assembly, men, women, and children, gathered to him from
Israel; for the people wept bitterly (Ezra 10:1, NASB).*

When Ezra began praying and confessing, he certainly was not
employing any strategy to win over the people. Instead, Ezra
was responding to sin in a way which came spontaneously to
one who had absorbed God's law in his innermost being.

The result was amazing. Rather than fearing Ezra or hiding
from him, the Judeans came to him. Almost before he knew it,
Ezra was surrounded by "a very large assembly" of people
weeping with him.

The reforms which the Judeans needed to make were not
imposed upon them by Ezra, but emerged from this group
experience of repentance and prayer. It was not Ezra, but a man
named Shecaniah, who proposed that the Judeans make a
covenant with God to put away their foreign wives and children. Although he asked Ezra to direct this process, Shecaniah
assured him that all those assembled would support him (Ezra
10:2–4).

The cooperation of the assembly is remarkable when one
realizes how difficult this task would be. Such a step may seem
cruel to us today. It is understandable only when one remembers how the entire book of Ezra pictures the Judeans as a tiny
minority floundering amid a sea of pagan cultures. Wives from
these cultures introduced idolatry and perverted social practices to Israel. Ezra foresaw that unless drastic steps were taken,
the nation of Israel might be wholly swallowed up.

In the end, Ezra emerges as a person who helped reform
Israel not simply through teaching the law. By bringing five
thousand unprotected people through a dangerous, lengthy
journey without mishap, Ezra witnessed to God's faithfulness
and power. By humbling himself and repenting, he brought the
Judeans to reform their lives.

Ezra: How Does This Apply to Me?
Seek, Do, Teach

■ ● ■

Judy Seabaugh

Statistics show that the Bible has been the world's best seller for many years. No other book can equal its record. Our family has more than twenty copies of the Bible in a host of translations, as well as the New Testament on cassette tape. Since we are surrounded by the opportunity to know God's Word, it should be our desire to give heed to this precious resource.

In the days of Ezra, God's Word was not nearly so accessible. But Ezra's hunger for the Word of God was strong enough to overcome the obstacles of its inaccessibility. Ezra 7:10 (KJV) best depicts how this scribe honored God's Word: "For Ezra had prepared his heart to seek the law of the Lord, and to do it, and to teach in Israel statutes and judgments."

As Christians, we should have the same goal: to honor God's Word. We can begin, as Ezra did, by seeking. We read in Psalm 119:2, "Blessed are they that keep his testimonies, and that seek him with the whole heart." Some time ago I struggled with an attitude that was not Christlike toward someone who I felt had wronged me. As I examined my heart, I knew that the desire to retaliate was growing inside me, and I did not want that attitude to remain.

As I asked the Lord to show me what I should do, he brought Psalm 37 to my mind. As I read, I realized there was an alternative to my desire for retaliation. Instead, I could trust the Lord to bring about his will in this situation. I could also rest from my yearning for revenge.

Unfortunately, we do not always have a Bible in our hands at every moment of temptation or in trying circumstances. One afternoon recently there was a knock at my door. On my front porch was a young woman who told me that my son had been in an accident on his bicycle. Her mother had been driving the car into which he had crashed.

There was not time to pick up my Bible and read. Yet, I felt strength and peace. Passages that I had memorized years

Judy Seabaugh is a pastor's wife, a homemaker, and a free-lance writer. She and her husband, Charles, have three sons and live in Cape Girardeau, Missouri.

before became a reality. One was Psalm 46:1 (KJV): "God is our refuge and strength, a very present help in trouble."

I did not sit down and recite those verses mechanically, but those words had been stored within me as a source on which to draw in that time of urgent need. The presence of the Lord and the reality of his Word gave me his peace and strength through those hours as I took my son to the hospital emergency room and his wounds were cleaned and stitched.

Seeking the law of the Lord goes one step beyond memorization: "Give me understanding, and I will keep your law and obey it with all my heart" (Psalm 119:34). We must seek to understand God's Word so that we can wisely apply it to each situation.

A seeking heart approaches daily Bible reading with anticipation. The first time I attempted to read the entire Bible through in one year, I read two or three chapters each day but often did not remember anything I had read when I finished.

I have learned that it is better for me to read only as much Scripture as I can take time to meditate upon to gain spiritual strength and guidance: "Your word is a lamp to my feet and a light for my path" (Psalm 119:105). In each day's reading we can learn something fresh that will light the path we walk.

We instruct children that it is improper to scribble in the Bible or tear its pages. Honoring God's Word, however, goes beyond our treatment of its printed pages.

We can handle the Bible with care, yet not honor it if we fail to put it into practice: "Do not merely listen to the word, and so deceive yourselves. Do what it says" (James 1:22).

As a pastor's wife, I receive many telephone calls requesting financial assistance or food assistance. One day the Lord gave me a tangible opportunity to be a doer of the Word. An elderly man came to our door asking for food. The first thing I did was to share with him the truth that Jesus wanted to be his Friend and make him a new person on the inside. No matter how limited our material resources, I could share the Good News about Jesus. After we talked, I gave the man a sack of groceries and offered him a ride home.

Jesus is the only One who can enable us to be a doer of God's Word. Just as a solar or light-powered calculator must have a constant source of light to function, we must have a constant relationship with Jesus to put God's Word into practice each day. If the light source is cut off from the calculator, it will not work. If our relationship with Jesus is cut off through busyness or neglect, we will experience failure in trying to live according to the Word.

As a doer of the Word, Ezra became upset when he saw that his people were not obeying God's commands. He became so irate that he plucked out his hair and his beard.

Ezra also prayed. His prayer resulted in repentance and change in the lives of the people. God has called each of us to fervent prayer for the rampant sin we see around us. We can pray faithfully in our own private devotions, as well as join other Christians in special times of fasting and prayer.

Making God's Word clear to those around us can range from formal teaching, such as Sunday school or home study groups, to informal teaching, which can be listening to the cares of those we meet wherever God has placed us. The knowledge of God's Word in the lives of many people is limited to what they observe in the lives of Christians. It is our responsibility to be sure they are witnessing authentic Christianity. We need to ask ourselves, "Are my non-Christian acquaintances learning from the way I live what God's Word teaches?"

A few years ago God spoke to me about becoming involved in areas where I could meet people who were searching for answers to life's problems, but who did not attend church to find those answers. The Lord opened several doors.

One of my opportunities was to volunteer one morning each week at a center that offers help to women who are experiencing crisis pregnancies. I have the privilege to speak words of hope to women whose lives are in turmoil.

We often overlook important chances to share God's Word because we are busy looking for the "big" openings. I was reminded recently of the woman who had prayed with me when I accepted Christ as Savior. I was an extremely shy six-year-old girl, and most people would have considered me too young to understand salvation. But this woman was sensitive to the opportunity to share the gospel with me, and I am so thankful that she was.

The large number of Bibles that are printed and distributed each year is important, but it is not enough. We must read and study God's Word—and allow it to make a difference in our lives. When God's Word is honored in our lives, as it was in Ezra's life, we will put God's Word into practice and look for opportunities to share the truth with others.

Ezra
Insights for Discovery
■ ● ■

1. In Ezra 1:1–4, read how Cyrus viewed his place in history in the will of God.

2. In Ezra 2:68–69, notice the response of family heads upon their arrival at the house of God. (Compare with the exiles' response in Ezra 8:35–36; examine also Ezra 3:11.)

3. In Ezra 3:3, observe how the people of Israel rallied around the purpose of rebuilding the temple in the face of opposition. (By also looking at Ezra 4:4–5 and then Ezra 7:28, see the relationship between courage in the Lord and doing the will of God.)

4. Meditate on the sovereignty of God, that he is always in control—see Ezra 5:5; 7:27–28; and 8:18–23, 31–32.

5. Observe in Ezra's prayer, following his being alerted to Israel's sin of intermarriage with foreigners (Ezra 9:1–3), the components of guilt over sin, consequences of sin, disdain for sin, judgment of sin, and God's forgiveness of sin.

6. Look closely at the people's reaction to Ezra's prayer (Ezra 10:1–4) and his challenge to confess and repent (Ezra 10:11–15).

7. Recognize the beauty of God's wonderful grace as shown in Ezra 9:13 and Ezra 10:2.

Peter:
He Became a Strong
Leader for Christ
■●■
W. Ward Gasque

Peter—I
A Man Called to Follow Jesus
—————— ■●■ ——————

"Come, follow me," Jesus said, "and I will make you fishers of men" (Mark 1:17).

Simon Peter was an ordinary working man, a fisherman by trade. We don't know a lot about his family background, but it was probably undistinguished.

We do know that Peter was married (Mark 1:30). He was also bilingual: among his family and friends he probably spoke Aramaic (the language of most Palestinian Jews of the day), and to his Gentile neighbors and the wholesale fishing merchants he would have spoken Greek. Peter had little formal education.

Peter and his brother Andrew had been disciples of John the Baptist, the one who had been sent to herald the way of the coming Messiah (John 1:35–42). Shortly after Jesus' baptism they became his followers.

Jesus' call to Peter was a challenge. "Come, follow me" was a call to a commitment of faith, to a new life. Peter was called to identify with the kingdom of God that Jesus proclaimed, and to assert its priority over all other claims in his life.

For Peter this challenge must have been difficult—it demanded personal sacrifice. However, Jesus walked before Peter and led him along the way. Peter's task was simply to follow.

Jesus' call to Peter also contained a promise: "I will make you fishers of men." Peter and his brother had learned the skill of making a living by catching fish from the Sea of Galilee. Now Jesus was going to teach them to find and captivate people for the kingdom of God.

Peter, the seasoned fisherman, would learn to "fish" in a new way he never dreamed of. His new task would dominate the rest of his life, taking him far from the fishing villages of his youth. And Jesus pledged not merely to teach him this new style of fishing, but to provide the enabling power to do it.

W. Ward Gasque is one of the founders of Regent College, Vancouver, British Columbia, where he has served since 1969. He and his wife, Laurel, have one child.

Peter—II
A Hesitant Confessor of Jesus

——— ■●■ ———

"But what about you?" he asked. "Who do you say I am?"
Simon Peter answered, "You are the Christ, the Son of the living
God" (Matthew 16:15–16).

When he followed Jesus' call, Peter entered a three-year intern-
ship program. He was one of the Twelve chosen to accompany
the Lord on his preaching and healing missions along the dusty
roads of Palestine.

Peter was also among the three closest associates of Jesus.
Peter and the two brothers, James and John, formed an inner
cabinet of the apostolic band. They were alone with Jesus on the
Mount of Transfiguration. They were again alone with Jesus in
the Garden of Gethsemane (Matthew 17:1; 26:36–37; Mark
14:32–33).

Jesus called him Cephas (Aramaic) or Peter (Greek), which
means "rock." Peter asked the questions that others dared only
to think, and he articulated the disciples' honest responses to
Jesus' words and deeds.

In the events of the last days of Jesus' life on earth, Peter was
the outspoken one who sometimes said the wrong thing and
was rebuked by his Lord (Matthew 16:22–23). Like the other
disciples, Peter had a difficult time understanding what Jesus
was trying to teach them about the necessity of the Cross.

Even after Peter confessed his faith in Jesus, he attempted to
rebuke the Lord for talking about his impending death. Yet
something of the significance of Jesus' person and mission was
beginning to dawn on Peter. In a moment of inspiration that
prefigured the full revelation to follow, he blurted out the
confession, "You are the Christ, the Son of the living God."

Jesus accepted Peter's confession and promised him a special
role in the building of the church. "You are Peter. . . . I will give
you the keys of the kingdom of heaven" (Matthew 16:18–19).
Beginning on the day of Pentecost and continuing for thirty-
five years, Peter used these keys to open the door of salvation
to thousands who repented of their sins and believed in the
Lord.

Peter—III
A Bold Witness of the Resurrection

■ ● ■

"Salvation is found in no one else, for there is no other name under heaven given to men by which we must be saved" (Acts 4:12).

In spite of his enthusiastic commitment to Jesus, Peter had failed. He had boasted that he would never deny his Lord, but he did just that (Mark 14:29, 31, 68–72). The three days between Jesus' death and his resurrection must have been agonizing for Peter since he was filled with remorse.

But the Resurrection changed everything. Peter was one of the first to hear the good news that Jesus was alive, and he was the first to investigate for himself. Rushing to the place where the body of Jesus had been laid, Peter was among the first to enter the empty tomb (Luke 24:12). And he became the first among the disciples to see the risen Lord alive (1 Corinthians 15:5).

His experiences, followed by the coming of the Holy Spirit on the Day of Pentecost, transformed a repentant but still frightened disciple into a fearless witness to Jesus Christ.

Peter's witness was empowered by the Holy Spirit. It was not the result of some plan formulated with his associates. As in Peter's call to discipleship, God himself took the initiative.

Peter's message focused on Jesus. He talked about who Jesus was, what he had done, and what God had done in raising Christ from the dead. Peter was a witness—one who told what he knew.

Peter called his hearers to repentance, literally a change of mind. He challenged those who heard him to identify with Jesus, to put their trust in him and submit to baptism, and to become part of the new community God was bringing into existence.

Peter—IV
A Faithful Shepherd of God's Flock
─────── ■ ● ■ ───────

You also, like living stones, are being built into a spiritual
house to be a holy priesthood, offering spiritual sacrifices
acceptable to God through Jesus Christ (1 Peter 2:5).

Eventually, probably in A.D. 40, Peter left Jerusalem for a wider
ministry among the thousands of Jews who did not live in
Palestine (1 Peter 1:1). Peter had been called to preach to the
Jews just as Paul had been called to minister to the Gentiles
(Galatians 2:7).

Of the two New Testament letters which bear Peter's name,
the first was written in the early days of the persecution of the
church under Nero. The apostle wrote to encourage believers
to remain true to their Lord, to live such exemplary lives among
the pagans around them that they would give glory to God in
the day of judgment (1 Peter 2:12), and always to "be prepared
to give an answer to everyone who asks you to give the reason
for the hope that you have" (1 Peter 3:5).

Peter used two illustrations to show the believers how God
called them to be his people in the world. First, the apostle
wrote that God is building a beautiful temple out of the most
interesting material: "living stones." All who put their trust in
Jesus as Lord become these living stones. Some are huge stones
which help hold up the walls while others are small stones in
some of the beautiful mosaics decorating the temple. Each has
an essential part to play in this "spiritual house" of God.

Peter added that believers are not just the building materials that God is using, but also the priests chosen by God to lead
the worship service. Second, the apostle wrote that God is
creating a new nation from among all the nations of the world:
"You are a chosen people, a royal priesthood, a holy nation, a
people belonging to God." The purpose of that call is to live
lives that "declare the praises of him who called you out of
darkness into his wonderful light" (1 Peter 2:9).

In other words, we are called to bear witness in worship,
word, and deed to what God has done for the world in the
Person and work of his Son.

Peter: How Does This Apply to Me?
Power That Transforms
■ ● ■
Laura W. Watts

Our youth minister slipped a piece of paper into my hand. "Take this home, think about it, and get back to me," he said resolutely, walking away. I turned the sheet over. The words "Youth Counselor Application" appeared in bold letters across the top of the page. As a youth counselor I would be leading six or seven junior high girls in weekly Bible study and prayer. I would be not only a teacher, I would be someone to whom the girls could turn for advice and spiritual guidance.

Me, of all people! I had been a failure in my Christian witness, and as a fashion model had once thought that success meant appearing on the cover of a high-fashion magazine. How could I be a role model for teenaged girls?

Perhaps that was how Peter felt when Jesus instructed him to "feed my sheep" (John 21:17, KJV). Yet instead of replying, "Who? Me?" Peter accepted Jesus' directive.

I thought about my own conversion, which had been much like Peter's. Immediately I began to walk with Christ, to learn from him, and to tell others of his love.

I thought I was willing to pay any price, but when it came to following Jesus in the hard places, the painful places, I often had said in my heart, and by my actions, "I know him not."

After the life-changing events of Pentecost, Peter was completely dedicated to Christ. Was the one who boldly proclaimed the message of salvation to the Gentiles the same Peter who had once so vehemently denied his Lord? What was it that had changed this ineffectual "fisher of men" into one of the greatest apostles?

Jesus' words to his disciples provided the answer: "You shall receive power when the Holy Spirit has come upon you; and you shall be my witnesses in Jerusalem and in all Judea and Samaria and to the end of the earth" (Acts 1:8, RSV). Peter's transformation was not due to mere human effort. It was due to the work and the enabling power of the Holy Spirit.

If I were to be an effective witness for Christ, I too would

Laura W. Watts is a free-lance writer and homemaker living in Raleigh, North Carolina. She and her husband, David, have twin daughters.

have to yield to the power of the Holy Spirit. That week I made an important phone call. "I'm volunteering as a youth counselor," I said brightly. "Is the position still open?"

From Peter we can learn the characteristics of a life transformed by the power of the Holy Spirit. The first characteristic is obedience. When standing before the Sanhedrin, Peter and the other apostles responded, "We must obey God rather than men. . . . We are witnesses to these things, and so is the Holy Spirit whom God has given to those who obey him" (Acts 5:29, 32, RSV).

Proclaiming God's Word isn't always easy. At times I feel inadequate or ill-equipped as a teacher.

"The Bible says that we're not to be unequally yoked," I announced at one of our weekly meetings.

Jenny said, "If I date only Christians, won't I be judging others?" I was taken by surprise, and my mind went blank.

After searching the Scriptures, I was later able to give Jenny an answer. "You're right," I told her. "We're not to judge others, but God does call us to be discerning."

Paul reminds us that we speak "not in words taught us by human wisdom but in words taught by the Spirit, expressing spiritual truths in spiritual words" (1 Corinthians 2:13). Whenever I'm obedient in communicating God's truth, his grace is more than sufficient to meet my needs.

Next, we see that a transformed life is grounded in the Word of God and bathed in prayer. Peter treasured the Word of God in his heart. In his Pentecost message he cited passages from David and the prophet Joel.

One day a girl in my group telephoned. "A friend of mine is going through a difficult time," she explained, "and I'd like to give her a few verses of Scripture. Can you help?" As we talked, I shared many verses relating to God's loving care.

Several days later my young friend called again. "The verses you gave me were perfect," she said. "But how did you find them so quickly? I want to know your secret!" My secret was simple: I had learned to hide God's Word in my heart.

Prayer was also of primary importance to Peter. In Acts 1:14, the apostles "joined together constantly in prayer."

Daily in prayer I intercede for each girl in my discipleship group. Without prayer, my labor for the Lord is in vain, for I am working from my own strength.

A third characteristic of a transformed life is that it is fruitful. Because Peter was empowered by the Holy Spirit, his witnessing resulted in many new converts. Luke records that at Pentecost more than three thousand were added to the disciples' number (Acts 2:41).

Two of the girls in my group invited me to dinner one evening. "We want to witness to our friends," Stacey said between bites, "but we're not sure where to start." So we spent the evening talking about "friendship evangelism" and practical ways to share Christ.

At a ski retreat the next weekend Stacey and several others shared their testimonies with more than forty teenagers. As a result, many of them made first-time commitments or rededicated their lives to Christ.

Not only was Peter faithful in his witness, but he was also obedient to Christ's call to "feed my sheep." In First and Second Peter, Peter exhorted and encouraged the believers entrusted to his care: "Be shepherds of God's flock that is under your care, serving as overseers—not because you must, but because you are willing, as God wants you to be" (1 Peter 5:2).

Rather than being a burden, overseeing the "flock" has been the joy of my life. As I have nurtured the girls in their faith, the Lord has blessed me beyond measure.

Finally, a transformed life is one that is increasing in Christlikeness. Luke records that when the Sanhedrin "saw the courage of Peter and John and realized that they were unschooled, ordinary men, they were astonished and they took note that these men had been with Jesus" (Acts 4:13).

I'm reminded of the little boy who talked with his pastor after the service one Sunday. "There's one thing I don't understand," the child said. "If I ask Jesus to come and live inside me, won't he stick out all over?"

The pastor smiled, then replied, "He certainly will!"

As a teacher, I need to make sure that Jesus "sticks out all over" my life. As I have yielded to the Holy Spirit, I have increasingly experienced his presence within me.

Peter ended his first epistle with a promise to all believers: "After you have suffered a little while, the God of all grace, who has called you to his eternal glory in Christ, will himself restore, establish, and strengthen you" (1 Peter 5:10, RSV).

These are the words of a man who had suffered the pain of denying the One whom he loved the most. But Peter became strong, firm, and steadfast—the "rock" that Christ intended him to be.

Peter
Insights for Discovery
■ ● ■

1. Study Peter's response to Christ (Matthew 4:18–20) and his continual fervent desire to be a part of Christ's kingdom (John 6:25–69; 13:7–9).

2. Peter draws his sword to defend Jesus at the time of his arrest (John 18:1–11), but only hours later denies him (John 18:15–27). Imagine the fear that caused Peter's denial and his sorrow at having failed his beloved Master and Friend.

3. In spite of his failure, Peter is able to identify himself as "an apostle of Jesus Christ" (1 Peter 1:1, KJV). What does this say about the Lord's willingness to forgive?

4. From Acts 4 and 5, what do you observe about the transforming power of God in Peter's life?

5. Peter learns to take a stand for, and even suffer for, Christ. What attitudes can result from our suffering (1 Peter 4:12–19)?

6. Read Acts 2 and reflect on how the Holy Spirit empowered Peter to evangelize. What do you learn about being acquainted with Scripture to tell others about Jesus Christ?

7. From the apostle's admonitions in 2 Peter, meditate on the importance of being holy before the Lord.

Nehemiah:
He Gave People a Mind to Work

■●■

James A. Davis

Nehemiah—I
Personal Involvement
■●■

Then I said to them, "You see the trouble we are in, how Jerusalem lies in ruins with its gates burned. Come, let us build the wall of Jerusalem, that we may no longer suffer disgrace" (Nehemiah 2:17, RSV).

Nehemiah occupied an esteemed position of honor, responsibility, and service in the court of Artaxerxes I, one of the most powerful political figures of the fifth century B.C. But instead of trying to retain his official dignity and remain aloof, Nehemiah chose to become personally involved with the people.

The tasks which he accomplished, along with his people, are remarkable. The walls of Jerusalem, razed and burned by the Babylonians in their conquest of the city over a century before, were rebuilt within fifty-two days. Economic policy and practice were considerably and beneficially reshaped. In cooperation with Ezra, the priest and scribe, the celebration of religious festivals was reinstated, and funding necessary to underwrite activities associated with worship in the temple was restored (Nehemiah 4–10).

Why and how were such enormous tasks undertaken and completed? Answers come in his initial address to the people of Jerusalem, in Nehemiah 2:17–18. For manifest in this address are Nehemiah's genuine concern for his people, his willingness to become personally involved in helping them, and the winsomeness of a transparent leader.

When Nehemiah hears about the dangerous and dishonorable vulnerability of the residents of Jerusalem, his concern for the people's welfare outweighs any concern for himself. When he arrives, he clearly communicates to the people that he does not intend to stand above them as a royal emissary, but to stand among them to share in their "disgrace" and to work with them to remove it (Nehemiah 5:15; Mark 10:42). Then he demonstrates his willingness to become involved by openly disclosing his prayers and plans for the work.

James A. Davis is currently serving in the pastorate in the Presbyterian Church (U.S.A.). He is the author of *Wisdom and Spirit,* and of a forthcoming commentary on 1 Corinthians to be published in *The Word Biblical Commentary Series.*

Nehemiah—II
Including Others

■ ● ■

Eliashib the high priest rose up with his brethren the priests and they built the Sheep Gate. . . . And next to him the men of Jericho built. And next to them Zaccur the son of Imri built (Nehemiah 3:1–2, RSV).

Nehemiah's next step was crucial. He enlisted the support and assistance of as many groups and individuals as possible to rebuild the walls. He then delegated to each of the workers a vital part of the project.

Nehemiah's willingness to be inclusive rather than exclusive in his planning and execution, and his delegation of work to those parts of the community having a vested interest in certain parts of the project, had a profound impact upon those who labored. This led to the quick completion of the entire wall.

Social, religious, or political status played little or no part in the assignment and conduct of the project. Priests were assigned with temple servants; rulers worked with tradespeople such as perfumers, goldsmiths, and merchants; and daughters worked alongside their fathers. The names of thirteen different groups and twenty-six other individuals are recorded here in what apparently is only a partial listing of those whom Nehemiah included in the work (Nehemiah 3).

It is significant to notice that one name is absent from this "list of credits"—that of Nehemiah himself (the Nehemiah named in 3:16 as the "son of Azbuk" is the "ruler of half the district of Beth-zur," a region located about thirteen miles to the south of Jerusalem). That he was involved cannot be contested, but the purpose of this record is not to show his personal contributions, but to provide a glimpse of Nehemiah's adeptness in including others in his work. Here was one who knew the importance of being inclusive when it came to giving people "a mind to work" (Nehemiah 4:6, RSV).

Nehemiah—III
Prayer and Planning
■●■

*We prayed to our God, and set a guard as a protection against
them day and night (Nehemiah 4:9, RSV).*

Much of the work of effective leadership needs to be done in
private long before it transpires in public. This is especially true
among God's people. Prayer which seeks out God's will, and
plans which formulate a response to his guidance, must take
precedence over the world's insistent demands for instant
response, direction, leadership, and motivation. Those who
direct the people of God need to take the time to pray and to
plan their acts of leadership instead of simply trying to react as
a leader to the myriad needs of the moment.

Nehemiah knew well that prayer and planning were necessary, he makes constant reference to these two activities as an
integral part of his personal life. In Nehemiah 1:4, for example,
a period of several days is summarized, during which Nehemiah prayed over the report he had received from Jerusalem.

He also spent some of this time planning his actions in
response to the call of God. In his closing prayer, Nehemiah
resolved to approach the king. He asks God to "give success to
thy servant today, and grant him mercy in the sight of this man"
(Nehemiah 1:11, RSV). In a similar way, after his arrival in
Jerusalem, Nehemiah spent a period of three days engaged
presumably once more in prayer. His agenda was crystallized
only after a night ride around the circuit of broken city walls
(Nehemiah 2:11–16).

Perhaps the most impressive demonstration of the importance of prayer and planning is found when the work had
progressed to the point where its opponents were actively
plotting its disruption. Instead of reacting by instinct, Nehemiah took the time to pray to God. As the consequence of his
prayers, he formulated defenses which frustrated his enemies
and at the same time allowed construction to progress.

Nehemiah—IV
Faces Opposition
———— ■ ● ■ ————

They all wanted to frighten us, thinking, "Their hands will drop from the work, and it will not be done." But now, O God, strengthen thou my hands (Nehemiah 6:9, RSV).

Nehemiah faced opposition both from within and from without. From within, some people withheld their personal financial support and old tensions surfaced between the common people and "the nobles and the officials" (Nehemiah 5:7).

From without, the opposition was much more concerted. Sanballat and Tobiah orchestrated an escalating campaign of opposition. They initially questioned the patriotism of those involved in the project, and then sought to belittle the possibility of achieving the goal. Finally, they attempted to sabotage the work and assassinate Nehemiah (Nehemiah 2–6).

In the face of such opposition it would have been easy for Nehemiah, or for his people, to become distracted or discouraged. But Nehemiah knew how to keep his mind and the minds of his people focused on the task.

Two lessons on leadership emerge. First, a leader cannot afford to ignore opposition. Instead, as Nehemiah did, the person must openly confront each onset of opposition with dialogue to determine its character, so that if possible reconciliation can be effected. Where reconciliation is not possible, prayer and planning must be implemented to ensure that the work continues to go forward.

Second, a leader cannot let opposition preoccupy his attention to the point that it becomes the predominant focus of one's energies. Instead, effective leadership must keep primary attention riveted on the effort rather than on its enemies.

By being willing to become personally involved, to involve others, to pray and plan, and to encounter opposition without becoming preoccupied by it, Nehemiah succeeded where others had failed. He rebuilt the city walls in only fifty-two days.

In his own final analysis, however, Nehemiah explained that his work had been accomplished "with the help of our God" (Nehemiah 6:16, RSV).

Nehemiah: How Does This Apply to Me?
Does a Leader Scrub Pots?

■ ● ■

Helen L. Challener

Washing towering stacks of dirty dishes has never been my idea of a fun time. However, for two summers while I was in college, I had the privilege—and I still consider it a privilege—to serve on the staff of a Christian camp.

My domain covered the dining room and dishwashing areas. The latter posed a hearty challenge and taught me more about serving the Lord. Not that I expected to be stimulated spiritually as a dining room hostess and a dishwasher! But God always uses a variety of training grounds and methods to teach his servants.

One major challenge was to recruit and motivate high school students to wash the hundreds and hundreds of dishes, pots, and pans. Two questions needed to be answered: How could I motivate workers to scrub a grungy pot or to dry the two-hundredth cup? And how could I give them a mind to work for the Lord, to lift their eyes off the earthly task, and help them see that they could glorify God even with a dishcloth in hand?

Looking back, I remember great frustrations as I feebly tried to encourage the members of each task force to do their work heartily for the Lord.

The book of Nehemiah presents the portrait of a leader who successfully gives his people a mind to work. Nehemiah motivated thousands to rebuild the Jerusalem wall during a bleak period of history when the Jews were recovering from the Babylonian captivity. Yet Nehemiah led the work force to complete the task in only fifty-two days.

To motive others a leader must be spiritually prepared for the task. A crucial first step is prayer. Nehemiah was in constant conversation with the Lord. When he first heard of the condition of the Jews in Jerusalem, he grieved and prayed. Though his heart was heavy, he faithfully carried out his daily work as a cupbearer. In the meantime he prayed for success and asked God to work in the king's heart.

Helen L. Challener is a homemaker and a free-lance writer. She and her husband, Bill, have two sons and live in Little Canada, Minnesota.

J. Hudson Taylor, missionary to China, often said, "God's work done in God's way will never lack God's supplies." Like Nehemiah, Hudson Taylor knew that he was not his own, that whatever service he would enter would have to be first directed by God. "To move man, through God, by prayer alone" was one of the slogans on which he depended. While he prayed and waited, he prepared. He studied Chinese and medicine so that when the call came, he would be equipped. Hudson Taylor was faithful in his responsibilities and practiced trusting God to supply all his needs.

A leader motivates others to serve by being willing himself to serve. Nehemiah modeled a servant's attitude in the king's court and in Jerusalem. Though he held an influential position as cupbearer under King Artaxerxes, he acknowledged a higher authority, a mightier King. As a leader, Nehemiah communicated his confidence that God was in charge of the task. Though God moved Nehemiah into a leadership position while the walls were being rebuilt, Nehemiah didn't forget how to serve. He worked alongside his task force.

Even in my dishwashing quarters at camp, I learned that the work was lightened when I, as a supervisor, worked beside the teams of workers. I needed to model that I was not above scraping mashed potatoes into the trash or using a dishtowel or a scouring pad. It also gave me an opportunity to demonstrate that even working for the Lord with dishpan hands can be a joyful experience.

A leader must be respected by those who serve under him. Nehemiah was a man of moral integrity. As governor over the land of Judah, he guarded the needs of the people and, unlike the previous leadership, refused to take advantage of the poor. Nehemiah admitted that a motivating factor in his righteous leadership was his fear of God. Furthermore, he did not stop at the task of wall construction, but recognized that the people needed a spiritual revival in their souls.

As a staff worker at the camp, I was fortunate to have a camp manager whom I could completely trust and respect. He modeled a lifestyle of godly integrity in his business dealings as camp manager and as overseer of the staff. Having such a godly leader motivated all of us to live up to his example and expectations.

A leader motivates others by not allowing them to be distracted from the task at hand. Because he knew his mission and had clear guidance from God, Nehemiah did not let short-term problems divert him from the long-term goal. He modeled for his workers a balanced reaction to opposition. When his enemies tried to frighten him and his workers into halting the work, Nehemiah led the people in prayer. He then took concrete steps to prepare the people for battle.

Although Nehemiah had physical enemies he could see and talk to, the distractions we encounter today are often more subtle. Perhaps we are tempted to pursue recreation before we have spent time in prayer or Bible study. Perhaps complacency has taken away a sense of urgency for God's work. Comfort and pleasure can become ends in themselves rather than rewards in the pattern of a Christian lifestyle.

Besides preventing distractions, a leader must communicate the goals of the work and why they are important. Nehemiah was realistic and straightforward with the workers (Nehemiah 2:17). As evidence of God's support of their goal, he then recalled God's prior involvement and blessing: "I also told them about the gracious hand of my God upon me and what the king had said to me. They replied, 'Let us start rebuilding.' So they began this good work" (Nehemiah 2:18).

When organizing a work force, and particularly a volunteer one, the workers must understand the overall goals at hand. Just as Nehemiah imparted the purposes of reconstructing the wall, our camp manager succeeded in helping us see how our individual jobs contributed to the spiritual welfare and ministry of the camp. We were often reminded that we were working for God and that he was prospering the work. Our camp director frequently shared with his staff evidences of God's working in our midst, and such encouragement strengthened our hands and hearts as we served.

More than ten years have passed since my summers as a camp staff worker. Today many applicants for volunteer service are ex-campers who have witnessed firsthand God's blessings on the camp's ministry. They have also experienced the benefits of serving the Lord in everyday settings.

When the wall was completed, the people joined Nehemiah in dedicating their labor to God. It was God, not man, whom Nehemiah aimed to please. This surely is the attitude we should have whether we are leaders or workers.

Nehemiah
Insights for Discovery
■ ● ■

1. Read Nehemiah 1–2. Trace Nehemiah's actions in determining what role God would have him play in rebuilding the wall around Jerusalem. What can you also learn from his prayer life?

2. None of us can do everything, but we need to be open to opportunities for ministry that come along our way. Is there a need at your church that you could possibly help meet? Pray about it, and if the Lord leads, act.

3. The more we have our eyes on others, the less we have on ourselves. Study Nehemiah 4:13–23; 1 Kings 12:1–17; and Mark 10:41–42. What is the impact of Nehemiah's servant leadership?

4. Why is Nehemiah 6:16 such a pivotal verse?

5. What does 1 Kings 5:1–6 teach you about battling complacency?

6. Meditate on Romans 5:1–5. What do you do when you don't feel like following God anymore? How can you better pace yourself to avoid burnout?

Part VI
A Firm Commitment
■●■

Dr. Robert Bellah wrote in *Habits of the Heart* that there is a "widely diffused" view of life in the "middle class mainstream" which "in its pure form . . . denies all forms of obligations and commitment in relationships, replacing them only with the ideal of full, open, honest communication among self-actualized individuals" (Harper & Row, 1985). I'm sure he is right, for in my experience I find that more and more people are disinclined to commit themselves deeply to persons, causes, or institutions. Granted, there is considerable ambivalence in the minds of those who deny obligation and commitment because they have seen the advantages it brings in committed lives, and often have themselves benefited from the commitments of others. But they have also seen the price of commitment and its abuses, too. Many of the younger generation marvel that their parents are "still married" after thirty-five years. They appreciate the commitment, but they have also seen the coolness, aloofness, and lack of honest communication in long-range marriages; and for them, communication rates above commitment. There is a serious problem here: It is not *either* commitment *or* communication; it is both/and. Accordingly, our society desperately needs the modeling and proclaiming of genuine, wholehearted commitment by those who are living life to the fullest.

Once again, Scripture comes to our rescue. It would be ludicrous to try to explain Christianity without showing that it is predicated on the Father's commitment to a fallen race; the Son's commitment to the Father's will—even to death on a cross; and the commitment of the Spirit to dwell in the lives of the redeemed until they arrive in glory. The dominant theme of the Christian gospel is God's gracious, faithful commitment to mankind and the resultant grateful commitment of the redeemed to their Lord and Master. We must get this across to the "mainstream."

The lives of the biblical characters give ample illustrations. Elijah, appalled at the practices of the priests of Baal which grated on his commitments to Jehovah, takes them on and wins. Daniel, far from home in a foreign land, does not waver when he is offered an easy way out of commitments he believed were right, and he stood so tall that even lions respected his space! Nathan, the prophet, aware that his beloved king had been involved in a murderous plot, is committed to telling the truth, fully recognizing the danger of rebuking the king. But David listened and repented. John the Baptist, who played second fiddle superbly, did the same thing as Nathan, but lost his life in the process.

These people were committed to the Lord which meant, practically, they were committed to what is good, right, and true. It's easier to be committed to what is profitable, popular, and comfortable. If you can do all six at once, blessings on you. But when these commitments clash, our choices show clearly what we're made of.

Elijah:
Calls Upon God With
Great Boldness

■●■

Thomas Finley

Elijah—I
Prophet of the True God
■●■

*"Then you call on the name of your god, and I will call on the
name of the LORD. The god who answers by fire—he is God"
(1 Kings 18:24).*

The prophet Elijah ministered to the kingdom of Israel at a
critical time. Ahab the king had married a Phoenician princess
and allowed her to worship Baal. Worse, he permitted her to
persuade the Israelites to worship this false god. With the
whole nation abandoning the Lord for foreign gods, the Lord
chose Elijah to be an instrument to demonstrate his power.

Baal was allegedly in charge of the rain; so to prove the
power of the true and living God over the false god Baal, Elijah
announced to King Ahab that the rain would stop until the Lord
gave the word for it to resume.

After three years of drought, Elijah challenged the prophets
of Baal to a great contest on Mount Carmel. First, two bulls
would be sacrificed and placed on an altar. Then the prophets
of Baal were to call upon their god and, in turn, Elijah would call
upon the Lord to send fire from heaven to burn the sacrifice.

Elijah believed that God would show his power at the
request of his servant. Elijah could be so bold because he knew
the limitless power of his God, even to do the seemingly
impossible. And indeed, Baal did not answer the prayers of his
prophets. It was the Lord God who sent the consuming fire,
thus showing himself to be the true God.

Thomas Finley is Associate Professor and Chairman of the department of Semitics
and Old Testament at Talbot School of Theology, Biola University, in La Mirada,
California. He and his wife, Robin, have one daughter.

Elijah—II
Discouraged Servant
————— ■ ● ■ —————

"Yet I reserve seven thousand in Israel—all whose knees have not bowed down to Baal and all whose mouths have not kissed him" (1 Kings 19:18).

One day Elijah called down fire from heaven, and then he ran in terror from a queen who had threatened his life (1 Kings 19:1–3). Apparently Elijah had not yet learned that he needed the strength of others to encourage and help him.

Elijah considered himself "the only one of the Lord's prophets left" (1 Kings 18:22). Tired, discouraged, and certain that the Israelites planned to kill him, he desired nothing more than for the Lord to take his life (1 Kings 19:4).

The Lord set up a graphic demonstration to teach Elijah a lesson. At Mount Horeb Elijah heard a mighty wind, felt a powerful earthquake, and shrank back from a hot fire. But the Lord was in none of these. The Lord was in a "gentle whisper" that called the prophet out of his cave to confront the haunting question, "What are you doing here, Elijah?" (1 Kings 19:12–13). While the Lord can and does work with mighty displays of his power, he also quietly persuades men and women to follow him. Elijah didn't know that God had called seven thousand followers to himself in Israel.

The Lord sent Elijah back the same way he came with a commission to anoint Hazael as king over Aram (Syria), Jehu as king over Israel, and Elisha as the next prophet. Elijah carried out only the last task personally. Elisha actually anointed Hazael and a third prophet was sent by Elisha to anoint Jehu (2 Kings 8:7–15; 9:1–10). While Elijah thought he was alone in serving God, the Lord already had a successor picked out.

What a lesson for Elijah! Not only were there seven thousand who had not bowed to Baal, but there were also others who were capable of carrying out the work. Through their efforts, Israel was eventually cleansed—at least temporarily—from Baal worship.

Elijah—III
Deliverer of Judgment
■●■

When Ahab heard these words, he tore his clothes, put on sackcloth and fasted. He lay in sackcloth and went around meekly (1 Kings 21:27).

Ahab conspired with his wife, Jezebel, to murder an innocent man merely to acquire a vineyard. At first the king tried to get Naboth's vineyard by buying it, but Naboth knew it would be wrong to give up land that was part of the family inheritance. According to God's law, it could not pass from the family permanently (Leviticus 25:23–34).

The king of Israel was not above the Law of Moses. When Naboth refused to give up his land, even the king could not ignore the demands of justice, and Ahab went to his home and sulked. But Jezebel told her husband to assert his rights as the king.

Bribes purchased the testimony of two false accusers, who said Naboth cursed God and the king, a crime that bore the death penalty in ancient Israel. With Naboth dead, Ahab took possession of the vineyard—an act of grave injustice that the Lord would not ignore.

At the Lord's command, Elijah confronted Ahab and delivered a stinging prophecy of judgment against the descendants of Ahab and against Jezebel. Ahab could have seized Elijah and thrown him into prison. Instead, the king humbled himself before the Lord by tearing his clothes, putting on sackcloth, and fasting. Each of these actions was an outward sign of mourning. In this case, the king mourned because he recognized he had sinned before God.

Unfortunately, Ahab's change of heart was short-lived. Only a few years later he reverted to his habit of refusing to listen to a prophet of God (1 Kings 22). Yet for at least a short while he humbled himself before the Lord and temporarily averted a disastrous judgment. And Elijah learned that the Lord was very much in the business of changing the hearts of people through the inner persuasion of the Holy Spirit.

Elijah—IV
Humble Instructor
——— ■ ● ■ ———

The prophets from Jericho, who were watching, said, "The spirit of Elijah is resting on Elisha." And they went to meet him and bowed to the ground before him (2 Kings 2:15).

When we look on the drama of the final hours of Elijah on earth, we see something unusual. Three times Elijah told Elisha to stay put; three times Elisha refused to leave the older prophet's side (2 Kings 2:2–6). From the context of the whole chapter, it seems that Elijah was actually testing Elisha to see if he was ready to travel by himself the road of a prophet of God.

At last the two men found themselves at the Jordan, where Elijah rolled up his cloak and struck the water. Elisha had passed the test; the old prophet could now be sure that the work would be left in good hands. After both men passed through the dry channel that opened up, Elijah said, "Tell me, what can I do for you before I am taken from you?" (2 Kings 2:9)

Was Elijah surprised that Elisha asked for "a double portion of your spirit"? Evidently not, though it was "a difficult thing" that Elisha had asked (2 Kings 2:10). It would require a new demonstration of God's power; only God could make a prophet! Surely Elijah spoke under divine inspiration, "If you see me when I am taken from you, it will be yours—otherwise not" (2 Kings 2:10). That is, if Elisha was willing to endure even to the point of facing the Lord's appearance on earth, the young man would become full heir to the ministry.

When the chariot of fire came to receive Elijah, the young prophet did witness it and was stricken with grief, knowing that he would no longer see his spiritual father on this earth. Then he arrived back at the Jordan and took Elijah's cloak and once again struck the water, saying, "Where now is the Lord, the God of Elijah?" (2 Kings 2:14)

In the sight of a company of prophets the waters parted, and everyone recognized that the spirit of Elijah was resting on Elisha. Because Elijah had been bold with God to the point of committing everything to him, there now was an Elisha who would carry on the same ministry.

Elijah: How Does This Apply to Me?
Learning Obedience in Difficulty
■●■
Betty Pharris

"I'm giving my thirty-day notice next week," my husband told me after working twenty years with the same company.

"I want you to be happy," I said, knowing that Charles had thought about a move into real estate for more than a year. However, this was about the extent of our conversation.

Although we were both Christians, we often experienced communication roadblocks in our marriage. We also harbored blind spots in our relationships to God. We were ignorant of many biblical principles and were disobedient to others.

While our life together had previously run along fairly smoothly, the real estate venture brought us to a head-on collision. Now it appeared that we must learn to work together to survive financially.

As Charles bought, sold, rented, and maintained the houses, the load fell on me to set up a bookkeeping system. I knew nothing about business as I had spent my adult life being a wife, mother, and homemaker. Frustration and anger grew in me as I labored over work that was beyond my abilities and desires.

To add to our trouble, the Tulsa real estate market began to collapse because of falling oil prices in 1982. As business consumed us, the gradual financial bondage, emotional anguish, and spiritual upheaval devastated me.

"Please, God," I prayed, "give me the right attitude toward this nightmare."

At that time I was studying Israel and the minor prophets in my Bible Study Fellowship class. I found that Elijah presented a dramatic lesson in prayer and obedience to the Lord. Elijah didn't hesitate to obey God's command to confront the wicked King Ahab with news of the approaching drought. Afterward the Lord told Elijah to move on to Zarephath, where he was to ask a poor widow for food, and again Elijah obeyed.

The widow had only a handful of meal in a barrel and a little oil in a jug. When Elijah met her, she was preparing what she believed would be the last meal for her son and herself. After

Betty Pharris is a free-lance writer. She and her husband, Charles, have two grown children and six grandchildren. They make their home in Broken Arrow, Oklahoma.

that there would be no food left, and they would die. But as she too obeyed, acting on God's promise that the food would not run out, she found that the flour and oil were continually replenished (1 Kings 17:10–16).

Her faith was tested, however, when her son later fell ill and died. But Elijah took her son and prayed to the Lord who answered the prayer, and the boy was returned to life. New power and life surged through all three of them.

I learned from Elijah that I needed God's power to change my attitude toward my situation. I observed many problem areas, including fearfulness, worry, impatience, anger, and pride. I longed for Elijah's kind of courage that produced security in eternal things, patience, meekness, and humility. I knew that these qualities could not grow in me in my own natural strength.

I made a personal commitment to rise daily at 5:00 A.M. to study God's Word and pray. As God enabled me to do this, as well as memorize Scripture, I was sustained in my daily responsibilities. Also, Charles and I began to read our Bible together more often.

It was a comfort to read in James 5:17 (KJV) that Elijah was "a man subject to like passions as we are." The difference was that Elijah persevered in earnest prayer and was sensitive to obey God's truths. Thus Elijah could pray valiantly at Mount Carmel for the fire to fall because his every action and word was in obedience to God's direction. I began to realize that only by total obedience to God would I see his power manifest in my life.

Meanwhile, 1 Kings 18:21 (KJV) queried me: "How long halt ye between two opinions?" I longed to be free from my "office prison" and at times even from my marriage. I wanted to serve God and Baal too. But finally the sobering thought hit me that God was asking me to yield the real estate business and my husband to him.

Elijah also challenged me with his injunction, "If the Lord be God, follow him" (1 Kings 18:21, KJV). I continually asked myself, "Are we choosing God's way, like Elijah; or our way, like Ahab?" If we were choosing our own way, it would be like pouring water on the altar fire in the name of Baal. If we were choosing God's way and appropriating our faith, this would please the Lord.

Even as Elijah persisted in his wait for rain, his faith never faltered. In 1 Kings 18:41–43, Elijah told Ahab that he heard rain. Then, after he climbed to the top of Mount Carmel and cast himself to the earth with his head between his knees in prayer, he sent his servant to look toward the sea for clouds. Elijah's focus was on God and not the surrounding weather conditions.

Our business situation has not changed, but while Charles and I wait for our "life-giving rain" of financial freedom, we too are focusing on God and prayer. As we await his timing, we choose to believe by his grace and mercy that it is to teach us new lessons in faith and to develop in us new character qualities.

With Elijah, despondence and fear came after the great public miracle of rain and his race to Jezreel. In 1 Kings 19:2, when news reached him that Jezebel would have him killed within twenty-four hours, he ran for his life.

In 1 Kings 19:4, Elijah runs a day's journey into the desert and sits down under a juniper tree. There he prayed that he might die, but God sent an angel to minister to him.

In the midst of our own despondency and fear, Charles and I have experienced God ministering to us in a special way through biblically sound seminars and Bible classes we have attended. Although we have been church members all our married lives, we have found ourselves refreshed by new spiritual insights.

After Elijah wandered in the wilderness for forty days and forty nights, God revealed himself to the prophet in a still, small voice (1 Kings 19:11–12). Charles and I are discovering the still, small voice of the Holy Spirit as we study the Bible together. We also find that the tensions in our marriage lessen as we heed the instructions and commands—and hold to the promises—that the Bible contains.

We have made a commitment to God to be free of debt, knowing that humanly speaking this is impossible. We have given God ownership of what actually was his all along. We are claiming Romans 8:28–29 (KJV), "all things work together for good to them that love God" that we might be ". . . conformed to the image of his Son."

Elijah's great boldness teaches us that if we will give all our rights to God, he will assume all responsibility for us.

I used to think that security was money in the bank. Now I am learning that godly security and true riches emanate from humility and fear of the Lord.

Elijah
Insights for Discovery
■ ● ■

1. Consider the state of the people of Israel by reading the accounts of the kings who ruled before and during Elijah's life (1 Kings 15:25–16:33). Now read 1 Kings 17:1. Think of the faith Elijah needed to approach King Ahab. What effect do you think Elijah's prophecy had on the king?

2. After studying 1 Kings 17:2–24, reflect on the woman's conclusion about Elijah (verse 24).

3. Read 1 Kings 18. What do Elijah's actions and words reveal about his relationship with God? His confidence in God's faithfulness? His communication with God? His jealousy for God? (See also 2 Kings 1:1–2:11.)

4. Taking into account all that you've studied about Elijah, what encourages you as you read James 5:17–18?

5. Look at other instances where the power of God was released when people called upon him in prayer (see 2 Kings 19:14–36; 2 Chronicles 14:2–15; and Acts 12:1–19).

6. Read what Jesus said about prayer in Matthew 7:7–11; 18:18–20; 21:18–22. In the context of these verses and Psalm 66:17–20, identify the conditions required for God to answer our prayers.

7. Meditate on Psalm 5:1–7 and Psalm 42:1–8. Think about how you can improve your personal communication to God.

Daniel:
He Remained Holy in a Stern Test
■ ● ■

David H. Engelhard

Daniel—I
Resisted Royal Rations
■ ● ■

Daniel resolved not to defile himself with the royal food and wine, and he asked the chief official for permission not to defile himself this way (Daniel 1:8).

Daniel's circumstances were a curious mixture of the worst of times and the best of times. The armies of Babylonian King Nebuchadnezzar had besieged and captured Jerusalem, carried off some of its citizens, and taken articles from the temple.

The Babylonian king sought to maximize the strength of his kingdom by using the talents of the most-qualified captives for his benefit. Daniel was fit physically, mentally, and spiritually for his role as one of the king's advisers (Daniel 1:4). Daniel had received the best education available in Jerusalem, but before he could actually function for the king, he needed to be indoctrinated in the Babylonian way of life.

While we read nothing of Daniel's resistance to learning the Babylonian language and literature, we are told that he "resolved not to defile himself with the royal food and wine."

This was more than a cross-cultural repulsion for food that looked and tasted unusual. Daniel was a covenant child, and he had learned early that some food was not pleasing to God, and therefore improper to eat.

The young prophet's obedience reaped special results. His diet of vegetables and water made Daniel and his three friends look "healthier and better nourished than any of the young men who ate the royal food" (Daniel 1:12, 15). Further, they received knowledge and understanding from God. Because of their faithfulness, the Lord would entrust to them yet greater responsibilities (Daniel 1:17).

In our own lives religious resolve and moral conviction can be difficult to maintain even under the best of circumstances. When difficulties and testings arise, commitment to our beliefs can become fragile. Or such circumstances can, by the grace of God, bring out our best and strengthen our convictions.

David H. Engelhard is Professor of Old Testament at Calvin Theological Seminary in Grand Rapids, Michigan. He and his wife, Jeanne, have three grown children.

Daniel—II
Humble in Achievements
———— ■ ● ■ ————

"This mystery had been revealed to me, not because I have greater wisdom than other living men, but so that you, O king, may know the interpretation and that you may understand what went through your mind" (Daniel 2:30).

God had given Daniel knowledge, understanding, and favor, and the prophet exhibited a humility that allowed the Lord to shine through. As a result, those who benefited from his ministry not only praised Daniel, but also praised God (Daniel 2:46–47).

The king's dreams and resulting insomnia had so disturbed him that he asked his astrologers to perform an impossible feat: telling the king what he had dreamed as well as interpreting it. "Unfair!" they cried. "Only the gods can do that!" (cf. Daniel 2:10–11)

Their response filled the king with such blistering anger that he ordered the execution of all his wise men. Before this order could be carried out, Daniel sought additional time to solve the mystery of the dream.

Daniel explained to his three friends the life-threatening situation they faced. They pleaded with God for mercy so that they might know the mystery of the dream and have their lives spared (Daniel 2:17–18). Daniel and his friends knew the true God whose message was contained in the dream.

The results of Daniel's humble submission to God were truly remarkable. He revealed the content of the king's dream and its interpretation. Joy and awe filled the king, and he honored both Daniel and God: "Surely your God is the God of gods and the Lord of kings" (Daniel 2:47).

Like Daniel, we need to strive for an attitude where our hearts and minds are properly attuned to God. If we humbly submit to God, we can know and do his will. We cannot succeed on our own insight. Unless we rely on wisdom from above and accept our role in the building of his kingdom, we will find ourselves no better prepared to give answers to the world's questions and perplexing situations than were Nebuchadnezzar's pagan astrologers.

Daniel—III
Persistent in Prayer
■ ● ■

When Daniel learned that the decree had been published, he went home to his upstairs room where the windows opened toward Jerusalem. Three times a day he got down on his knees and prayed, giving thanks to his God, just as he had done before (Daniel 6:10).

Persistent prayer was a mark of Daniel's life. Power from prayer gave him the wisdom and courage to act in the face of personal danger. Daniel had matured into a man of God. He had so distinguished himself as an official of the land that he was in line for a promotion (Daniel 6:3). His excellence had produced jealousy in Daniel's Babylonian co-workers. When they looked for a flaw in his character, they discovered that he was neither corrupt nor negligent, but completely trustworthy (Daniel 6:4). This was high praise from worldly leaders. But instead of affirming Daniel's godly character, they sought ways to bring him into disfavor with the king.

According to Daniel's fellow workers, his only flaw was his commitment to his God. Their plan to cause this holy and righteous man to "fail" was to create a conflict of loyalties. They knew that Daniel would never bow down to an earthly king.

The new king, Darius the Mede, was easily swayed by the suggestion of this special interest group. He issued a decree that prohibited the worship of anyone except himself. But Daniel did not participate in this idolatry. Instead, he boldly opened his windows and prayed to his God. God's sustaining grace gave Daniel a courageous confidence to remain faithful and holy in spite of the certain punishment he would receive.

God did not disappoint Daniel. When Daniel was placed in the lions' den, the lions' mouths were shut and the prophet was spared.

Once again a pagan king praised God when his power was demonstrated. Darius decreed that all should fear Daniel's God: "For he is the living God and he endures forever; his kingdom will not be destroyed, his dominion will never end" (Daniel 6:26).

Daniel—IV
Dreamer of Dreams

———— ■ ● ■ ————

In my vision at night I looked, and there before me was one like a son of man, coming with the clouds of heaven. . . . He was given authority, glory and sovereign power; all peoples, nations and men of every language worshiped him. His dominion is an everlasting dominion that will not pass away, and his kingdom is one that will never be destroyed (Daniel 7:13–14).

Daniel's dream came several years before he was put into the den of lions. He understood that none of Darius' political plans could ever shake the foundation of God's kingdom plans.

Daniel's dream was realistic. When the fourth beast appeared, it was more terrifying and frightening than the three other beasts, and it had more power than thought believable. Surely this beast would last forever and consume everything in its path. But it too met its end. All its boastful and arrogant talk could not prevent its destruction in the blazing fire (Daniel 7:7–11).

In Daniel 7, we receive a guide to redemptive history, but not a detailed roadmap. Still, the main thrust is unmistakable: Our exalted and everlasting God reigns in heaven and on earth, and no temporary kingdom is a serious threat to his sovereignty. Therein lies our hope.

Our hope is found in the one who was "like a son of man," who approached the Ancient of Days and received for us kingdom authority, glory, and power. He was given dominion by God over people, nations, and languages, and his dominion will never diminish or fail.

Jesus repeatedly identified himself as the Son of Man so that his disciples and we would know that he is the rightful heir of the eternal throne.

Our eternal hope and home is secure, a gift of grace from the King of Kings and Lord of Lords. If we know and believe in this hope, we can face the doubts, dilemmas, and disappointments of each day with a confidence rooted in God's victory over sin and evil.

Daniel: How Does This Apply to Me?
Facing the Lion in My Office
■ ● ■
Norma Sanders Mezoe

My supervisor, Gloria, sat busily working at her desk as usual. And as usual she didn't look up when I entered the office. The scowl on her face was a clear warning of another bad day—a day of working in a tension-packed atmosphere.

Working with Gloria hadn't always been that way. Though she was a perfectionist, my work as her secretary had met her approval in the past. A few months earlier she had told our board of directors that I was a valuable asset in our office.

Now I was beginning to face each workday with apprehension. Even my phone calls were open to Gloria's criticism. After I completed a telephone conversation, Gloria would inform me of additional information she thought I should have included. I tensed whenever the phone rang. I knew she would be listening closely as I spoke.

I had worked for other supervisors before, but never with this kind of conflict.

I needed my job and I didn't want to lose it. I enjoyed the work and firmly believed that God had opened the door for me to be working here. Just weeks after my husband left me, the position opened up, and my lifestyle changed from that of a homemaker to that of a secretary.

During this time of change, my thoughts were similar to those that I imagined young Daniel had. His roots had been torn from Jerusalem and transplanted in Babylon. His heart must have ached as he thought of his family and the familiar environment of his youth. But Daniel adjusted. In fact, by allowing God to be in control, Daniel thrived. He became one of three administrators in the kingdom of Darius (Daniel 6:1–2).

I certainly didn't have similar acclaim, but over the years I had sharpened and increased my abilities as a secretary. Now it seemed that the confidence I had acquired was being eroded by Gloria's constant criticizing and nit-picking. I knew that she was struggling with personal problems as well, but it seemed that I had become her scapegoat.

Norma Sanders Mezoe is a homemaker and a free-lance writer. She has three grown children. She and her husband, Gene, attend Sandborn Baptist Church.

I shared my problem with Christian friends who I knew would pray faithfully for me. I was praying too—not only for myself but for Gloria and our relationship. Each morning I sought God's guidance for that day. Each evening I offered thanksgiving that he had brought me through another day and had smoothed the rough spots.

Like the prophet Daniel, I knew that my strength and guidance came from God. Daniel was persistent in his prayer life. He chose to kneel before his open window three times daily to talk with God. Even after King Darius passed an ordinance forbidding the asking of petitions from anyone other than himself, Daniel remained steadfast in his prayer life (Daniel 6:6–11).

After working with Gloria for many tension-filled weeks, she stood before me one day with a letter which I was to type. The letter, detailing what Gloria claimed to be my most serious faults, would be sent to our organization's headquarters.

It was a humbling task to type the incriminating words, knowing that they might even result in my being dismissed from my job. But I swallowed my pride and typed the letter.

By the end of that day my emotions were frazzled. I was close to despair. However, God remained faithful; he did not allow my faith and self-respect to be devoured. His plans for my life would not be destroyed.

During this testing time, Pam, a Christian friend of mine, told me of a similar trial that she had faced. She too had been criticized unfairly in her work. Out of desperation she sought other positions. But then it seemed that God was leading Pam to remain in her present job and endure the frustrations. She stayed even though it was tough, and eventually the problems were smoothed out. Her positive Christian witness radiated throughout that difficult period. Pam's testimony challenged me to continue praying for Gloria and to try even harder to perfect my work.

Slowly the atmosphere at work changed. Gloria and I talked more. From time to time I told Gloria about what God was doing in my life: of his plans for creating joy from sadness and of the peace he offered. I didn't play the role of a preacher of judgment. Simply but boldly I tried to proclaim the Good News of God's love.

Months passed and Gloria's respect returned for me and my work. Then problems began to develop in her job. She had been expecting a promotion; instead, she was asked to leave the organization.

In the weeks before she left, I let Gloria know that I cared about the heartaches in both her professional life and in her personal life. A few days before she left, she approached my desk.

"There is something I don't understand," she said. "Even though I will be out of work soon, I have a strange feeling of peace."

"Gloria," I quietly said, "I've been praying for you. I think God is answering those prayers."

This opened a discussion about the timing of answered prayers—that we must wait for God's timing and not try to control situations on our own. We agreed that we don't always understand God's timing, but we know his timing is best.

Daniel must have believed in God's perfect timing for answering prayers. When the prophet faced the hungry lions, the prayers which he had courageously prayed before his open window had long before reached the ears of his loving God. And God closed the mouths of the lions.

When Darius stood fearfully before the lions' den on the morning after Daniel had been thrown in, the king cried out, asking Daniel if his God had been able to save him. Darius must have been both relieved and amazed to hear Daniel's voice in reply (Daniel 6:19–23).

Daniel not only passed his test in the lions' den, but his actions convinced King Darius that Daniel's God was the true and living God. Darius then decreed that all of his kingdom must serve Daniel's God (Daniel 6:25–27).

I passed my test as well. God walked with me through those tension-filled days when it seemed that a lion's breath was hot upon me. And because I had passed my test, I was able to offer encouragement to Gloria when she battled her own enemy.

The day after Gloria left, a large bouquet of colorful fall flowers was delivered to my office. The message: "In appreciation. Thanks for everything. Gloria."

Even in the lions' den—or especially in the lions' den—God can use us to demonstrate his power and love to those who need encouragement.

Daniel
Insights for Discovery
■ ● ■

1. Look at the qualities and the habits that Daniel possessed, as revealed in Daniel 1:8–21; 2:14–23; 6:1–10.

2. Take note of Daniel's reputation among the kings of his day (Daniel 2:46–49; 5:10–16, 29; 6:1–3, 38).

3. Read Daniel 6 and consider the reasons for Daniel's suffering and for his overnight survival in the lions' den. See a related passage in 1 Peter 2:19–24.

4. Meditate on Psalm 34:15–22 and focus on God's response to faithful prayer in your life.

5. How should we react to persecution and suffering, according to Matthew 5:10–16; John 15:18–16:4; Philippians 1:27–2:11; and 1 Peter 4:12–19?

6. Hebrews 11:1–12:2 tells us that many of our spiritual ancestors suffered for their commitment to the Lord. What challenges you most about this passage of Scripture?

7. From 2 Corinthians 1:3–11 and James 1:2–12, reflect on the spiritual growth and the ministry that suffering brings about. Ask God to use you in another person's time of suffering.

Nathan:
He Dared to Confront
■●■
Robert L. Alden

Nathan—I
The King's Confidant
■●■

*After the king was settled in his palace and the LORD had given
him rest from all his enemies around him, he said to Nathan the
prophet, "Here I am, living in a palace of cedar, while the ark
of God remains in a tent" (2 Samuel 7:1–2).*

Prior to the events in 2 Samuel 7, King David of Israel had con-
quered a series of surrounding nations. The victories allowed
David to settle into his palace. This palace is apparently the one
mentioned in 2 Samuel 5:9, "David then took up residence in
the fortress and called it the City of David." The building of a
palace by a successful king was a virtual necessity in the ancient
Near East. It was, to some extent, a token of achievement that
the people expected, but not necessarily a monument to the
monarch's pride.

In this new residence the prophet Nathan apparently had
access to David. In chapter 7, he delivers God's words to the
king regarding the continuation of the Davidic dynasty. In
2 Samuel 12, Nathan confronts David about his affair with
Bathsheba. And in 1 Kings 1, Nathan plays a central role in the
selection and coronation of Solomon as David's successor.

The fact that the prophet is present, not summoned from
somewhere else for an opinion, indicates that he was likely the
king's confidant. We know that other prophets were close to
kings and served as their spiritual advisers, chaplains, or
confessors. Isaiah served King Hezekiah in such a capacity.
King Ahab of the ten northern tribes had four hundred such
prophets to give him counsel (2 Chronicles 18:5). None of these
prophets, however, was a true prophet of the Lord, so the
advice they gave was essentially what the wicked king wanted
to hear, though it was false (2 Chronicles 18:1–27).

Unlike Ahab, David was a godly man, and the prophets he
chose as advisers were also godly. Just how much advice
Nathan had given in the past we do not know. But he spoke
with an authority that David never contradicted. Undoubt-
edly, Nathan had earned the respect of the king.

Robert L. Alden is Professor of Old Testament at Denver Conservative Baptist
Seminary in Denver, Colorado. He and his wife, Mary Jane, have two children.

Nathan—II
The Lord's Spokesman

■ ● ■

*"Go and tell my servant David, 'This is what the LORD says:
Are you the one to build me a house to dwell in?'" (2 Samuel 7:5)*

Advisers who tell us the truth are rare indeed. That is why Nathan, as a prophet to David, was so exceptional.

David grew restless as he considered the contrast between his own palatial residence and the well-worn tabernacle that housed the ark of God. He needed some word from God.

Nathan had initially concurred with the king, telling him to go ahead and do whatever he wished. The following night, however, God's word came to Nathan. It compelled Nathan to revise his earlier advice to the king.

David's concern was the house of God, but the focus of the revelation to Nathan was the house of David. *House* means dynasty, ongoing family, or succession of heirs to the throne. Second Samuel 7:11–12 says: "'The Lord declares to you that the Lord himself will establish a house for you: When your days are over and you rest with your fathers, I will raise up your offspring to succeed you, who will come from your own body, and I will establish his kingdom.'"

Thus, Nathan adjusted his advice. From his earlier counsel David might have gone ahead and built the temple. But when the obedient prophet faithfully retold the message that God had given him, David got a promise that was better than any building.

The temple that David's son Solomon eventually built vanished long ago. At best, only a few rows of the outermost retaining walls are still visible. As Nathan predicted, the "house" of David is still with us. Indeed, about twenty successors followed David to the throne in Jerusalem, but the final fulfillment of Nathan's promise came when an angel of the Lord appeared to some shepherds and announced, "Today in the town of David a Savior has been born to you; he is Christ the Lord" (Luke 2:11).

Nathan—III
The Prophet Who Confronted
——— ■ ● ■ ———

*The thing David had done displeased the LORD. The LORD sent
Nathan to David (2 Samuel 11:27–12:1).*

David sinned against the Lord when he committed adultery
with Bathsheba, the wife of one of his finest soldiers. He added
to that sin by arranging a furlough for Uriah to make it appear
that the child fathered by David himself would be Uriah's. And
David compounded those sins with a scheme whereby Uriah
would die in battle.

Nathan, who years before had brought to David the promise of a glorious future, now had to bring rebuke: God's stinging
indictment against the king who was in deep sin.

To do this, Nathan tells David a parable: There were two
men, one poor and one rich, one who owned a single sheep and
one who had many. Then one day the rich man took the sheep
of the poor man and killed it to prepare a meal for a traveler.

At first David did not understand the point of the story.
Rather, thinking it was a real case, he immediately offered a
verdict: "The man who did this deserves to die!"

Then Nathan said, "You are the man!" He went on to
explain all that God had given David. The king had several
wives. He was surrounded by luxury and honored with
success, he enjoyed all good things; yet he had burned with lust
for what God's law had strictly forbidden—another man's wife
(2 Samuel 12:1–5, 7).

There was no justification David could offer, and he did not
try. David simply confessed, "I have sinned against the Lord"
(2 Samuel 12:13).

The law of Moses prescribed death for those guilty of
adultery and murder (Leviticus 20:10). God did not implement
that law in this case. His brief but blessed verdict given through
Nathan was: "The Lord has taken away your sin. You are not
going to die" (2 Samuel 12:13).

When David acted contritely, it must have been a great
relief to Nathan. Other prophets lost their lives for rebuking
kings for their sins. Nathan should be commended for his
courage in carrying out this unpleasant task.

Nathan—IV
Messenger of Comfort
■ ● ■

And because the LORD loved him, he sent word through Nathan the prophet to name him Jedidiah (2 Samuel 12:25).

The first son of David and Bathsheba, the one conceived illegitimately through their adulterous affair, died soon after he was born. That happened in direct fulfillment of God's word of judgment through Nathan: "But because by doing this you have made the enemies of the Lord show utter contempt, the son born to you will die" (2 Samuel 12:14).

When Bathsheba was properly married to the king, she bore him a second son who was called by two names. The royal parents named him Solomon, but God gave him another name, Jedidiah. This is not an unusual practice in the Bible. God renamed Abram, Abraham. He renamed Sarai, Sarah. He changed Jacob to Israel and Hoshea to Joshua. In Isaiah 7:14 Jesus was called Immanuel.

Often these names have spiritual significance. That is the case with Jedidiah, which means "beloved of the Lord." *Iah* is the shortened form of God's name Yahweh. *Jedid* comes from the same root as the name David, so there is a certain memory of the father preserved in the name of the son.

Unlike the rebuke that Nathan had brought to David, this is a pleasant message to deliver. The prophet who had needed the courage to confront the sinning king now has the happy task of comforting the chastened king. He assures him that with the use of this name, God's promises are still in effect. David's dynasty would continue and it would continue with God's blessing and love.

This newborn child one day became king of Israel, and Nathan played a crucial role in bringing that about (1 Kings 1). As a faithful prophet, Nathan did his job well. He was true to his king, but more important, he was true to his God.

Nathan: How Does This Apply to Me?
Seeking God's Interests
———— ■ ● ■ ————
Marilyn N. Anderes

My six-year-old son and I made a quick stop at the art store where I regularly buy calligraphy supplies.

"Why is that ugly picture there, Mom?" my son asked. He pointed to the store's front window where a print rested on an easel. I was startled to see a picture that to me seemed pornographic. In many previous visits to this retailer I had enjoyed quality merchandise, helpful sales personnel, and a pleasant store atmosphere. But now I wondered what had happened that they were displaying what I believed to be tasteless and offensive.

I debated how to respond. I could ignore the picture, but my son's probing question and pointing finger wouldn't allow that. I could boycott the store, but it was the nearest source for my supplies. Another option frightened me: I could speak with the manager about removing the print.

I decided to approach a saleswoman who looked friendly. Bracing my shoulders and straining to have a soft voice and sweet smile, I asked, "May I speak with you about something important?"

"Of course," she answered.

I gulped. My smile melted as my quivering voice increased in decibels. My cheeks flushed, and I silently questioned my willingness to become involved.

"I've told my friends about your excellent store," I blurted. "But I'm concerned about the picture that greets your customers today." Clearing my throat, I continued, "I find it inappropriate to be in a family shopping mall and improper for the eye level of my first-grader. Will you consider removing the picture?"

The clerk's reply stunned me: "That's our best seller. Too bad."

On the way to the parking lot my shoulders sagged and my hands fell limp. "I did the right thing," I thought, "but why do I feel so stupid?"

Marilyn N. Anderes is a homemaker, women's retreat speaker, and free-lance writer living in Mitchellville, Maryland. She and her husband, John, have three children.

I thought about how the prophet Nathan must have felt when the Lord dispatched him into action. King David had committed grievous sins and offended God. Idleness, lust, adultery, murder, and lying all demanded confrontation, and the Lord called on Nathan to help David remember God's ways.

A job description for prophets is found in Deuteronomy 18:18: "I will raise up for them a prophet like you from among their brothers; I will put my words in his mouth, and he will tell them everything I command him."

Nathan was faithful to the challenges of his position as a prophet of God. He listened to God and "reported to David all the words of this entire revelation" (2 Samuel 7:17). Nathan's daily concerns were points of communication with the Lord, and he was trained by practice to see God's interests. Nathan was God's ambassador, seeking reconciliation between a sinner and his Lord. David's sins didn't just irk Nathan; they were offenses to the Almighty, the One whom Nathan represented.

In much the same way, the store display was not just an insult to my artistic eyes. It wasn't the colors or the symmetry that outraged me. Because of my relationship with God, I believed that the picture was a moral affront to him. I was convicted of my responsibility to uphold his standards.

Nathan was able to confront David because their relationship was based on openness, and he had established credibility with David.

Similarly, my frequent visits to the store had provided the opportunity to develop a relationship with the retailer. Most of the sales people knew me as a congenial face in a busy day, not as a crank or a stranger. I had earned some credibility before the day of confrontation.

Nathan was also sensitive to God's timing. After David's affair with Bathsheba, "the Lord sent Nathan to David" (2 Samuel 12:1). Nathan obeyed. The prophet was in tune not only with what God wanted to accomplish, but with when he wanted it done.

I'm not sure when the store first displayed the picture, but I sensed God prodding me to take action the first time I saw it. As God's Spirit moved me, I was willing to speak his truth.

Nathan was also careful in his approach to the king. He told the story of a rich man who took the only thing owned by a poor man. David was incensed. Even when he asserted, "You are the man!" (2 Samuel 12:7), Nathan invited repentance; he didn't demand change. As a loving confronter, Nathan appealed to David's sense of right and wrong.

Nathan left the results in God's hands. He didn't know how David would respond, but Nathan's mission was successful because David saw that he had grieved God. David cried for forgiveness, cleansing, and restoration (Psalm 51).

In my situation I had a chance to call upon the retailer's sense of good business practice. I didn't say, "you should throw away that filthy thing," forcing a fists-up posture. The response from the sales people at the store wasn't immediate, but the print was moved to an inside wall and eventually disappeared altogether.

Nathan was more complete in his reproof. After God's message was spoken by the concerned prophet, David knew with certainty that his sin had affected others and the consequences were inevitable. The Lord's Word was trampled, and God's enemies were given an occasion to mock him. Even generations following David would feel the effects of his immoral choices, beginning with the death of his newborn infant (2 Samuel 12:9, 14, 19).

Nathan also slowed the king down. The prophet helped David to think about his past actions and to reconsider his present course. The consequences remained, but David's relationship with the Lord was restored and he could continue in God's way.

Likewise, I had a chance to help the retailer slow down so that he could rethink his position and consider his actions from a consumer's point of view.

David struggled with God's complaint, but then he agreed and turned himself around. When the episode was behind him and the good news of Solomon's birth was to be declared, Nathan was given the announcement honors. He continued his caring relationship throughout the king's old age. By making sure that Solomon was crowned as the rightful successor to the throne, Nathan assured the continuity of God's covenant—the same promise he had proclaimed to David years earlier.

With care we can confront both Christians and nonbelievers. Nathan inspires us to seek God's interests in God's way, acting with his wisdom in his time. When we sense God's leading, we can and should "speak the truth in love" (cf. Ephesians 4:15).

Nathan
Insights for Discovery
■ ● ■

1. Study how Nathan confronted David (2 Samuel 7:5, 8; 12:7, 11). Think about the significance of the phrase, "This is what the Lord says."

2. Contrast the mood swings that Nathan must have experienced in his appearances before the king in 2 Samuel 12:14 and 2 Samuel 12:25.

3. Read Psalm 51:1–13 and witness David's reaction to the uncovering of his sin. (See related verses in Proverbs 9:9 and 16:13.)

4. Consider David's prayer for God's protection in Psalm 19:12–13. How does this action apply to you?

5. Reflect on Jesus' warning about judging in Matthew 7:1–5. (See also Luke 17:3–4.)

6. From Romans 15:1–2 and Galatians 6:1, notice our obligation to the weak and to a fallen believer. (Observe in Romans 12:10; Ephesians 4:2; and Philippians 2:3–4, what is crucial for this ministry.)

7. Study Isaiah 6; Jeremiah 1; and Ezekiel 2. Examine the calls of these other prophets.

8. In light of Christ's Great Commission to preach the gospel (Mark 16:15), note Romans 10:12–15 and 2 Corinthians 5:16–20. Meditate on your role in challenging your family and friends with the claims of Christ, to repent of their sins, and to commit their lives to the Lord.

John the Baptist: He Led the Way to the Savior

■●■

Andrew C. Ross

John the Baptist—I
Prophet and Baptizer

─────── ■ ● ■ ───────

"Bear fruit that befits repentance, and do not presume to say to yourselves, 'We have Abraham as our father'; for I tell you, God is able from these stones to raise up children to Abraham" (Matthew 3:8–9, RSV).

John the Baptist came out of the desert proclaiming news of the coming of the kingdom of heaven. This had been referred to by Old Testament prophets, most sharply by Amos: "Woe to you who desire the day of the Lord! Why would you have the day of the Lord? It is darkness, and not light; as if a man fled from a lion, and a bear met him" (Amos 5:18–19, RSV).

This day was seen by John as one of sharp judgment: "The ax is laid to the root of the trees" (Matthew 3:10, RSV). He said that the Messiah would come with his winnowing fork in his hand (Matthew 3:12, RSV). A winnowing fork was used to toss threshed grain into the air so that the chaff was blown away and only the grain was left.

John called the people to confess their sins and repent. Huge crowds came to hear him, recognizing in him the authentic voice of prophecy which had long been silent in Israel. Those who confessed and repented were baptized by John in the Jordan River. This baptism was not a vehicle of God's grace; rather, it was a symbolic act of sinners turning away from the sin of the past toward a future of service to God.

The message of the coming day of the Lord was resonant with notes from the prophets of the past, but the action of baptism was new. The rabbis of the school known as the House of Hillel had taught that baptism by immersion was an essential part of the initiation of Gentile converts into the community of Israel, along with circumcision for men. However, it was the children of Abraham who now had to be baptized. This was a radical departure from the traditional understanding of the relationships between God's people and outsiders. Yet Jesus endorsed this teaching by requesting to be baptized by John.

Andrew C. Ross is Senior Lecturer, Faculty of Divinity, at the University of Edinburgh, Scotland. He and his wife, Joyce, are the parents of four grown children.

John the Baptist—II
Forerunner

■ ● ■

"This is he who was spoken of by the prophet Isaiah when he said, 'The voice of one crying in the wilderness: Prepare the way of the Lord, make his paths straight'" (Matthew 3:3, RSV).

John was believed to be a prophet by many of the thousands who flocked to hear him. Others saw him as Elijah come back, as had been promised by Malachi, to prepare the people for "he who was to come" (cf. Malachi 3:1; 4:5–6). The angel had told John's father, Zechariah: "He will go before him in the spirit and power of Elijah, to turn the hearts of the fathers to the children, and the disobedient to the wisdom of the just, to make ready for the Lord a people prepared" (Luke 1:17, RSV).

From his youth John accepted the task to which his parents had dedicated him. He went to live in the desert to prepare himself. In the Israelite tradition, the desert was associated with being close to God. From the harshness of the desert had come the prophets to bring the people back to their God.

Eventually John's call to action came, and he emerged from the desert. In the Jordan valley and on the borders of Judea, he preached not only the message of God's coming judgment but also the imminence of the arrival of "he who is to come" (Matthew 11:3, RSV). Many who waited for the Messiah saw him as a divine figure who would overthrow the powers of the world and rule the earth through a restored Davidic kingship. Yet others saw him as coming to bring God's judgment on Jew and Gentile alike.

As Amos had warned, the day of the Lord was to be feared. John preached of God's righteous judgment arriving with and through the One who was coming. Yet many understood Isaiah as teaching that the coming of the Messiah was a matter for rejoicing (Isaiah 40).

John was certain that he was the forerunner of the One who was to bring terrible judgment, and John was overwhelmed with joy when he recognized in Jesus, the young Galilean of David's clan, the One "who is to come" (Matthew 11:3, RSV).

John the Baptist—III
Doubter

■ ● ■

When John heard in prison about the deeds of the Christ, he sent word by his disciples and said to him, "Are you he who is to come, or shall we look for another?" (Matthew 11:2–3, RSV)

John, God's special messenger to whom thousands came to confess, repent, and be baptized, was now in prison—Herod's dungeon. There, as he heard from his disciples of the ministry of Jesus, John became deeply disturbed and began to doubt the Jordan experience.

With all the righteous passion of Amos, John warned of the coming judgment, saying that the Messiah would baptize the truly penitent with the Holy Spirit and destroy the unrepentant. It was clear from what John heard that Jesus was not acting in this way. Nor was Jesus acting out the messianic role that many others desired, the divine warrior destroying the Romans while restoring the Davidic kingship. Far from it. The Romans continued to rule the Mediterranean world; Herod dwelt in his luxurious palace; and John, God's prophet, the forerunner of the Messiah, lay in a dungeon.

Jesus sent an answer back to John with his disciples. Just as both Matthew and Luke had introduced John with words from Isaiah (Matthew 3:3–4), Jesus pointed to his deeds (Matthew 11:4–6) in terms that specifically recalled the prophecies of Isaiah (Isaiah 29:18–19; 35:5–6). At the end of Jesus' list were the words: "And the poor have good news preached to them" (Matthew 11:5, RSV).

The message to John from Jesus ended with a beatitude: "Blessed is he who takes no offense at me" (Matthew 11:6, RSV). Jesus was saying that his humility and his association with the outcast and the poor, which puzzled John, have caused many to take offense even to this day.

John the Baptist—IV
More Than a Prophet
————— ■ ● ■ —————

"All the prophets and the law prophesied until John; and if you are willing to accept it, he is Elijah who is to come" (Matthew 11:13–14, RSV).

"All the prophets and the law" was a traditional way that Jewish teachers referred to the Scriptures. Jesus was saying that John's ministry was the climax and the end of an age. Equally, because he was the messenger who would prepare the way of the Lord (Malachi 3:1; 4:5), John's ministry was also the beginning of God's new age. "Yes, he is Elijah," said Jesus—the same Elijah whose coming announced the arrival of the Messiah.

Jesus had gently but firmly corrected John's inadequate vision of the Messiah's ministry. In his reply to John's disciples, Jesus mentioned the limitations of John's understanding and of his ministry. Then Jesus turned to the multitude to pay tribute to John as a prophet—indeed, "more than a prophet" (Matthew 11:9, RSV). John was Elijah, the forerunner of God's new age.

This was difficult for Jesus' hearers to accept. An Elijah in prison was not at all a part of their understanding of the role to be played by the returning Elijah. In the same way, later, the idea of a crucified Messiah was also bewildering and difficult to accept. But Jesus did not mean that John was literally Elijah come back through some form of reincarnation, but John fulfilled the Elijah role as the forerunner of the kingdom of heaven.

Jesus fully acknowledged John's greatness, but then added, "He who is least in the kingdom of heaven is greater than he" (Matthew 11:11, RSV). This did not mean that John and all the prophets and saints of old were excluded from God's salvation. It meant that their vision of God and his purposes for humanity was less complete than that of those who are brought by Jesus into his new kingdom. John's vision of radical judgment was true, but it must be seen in the light of Jesus, who preached Good News to the poor and died on a cross, despised and rejected.

John the Baptist: How Does This Apply to Me?
Whether Small or Large: Faithful to the Task

———— ■●■ ————

William A. Bembeneck

In a world in which big seems to be best, it is easy for me to feel misplaced or insignificant as I survey the small sanctuary of the church where I serve as pastor. God surely is interested in the large churches and big ministries, but does he see me and my attempts to do his bidding? Does God recognize my name when he looks over his churches? Are there rewards for small ministries?

As I pondered these questions, a man emerged from the pages of the Bible and caught my attention. He was a fearless proclaimer of truth, challenging the religious leaders of Israel and the political leaders of Rome. He called the nation of Israel to repentance. But he was a man who lived alone in the wilderness. His food was locusts and wild honey. His clothing was made of coarse camel's hair. He backed down to no one, and he was imprisoned and lost his head for it. The man was John the Baptist.

No record is given of John the Baptist's being invited to preach his message in Israel's synagogues. He was not in demand to travel from town to town for speaking engagements. Those desiring to hear John had to leave the city and journey into the wilderness where he was preaching and baptizing.

One day messengers from Jerusalem arrived, seeking an interview with John the Baptist. They questioned him as to his identity. No, he was not the Christ. Neither was he the promised prophet nor Elijah.

"Who are you?" they probed.

"A voice," he declared.

A voice? There was not even a name attached to the voice; he was simply a voice.

William A. Bembeneck is the pastor of Christian Bible Fellowship (nondenominational) in Farmington Hills, Michigan. He and his wife, Elizabeth Anne, have two children.

How could he ever become well known apart from promoting his name?

I looked carefully at John the Baptist's responses to his interrogators. His statements reveal his humility. Recognizing the supremacy and Lordship of Christ over himself, he said, "He it is, who coming after me is preferred before me (John 1:27, KJV). The world needed to see Christ, not John. He described Christ as One "whose shoe's latchet I am not worthy to unloose" (John 1:27, KJV). And John's inspiring conclusion revealed his attitude toward his ministry: "He should be made manifest to Israel, therefore am I come baptizing with water" (John 1:31, KJV).

John never cared whether he became popular. His goal was to be faithful to his calling to proclaim the coming Messiah.

I studied further John the Baptist's philosophy on ministry and was encouraged at what I found. Three solid pillars supported John's humble attitude as he responded to his questioners.

First, John realized that capacity for service was given by God. All we have and all we are is determined by God's hand. God groomed John for the ministry as the forerunner of Jesus Christ. Paul taught that the church edifies itself in love "according to the effectual working in the measure [capacity] of every part" (Ephesians 4:16, KJV). Every member contributes to the development of the church by ministering in the capacity God has designed for each.

My responsibility before God is to seek him supremely. Then, based upon the capacity he has created in me, Jesus Christ can be made known through me. My ministry is secondary. That I work for God is important, but whether or not I am known for that work is unimportant. It is Jesus Christ only who is to be promoted. I may be left in obscurity, but in that obscurity, I will serve the best I can.

Second, John believed that the real joy in service is pleasing Christ. Every believer desires to hear, "Well done, thou good and faithful servant: . . . enter thou into the joy of thy Lord" (Matthew 25:21, KJV). When the master is pleased, the servant is satisfied.

Likewise, my joy must be found in pleasing Christ rather than in pleasing myself. My joy often fluctuates, depending upon the effectiveness of my ministry. A "good" sermon yields joy. A "poor" sermon yields sorrow. Seeking the pleasing smile of my Lord helps to stabilize my reaction toward my ministry. Knowing that I am doing all for his promotion protects me from despair during times of doubt and personal setbacks.

Third, John's purpose in ministry was to promote Christ. He never sought the accolades of people for himself. Rather, he lived constantly in the thought, "He must increase, but I must decrease" (John 3:30, KJV). Self was dethroned in John's life so that Christ could be enthroned. John the Baptist could be content in obscurity because he lived to advance the name of Christ. If being himself a nameless voice in the wilderness promoted the much preferred Christ, John determined to be the best nameless voice ever.

The lessons from John the Baptist's life have caused me to reevaluate my own priorities and values in the ministry. Whom am I seeking to please? Is obscurity such a bad place to be when centered in God's plan? Are my values in the ministry the same as my Lord's? Am I decreasing so that Christ may constantly increase?

Perhaps people place John the Baptist in obscurity, but the words of Christ bring promotion. Christ viewed John as "much more than a prophet" (Luke 7:26, KJV). He praised him by saying, "Among those that are born of women there is not a greater prophet than John the Baptist" (Luke 7:28, KJV). Christ knows his servants, large and small, popular and anonymous, and he is pleased with their self-sacrificial service.

John the Baptist
Insights for Discovery

———— ■ ● ■ ————

1. Understand Zechariah's elation at the birth of his son, John the Baptist, by reading Isaiah 40:3–5 and Luke 1:57–79.

2. Think about John the Baptist's faithfulness in boldly proclaiming the gospel and preparing the way for Christ (Matthew 3:1–17; Mark 1:1–11; Luke 3:1–20; and John 1:19–34). Take note of the various reactions to John the Baptist and his message.

3. Study John 3:22–36 and notice how well John the Baptist knew his own purpose. Of what importance is his statement in verse 30? (See a related thought in Galatians 2:20.)

4. Read Luke 7:18–28. What can you learn from Jesus' tribute to John?

5. Look at Matthew 14:1–12 and Mark 6:14–29 and reflect on what it cost John the Baptist to be obedient. Meditate on Psalm 119:33–36.

6. Andrew (John's disciple) switched his allegiance to Christ (John 1:35–42). Consider Andrew's response to Jesus and his witness to his brother, Simon. Compare Andrew's response to the story of Philip and Nathaniel in verses 43–51.

7. According to Psalm 145, what are we to proclaim and why? From where do we receive our motivation to speak of God?

Julie Royer

Mini Toon

Les sirènes pleurent des bulles

boomerang

Catalogage avant publication de Bibliothèque et Archives
nationales du Québec et Bibliothèque et Archives Canada

Royer, Julie, auteure

    Les sirènes pleurent des bulles / Julie Royer.
    (Mini Toon)
    Pour enfants de 7 ans et plus.

    ISBN 978-2-89709-288-7

    I. Titre.

PS8635.O955S57 2018   jC843'.6   C2018-941797-8
PS9635.O955S57 2018

Texte : Julie Royer
Illustration de la couverture : Richard Petit
Illustrations des pages intérieures : Sabrina Gendron
Graphisme : Mika et Marylène Gingras

Dépôt légal : Bibliothèque et Archives
nationales du Québec, 4ᵉ trimestre 2018

ISBN 978-2-89709-288-7

Imprimé au Canada

Gouvernement du Québec – Programme de crédit d'impôt
pour l'édition de livres – Gestion SODEC
Boomerang éditeur jeunesse remercie la SODEC
pour l'aide accordée à son programme éditorial.

Financé par le
gouvernement
du Canada

Canadä

info@boomerangjeunesse.com • www.boomerangjeunesse.com

MIXTE
Papier issu de
sources responsables
FSC® C103567

Pour Léonie, Alex, Gaïa,
Jézabel et Stella-Rose

CHAPITRE 1
DES BULLES MAGIQUES

Pour son anniversaire, Mimi a invité ses amis à son chalet, au bord de la mer, à **Villedesvagues**.

– C'EST TROP COOL ! s'écrie Lulu en mettant des lunettes de

soleil qui lui donnent
l'allure d'une star.

– **VRAIMENT
GÉNIAL !**

s'exclame Léon,
son frère jumeau,
en plantant un
drapeau au sommet
d'un château
de sable.

– Je suis
tellement
contente qu'on
soit ensemble !
leur répond Mimi
tout en étalant
sa serviette sur
le sable, à l'ombre
d'un **parasol**.

Sophie, la mère
de Mimi, vient
rejoindre les enfants.
Elle a une bouteille
de **BOISSON
GAZEUSE**
dans une main
et des coupes
en plastique
dans l'autre.
Elle **s'assoit**
à côté de Mimi.

11

— **Léon, Lulu, venez vous désaltérer !**

Le frère et la sœur, qui ont très soif, viennent prendre place sous le parasol. Sophie décapsule la bouteille et verse du liquide bleu

12

pétillant dans
une coupe qu'elle
tend à Léon.

– Merci... **Miam !**
Quand les bulles
éclatent, ça
goûte la barbe
à papa !

Sophie offre
une autre coupe
à Lulu, qui la porte
à ses lèvres.

– Hum... Moi,
je trouve que
ça goûte plutôt les
**CORNICHONS
À L'ANETH.**
En tout cas,

c'est **vraiment**
bon et ça pétille !

Mimi prend
la coupe que
sa mère lui tend
et avale une gorgée
de **boisson.**

–

D'abord, ça goûtait

le pâté chinois.
Puis, il y a eu une
explosion de fruits
dans la fondue
au chocolat !

— **C'est spécial !**
Qu'est-ce
que c'est ?

Sophie sourit.

– C'est du **Splouf Cola**. En plus de rendre le cœur léger, ses bulles prennent le **goût de nos aliments PRÉFÉRÉS.**

Étonnés, les trois jeunes **ouvrent** grand les yeux.

17

18

– C'est un breuvage
MAGIQUE?
demande Mimi.

Léon RIGOLE.

– **LA MAGIE,
ÇA N'EXISTE PAS**,
Mimi, voyons !

Sophie hausse
les sourcils.

19

— **Moi, j'y crois. D'ailleurs**, voulez-vous savoir quel est l'ingrédient principal du Splouf Cola ?

— **OUI !!!**

— Les larmes de SIRÈNES.

– HEIN ?!?

Les filles
n'en croient
**PAS LEURS
OREILLES.**

Léon lève les yeux
AU CIEL.

— Franchement,
les sirènes **n'existent
pas !**

La mère de Mimi
sert à nouveau
DU COLA
AUX ENFANTS.

— Oh oui, elles
existent, affirme-
t-elle, et elles

22

pleurent des bulles.
À Villedesvagues,
il y a des cueilleurs
DE LARMES
DE SIRÈNES.
Tous les jours,
ils vont dans
un **endroit**
secret où vivent
les sirènes.
Là, **ils recueillent**
leurs bulles

23

à l'aide de bouteilles
spéciales.

QUELLE
HISTOIRE
extraordinaire!

– On le fabrique
comment, le Splouf
Cola? demande
Lulu, curieuse.

25

— Les cueilleurs
mettent les bulles,
une à une, dans
un sirop qu'ils
fabriquent à la main
et qu'ils transvident
ensuite dans des
bouteilles comme
celle-ci. Produire
cette boisson prend
BEAUCOUP
de temps.

C'est donc un produit rare et **précieux** qu'on ne trouve qu'à Villedesvagues...

– **MAIS...** s'inquiète soudain Mimi, pourquoi les sirènes pleurent-elles ? Est-ce qu'on leur fait **du mal ?**

27

Sophie **sourit**.

– NON. D'après
ce qu'un cueilleur
de bulles m'a
raconté, les sirènes
coupent des
oignons de mer,
ce qui leur fait
monter les **larmes**
aux yeux.

28

Lulu regarde
les petites bulles
qui remontent
à la surface
de son verre.

— Qu'est-ce que
les **sirènes** font
avec les **oignons
coupés** ?

— Elles cuisinent
de la soupe
aux algues et
à **l'oignon**.
Elles en raffolent.

À l'évocation de ce
mets, Léon grimace.
Il déteste
les oignons !
Ça pue et ça donne
mauvaise haleine.

POUAH !

Préoccupée
par le sort des
**PLEUREUSES
DE BULLES,**
Lulu demande :

— Est-ce que
les cueilleurs
donnent quelque
chose aux sirènes

31

32

en échange de leurs
LARMES ?

– Ils leur offrent
des PAILLETTES,
des MIROIRS,
des BRILLANTS
et des PERLES
avec lesquels
elles fabriquent
des BIJOUX.

33

Des bijoux de sirènes ! **WOW !**

— Oui, ajoute Nathan, le père de Mimi, **QUI VIENT DE SE JOINDRE AUX VACANCIERS.** Il paraît que les sirènes rangent leurs bijoux dans des coffres qu'elles

34

cachent sur la plage
quand la marée
est haute. Je viens
justement de trouver
une carte au trésor,
dans le grenier
du chalet.

UN TRÉSOR ?
Décidément,
LES VACANCES
commencent bien !

Le père étale la carte sur la serviette de Mimi. Léon, qui ne croit pas facilement tout ce qu'on lui raconte, **examine le document d'un œil** de **détective PROFESSIONNEL.** La carte est jaunie, ses bords sont déchirés.

36

Tout en haut, il est écrit, en lettres attachées :

« LE TRÉSOR DES SIRÈNES ».

À la fin de son examen, le garçon conclut : « C'est une VRAIE CARTE. »

— Regardez,
dit Nathan en
**indiquant du
doigt** un point
sur le document.
Nous sommes ici.
Devant nous, il y
a la mer. À l'ouest
se trouve l'île aux
Crabes, qui a été
longtemps déserte.
Il y a quelque temps,

un dénommé
Joe Lerichepafin
l'a achetée pour y
CONSTRUIRE
un château et
une usine. C'est
du moins ce que
j'ai lu dans le journal
de Villedesvagues
ce matin. En tout
cas... SUR LE
BORD DE L'EAU,

39

on reconnaît la
butte aux Goélands.
Il y a un X dessus.
D'après moi, le
trésor des sirènes
est caché là.
**Saurez-vous
le trouver ?**

— OH QUE OUI !
s'écrie Mimi.

Le trésor des sirènes

SUIVEZ-MOI !
**Les trois amis
se lèvent d'un
bond**, saisissent

leurs pelles et

partent à la course,

sous l'œil
ATTENDRI

de Sophie et
de Nathan.

Mimi, Lulu et Léon
ne le savent pas,
MAIS ILS
S'APPRÊTENT
À VIVRE
TOUTE UNE
AVENTURE.

CHAPITRE 2

LE TRÉSOR DES SIRÈNES

— C'est par ici !
s'écrie Lulu en
arrivant, essoufflée,
au sommet de
la butte.

— Si on se fie
à la carte, le trésor
se trouverait **ici**,
déclare Mimi en
désignant un point

du bout de son gros orteil. Creusons !

Les trois amis se mettent **aussitôt** au travail.

Creuse !
CREUSE !
Creuse !
Creuse encore !

48

Bientôt, une montagne de sable se dresse à côté des vacanciers. **Mais... aucune trace du trésor.**

— Passe-moi la carte, Mimi, dit Léon. Je ne suis pas certain qu'on soit au bon endroit.

50

– **OUAIS**, renchérit Lulu. J'ai l'impression que si on continue à creuser comme ça, **ON VA SE RETROUVER EN CHINE**.

Mimi, qui veut à tout prix mettre

la main sur les
joyaux des sirènes,
saute dans le trou.

– Mon petit
doigt me dit
qu'on **Y EST
PRESQUE...**

Tout en parlant,
elle donne de petits
coups de pelle

par-ci, par-là,
et tout à coup...

— J'ai touché
**QUELQUE CHOSE
de dur !**

La jeune fille lâche **SON OUTIL** et, à l'aide de ses mains, déterre un petit coffre en bois.

– HOURRA !
crie Lulu.

– C'est vraiment trop, **TROP**

COOL !

s'exclame Léon.

Mimi tend le coffre à ses amis, qui le prennent et le posent sur le sol. Ils aident ensuite la jeune fille à **sortir du trou**.

— Qui va ouvrir
le coffre ? demande
Léon, impatient
de découvrir
ce qu'il contient.

— Ça devrait
être Mimi, fait
valoir Lulu. Après
tout, c'est son
anniversaire !

LES AMIS se mettent d'accord.

Mimi prend la boîte, inspire, l'ouvre...

– **WATATOW!** s'écrie Lulu en **apercevant** des **colliers**, des **bracelets** et des **boucles d'oreilles** qui brillent sous le soleil.

— Wouah ! s'exclame à son tour Mimi. Avez-vous vu les couronnes ? Les pierres précieuses ? Il y a même des pièces d'or !

— C'est des fausses !
lance Léon, déçu.
Les pierres sont en
fait des morceaux
de verre. ET
LES PIÈCES
SONT EN
PLASTIQUE.
On en trouve
des pareilles au
Pas-Cher-Rama.

– Mais non !
lui assure Mimi.
OH ! Il y a une
feuille, au fond !
Tiens le coffre, Lulu !

Une fois qu'elle
a les mains libres,
la jeune fille prend et
déplie le message.
Dessus, il est écrit :

« Joyeux anniversaire, Mimi! Nous espérons que tu passeras de BELLES vacances avec tes amis à Villedesvagues.

Sophie et Nathan XX »

– **Je le** savais **que tout était** faux **!** grogne Léon. Les trésors, c'est comme les sirènes et la magie : **ça ne se peut pas ! Bon !**

Fâché, il donne un coup de pied **dans le sable.**

63

– Eh bien moi, j'ai beaucoup aimé cette course, répond Mimi en souriant. C'était **UNE VRAIE belle surprise**.

– Je suis d'accord, DÉCLARE Lulu en enfilant une

ÉNORME bague. J'adore les bijoux! Tu devrais prendre quelques pièces, Léon. TU N'EN AS PAS DE SEMBLABLES à celles-là dans ta collection.

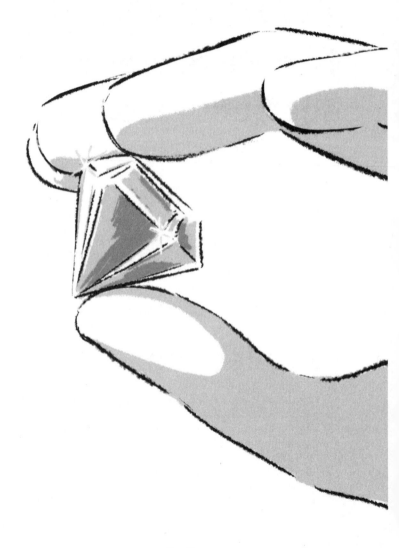

66

— Elles n'ont
aucune valeur !
ronchonne le garçon
en jetant un œil
au coffre. Et puis,
DES PIERRES
EN VERRE,
ça ne sert à rien !

Mais, à y regarder
de plus près,
il réalise que

67

plusieurs pierres ont des **formes intéressantes**. Aussi, il finit par en choisir une, **deux, cinq, neuf, TREIZE**. Il évite tout de même d'avoir l'air d'y prendre plaisir, pour ne pas donner raison à sa sœur.

– Bon, est-ce qu'on va se baigner ? demande brusquement le garçon. Creuser comme ça, ça m'a donné chaud !

– OUIIIII !

Parées comme
de riches princesses,
les filles dévalent
la butte et
COURENT
vers la mer. Léon
prend soin de
REMONTER
les fermetures à
glissière de ses
poches débordantes
de PIÈCES et de

70

PIERRES avant
de partir à la suite
de sa sœur et
de son amie.

— Le dernier
qui saute à l'eau
est une **BOULE
MOUILLÉE !**
crie Lulu en tenant
sa couronne.

– UNE POULE,
on dit une poule,
la corrige Léon.

– En tout cas,
c'est toi qui l'es !
rigole Lulu avant
de rejoindre Mimi
dans les vagues.

SPLIF !
SPLOUF !
SPLASH !

— **Brrrr ! L'EAU EST FROIDE !** se plaint Léon, qui est le dernier à mettre le pied dans l'eau salée.

– Oui, mais elle est bonne, dit Mimi. **HÉ ! REGARDEZ !** Je sais faire l'étoile de mer !

La fêtée se laisse tomber sur le dos. **Les bras et les jambes en croix**, elle flotte

gracieusement sur les flots. Comme elle est jolie, avec son collier de perles et ses bracelets **multicolores** !

– **BRAVO !** lui lance Lulu. Moi, **je peux faire des culbutes.**

La jeune fille pince
son nez avec ses
doigts, descend
dans l'eau et fait
une, deux, trois
pirouettes.

– **SUPER !**
la félicite Mimi.
En plus, tu n'as
même pas perdu
ta couronne !

– **OUAIS, pas mal !** s'exclame Léon. Moi, je peux marcher la tête en bas. Et contrairement à toi, je n'ai pas besoin de me pincer le nez !

Lulu soupire. Son frère a tendance

À SE CROIRE MEILLEUR QU'ELLE.

Le garçon plonge et sort les jambes de l'eau avant de remonter à la surface en catastrophe.

79

— Qu'est-ce qui se passe ? lui demande Lulu, moqueuse. **TU AS PRIS un bouillon ?**

— **NON !**

— Oh, laisse-moi deviner, dit à son tour Mimi en se retenant

80

de rire : tu as
perdu tes pierres
et des pièces ?

– **NON !**

Les filles haussent
les épaules.

– **BEN QUOI,
ALORS ?**

Le garçon regarde
tour à tour Mimi
et Lulu.

– Il y a quelqu'un
sous l'eau...

– **HEIN !?**

Le garçon plonge
à nouveau. Les deux
filles prennent une

bonne respiration
et le rejoignent.

C'EST ALORS QU'ILS SE RETROUVENT FACE À...

CHAPITRE 3
S.O.S.! SIRÈNE EN DÉTRESSE!

De la main,
la **créature sous-marine** fait un signe
aux enfants pour
qu'ils remontent
à la surface.
Ce qu'ils font.

Dès qu'elle a **la tête
HORS DE L'EAU**,
la sirène s'écrie :

– ENFIN, JE VOUS TROUVE !

Léon, qui, tantôt, était impressionné, fronce maintenant les sourcils.

– AHHH ! J'AI DEVINÉ !

Vous êtes déguisée et vous êtes là pour **animer la fête de Mimi...**

— **Pas du tout!** répond la fille-poisson. Je m'appelle Perla et j'ai nagé jusqu'ici pour vous demander de l'aide!

— De l'aide pour quoi ? demande Lulu, sous le choc.

Perla regarde les enfants en **se mordant la lèvre.** Visiblement, elle est aux prises avec un problème très grave.

— **BELLANIE**,
ma petite sœur,
a été enlevée !

– PAR QUI ?
l'interroge Mimi,
les yeux ronds.

– **PAR JOE**
Lerichepafin !

Léon se gratte
la tête. Il lui semble
avoir déjà entendu
ce nom.

– **HÉ !** C'est
de lui que parlait
ton père tantôt,
Mimi. C'est l'homme
qui a acheté l'île
aux Crabes !

96

La sirène s'agite,
donne des coups
de queue nerveux
dans l'eau.

– EXACT !
confirme-t-elle.
Il y a construit
un **château**
et il souhaite
maintenant y bâtir
une grande usine !

Les trois
amis écoutent
attentivement
Perla, qui poursuit,
paniquée :

— Il veut y fabriquer
des **BOISSONS
GAZEUSES**
à base de **larmes
de SIRÈNES**

qu'il compte vendre **dans les supermarchés DU MONDE ENTIER !**

Soudain, Mimi et Lulu comprennent tout.

— Pour réaliser son plan, dit Mimi,

il aura besoin de
plein de larmes...

– Et de BEAUCOUP
DE SIRÈNES,
ajoute Lulu.

À ces mots, le rouge
monte aux joues
de Perla.

— **OUIIII!** C'est pour cette raison qu'il a kidnappé ma sœur! Mais il a l'intention de capturer **TOUTES** les sirènes de Villedesvagues. **CE QUI VEUT DIRE QUE NOUS SOMMES EN GRAND DANGER!**

Vous devez m'aider
à libérer Bellanie
et à arrêter Joe
Lerichepafin !

**LES TROIS AMIS
SE CONSULTENT
DU REGARD.**

Puis, Mimi toussote.

103

— On voudrait
bien vous aider...
commence-t-elle.

Baissant les
yeux, Lulu termine
la phrase de
son amie :

— ... SI ON
LE POUVAIT.

Quant à Léon,
il ajoute, pas
encore tout
à fait convaincu :

— Qu'est-ce qu'on
peut faire contre
un **HOMME
AUSSI RICHE ?**
D'ailleurs, qui nous
dit que vous êtes
une vraie sirène ?

– Mais... mais... réplique Perla, qui ne s'attendait pas à cette question, je suis une vraie sirène ! **Si vous ne m'aidez pas, QUI LE FERA ???**

Lulu, qui réfléchit
en faisant tourner
une bague ornée
d'un gros diamant
autour de son index,
finit par demander :

— **Pourquoi vous
adressez-vous
à nous ?**

Les lèvres de la sirène se mettent à TREMBLER, signe qu'elle est sur le point de pleurer.

— **PARCE QUE VOUS AVEZ DES JAMBES !** Moi, je n'ai qu'une queue de poisson.

Je ne peux donc pas sortir de l'eau pour secourir ma sœur !

DÉSESPÉRÉE,
elle ajoute :

— **Ne m'abandonnez pas !!!**

110

Incapable de se
retenir davantage,
elle se met
à pleurer.
Alors, il se passe
quelque chose
d'extraordinaire :
ses larmes se
transforment en
BULLES QUI
S'ENVOLENT
VERS LE CIEL.

111

À cet instant précis, Léon comprend que **la magie et les sirènes EXISTENT** bel et bien et qu'on a réellement besoin de lui.

— **Ne pleurez pas comme ça,** dit-il, gêné.

Tandis que Léon
et Lulu tentent
de consoler Perla,
Mimi jette un
œil à Sophie
et à Nathan.
**Ils discutent
joyeusement
sur la plage**
en dégustant
une coupe de
Splouf Cola.

– On voudrait vraiment vous aider, mais je ne suis pas certaine que mes parents nous laisseront faire... objecte la jeune fille.

La **créature marine** claque des doigts.

– Ah bon ?
Ils semblent
pourtant partis
pour faire une
longue sieste...

Les enfants
se retournent.
**Les deux adultes
dorment sous
LE PARASOL !**

— Comment avez-vous fait ? demande Léon, qui n'en revient pas.

— C'est ce qu'on appelle de la **MAGIE MARINE**, répond la sirène en haussant les épaules.

— C'EST D'ACCORD, dit finalement Mimi, qui a l'esprit d'aventure. **ON VA VOUS AIDER.**

— Vraiment ? Dans ce cas, **IL N'Y A PAS DE TEMPS À PERDRE !**

La sirène enfonce
ses doigts dans
sa bouche et siffle
trois petits coups,
trois grands coups,
puis à nouveau
trois petits coups.

— **Fouit-Fouit- Fouit !**
FOUIT-FOUIT-
FOUIT ! Fouit-
Fouit- Fouit !

119

— C'est du morse, explique aux filles Léon, qui s'y connaît dans les affaires de détectives et de capitaines. **ELLE ENVOIE UN S.O.S.**

— **À QUI?** demande Lulu.

— Sûrement à ses amis, répond Mimi.

Au loin, de la mousse blanche se forme au-dessus des vagues. De quoi s'agit-il ? **Oh !** **Quelque chose se rapproche d'eux à grande vitesse.**

Qu'est-ce que la sirène a déclenché en lançant son appel à l'aide ?

Les trois amis sont fixés quand ils voient surgir des ailerons dans l'eau...

122

– DES RE-RE... DES **REQUINS ?** bafouille Léon, qui ne se sent pas très brave, tout à coup.

– **MAIS NON !** répond Lulu, émerveillée. Ce sont des **dauphins !**

124

– OUI ! s'exclame **Perla.** Ils vont vous mener à l'île aux Crabes. On va y arriver plus vite ainsi qu'à la nage.

Les mammifères se dirigent vers le groupe en faisant des bonds hors

de l'eau, ce qui
permet aux amis
de voir leurs petits
yeux noirs
et leur nez effilé.

– WOW !

Ils sont trop beaux !
s'extasie Mimi,
qui n'avait encore
jamais eu la chance

D'OBSERVER des **dauphins** d'aussi près.

HI-HI-HI-HIHIHI HIHIHI !

fait le premier **DAUPHIN** en se présentant devant Perla.

127

Ses deux amis restent un peu en RETRAIT. La sirène leur sourit avant de leur répondre par un « crɾɾrcrrr » sonore. Elle se tourne ensuite vers les enfants.

129

– Ils disent qu'ils sont **HEUREUX** de vous rencontrer.

– **HO-HI-HI-HUHUHU-HI-CRRR !** chante le second dauphin en s'ébrouant.

La sirène **hoche** la tête.

— Il dit de prendre place sur leur dos. Ils vont vous mener à destination. Quant à moi, **JE VAIS VOUS SUIVRE.**

Les dauphins s'approchent des enfants, qui sont **ENTHOUSIASTES**

à l'idée du voyage
qui les attend.

ET C'EST PARTIIIIII !

CHAPITRE 4
L'ÎLE AUX CRABES

Quelle équipée !

« LA MER,
LE TRÉSOR,
LES SIRÈNES,
LES DAUPHINS...
Je ne pensais jamais
vivre un anniversaire
aussi fantastique »,
se dit Mimi,
AUX ANGES.

137

– **Waouuuuuh !**
s'écrie Lulu, au
comble de la joie,
tout en vérifiant
de temps à autre
si sa couronne tient
toujours en place.

– **PLUS
VITE !** PLUS
VIIIIIIIITE !

138

hurle Léon, qui
voudrait dépasser
tout le monde
et qui, à force
de crier, finit par
avaler **une tasse
d'eau salée.**

EUH-EUH-
EUH !
PEUH !

Dans le temps de
le dire, la traversée
est finie.

Bientôt, la troupe
se retrouve près
de la **plage de
l'île aux Crabes.**
Perla remercie
alors les dauphins,
les priant de rester
dans les environs,

ce qui, dans la langue de ces mammifères, sonne à peu près comme ceci :

CRRRRRR-CRRR-HI-HI-HI-HUUUU-HI !

Ensuite, elle sort d'une sacoche en forme de coquillage **une paire de CASTAGNETTES** et entame une conversation avec UN CRABE qui se trouve là par hasard. Décidément, **Perla connaît toutes les langues !**

– Clac-clac-
clac-clac-clac ?

– CLA-CLA-
CLAAAAAC !

– **Cla-clac !** Le crabe
salue la **sirène** avant
de poursuivre
sa route. Perla se
tourne alors vers

les enfants et leur dit, tout en rangeant ses instruments :

— Vous vous rendrez facilement au CHÂTEAU DE JOE LERICHEPAFIN. C'est le seul de l'île, qui est très petite.

Vous n'avez qu'à suivre le chemin pavé et à lire les affiches. **C'est bien indiqué**, selon ce que le crabe m'a dit.

Les trois amis hochent la tête.

Perla continue :

— Une fois sur place, vous devrez entrer dans le château, trouver l'endroit où Lerichepafin a enfermé ma sœur, la libérer et venir me rejoindre **ICI MÊME**, le plus vite possible.

Les enfants écoutent attentivement LES CONSIGNES DE LA SIRÈNE.

— En ce moment, Lerichepafin se fait BRONZER à l'autre bout de l'île, toujours selon le crabe.

Alors, c'est le
moment d'agir.
Bonne chance !
Et n'oubliez pas
que Villedesvagues
compte sur vous !

Sans perdre une
seconde, Mimi
et Lulu sortent
de l'eau pour partir
en direction du

château. Mais Léon,
lui, reste dans l'eau.

– **Qu'est-ce que tu
FABRIQUES ?**
demande Lulu.
On a une mission
à accomplir,
je te signale !

LE GARÇON RESTE MUET.

Il semble mal
à l'aise.

– JE LE SAIS !
s'exclame Lulu.
Tu voudrais
retourner au chalet !
Peureux, va !

Léon rougit.
Furieux, il croise
les bras :

— Je ne suis
**PAS UN
FROUSSARD,
BON !**

— **Qu'est-ce que
tu fais, alors?
VIENS-T'EN !**

153

154

crie Mimi. On est super pressés !

Mais Léon demeure immobile, le visage fermé. **IL A DE L'EAU JUSQU'À LA TAILLE.**

Personne ne comprend ce qui se passe, jusqu'à

ce que Perla
mette la main
sur un objet flottant
non identifié...

– SON MAILLOT
DE BAIN! crient
Lulu et Mimi dans
un grand éclat
de rire.

***

– **O.K.**, ce n'est pas si drôle que ça, grogne Léon en sortant enfin de l'eau. J'ai dû perdre mon maillot **pendant la course, tantôt.** Les dauphins nageaient vite, et je n'avais probablement

pas assez serré
mes cordons...

– En tout cas,
tu aurais dû te voir !
rigole Lulu. Tu étais
rouge comme
un têtard !

– Un homard, Lulu !
On dit « **ROUGE**

COMME UN HOMARD ».

Là, si tu n'arrêtes pas de te moquer de moi, je vais...

Mimi interrompt ses amis en attirant leur attention sur une affiche placardée en

bordure de la petite
forêt de palmiers
qui sépare la plage
du château.

– REGARDEZ !

Sur la pancarte,
il est écrit :

« CHÂTEAU DE JOE LERICHEPAFIN PAR LÀ ».

— On est près
du but, affirme Mimi
en s'engageant
entre les arbres.
C'est **EXCITANT,**
mais **effrayant**
en même temps.
J'ai le cœur qui
bat très fort.

— Moi, répond
Lulu, j'adore nager

dans les mystères,
les missions et
le danger. **En
ce moment,
je me sens
heureuse
COMME UN
POTIRON
DANS L'EAU.**

Son frère soupire
bruyamment en

levant les yeux
au ciel.

– **Un poisson,
Lulu !** Tu aurais
dû dire « heureuse
comme un poisson
dans l'eau » ! **Tu
M'ÉNERVES,
à la fin !!!**

Mimi les interrompt
à nouveau.

– **OH !**
Une autre !

Devant eux se
dresse une nouvelle
affiche, sur laquelle
on peut lire :

« Fin de la forêt :
CHÂTEAU DE
LERICHEPAFIN
DANS CENT
PAS ».

D'un commun
accord, les jeunes
REPRENNENT
leur marche en
comptant leurs

166

FiN DE LA FoRÊT:
CHÂTEAU DE
LERiCHEPAFiN
DANS CENT PAS

167

pas afin de vérifier si l'affiche dit vrai. Toutefois, à partir de **soixante-dix-huit**, Léon et Lulu perdent le compte exact de leurs ENJAMBÉES, puisqu'ils ne **S'ENTENDENT PAS** au sujet de leurs calculs.

– **TU FAIS DE TROP GRANDS PAS**, Léon, affirme Lulu.

– **Puis toi, tu comptes TROP fort !** Je suis tout mêlé. Pour bien faire, il faudrait recommencer !

169

170

– On n'a pas le temps, figure-toi!

Mimi coupe court à leur discussion en attirant leur **ATTENTION** sur une troisième affiche. Cette fois, on peut y lire :

« VOUS ÊTES ARRIVÉS AU CHÂTEAU DE JOE LERICHEPAFIN ».

Les jeunes LÈVENT les yeux. C'est alors qu'ils aperçoivent le château en question.

172

– **WOW !**

souffle Léon.
Il est gros...

– OUAIS !
Et il est beau...
ajoute Mimi.

– Il ressemble
pas mal à celui

de la **PANCARTE**, conclut Lulu.

Soudain, derrière eux, une voix les fait sursauter.

– On peut vous aider ?

– **Ouaaaaaahhhh !**

Joe Lerichepafin !
QU'EST-CE QU'IL FAIT LÀ, LUI ?
Il ne devait pas être à la plage ?

CHAPITRE 5

JOE LERICHEPAFIN

C'est Mimi qui reprend ses esprits la première.

« **VITE**, pense-t-elle, il faut trouver quelque chose à lui dire pour qu'il nous laisse **ENTRER** dans son château! »

– BONJOUR, MONSIEUR !

C'est tout un honneur de vous RENCONTRER.

Nos parents nous parlent souvent de vous. En fait, vous êtes notre idole depuis **toujours.**

180

En robe de chambre et en gougounes, le visage luisant de crème solaire, **l'homme regarde tour à tour** les trois enfants. Il est curieux de savoir ce qu'on leur a dit à son sujet. Il aime

182

tellement que les
gens parlent de lui !

– AH OUI ?
Qu'est-ce
qu'ils disent ?

Lulu et Léon
retiennent leur
souffle. Quant
à Mimi, **elle bat**
des cils.

— Ils disent qu'on
devrait prendre
exemple sur vous
pour construire
des **châteaux**
et des **USINES**.
Ils nous ont laissés
ici tantôt en nous
disant de faire
connaissance
avec vous, puis
ils sont repartis

184

à bord de leur yacht.
Ils vont revenir
nous chercher
à la fin de l'après-
midi. Ils sont très
riches eux aussi,
vous savez...

WOUAH!

Les jumeaux
admirent leur amie.

Ils ne savaient pas qu'elle avait autant d'imagination. **Elle a un air si NATUREL...** Un peu plus et ils croiraient son histoire. Pour sa part, Lerichepafin a été intrigué par les derniers mots de Mimi.

— Comme ça,
vos parents sont
très riches...

— OUUUUUI,
dit Lulu, qui entre
dans le jeu. On est
des princesses et
notre frère est
un prince. C'est
pour ça qu'on a
plein de bijoux.

CLING !

CLING !

En parlant, la jeune fille **agite ses bracelets** et passe ses bagues sous le nez de l'homme pour attirer son attention.

— C'est vrai, ajoute
Léon. Nos parents,
la reine et le roi
du royaume de...
de... la Pépite dorée,
nous ont donné
beaucoup d'argent
de poche, au cas où
on voudrait s'acheter
une collation ou...
euh... une boisson
GAZEUSE...

ZIIIIIIP!

Le garçon ouvre
la fermeture
à glissière de
l'une des poches
de son maillot
et en SORT
UNE FAUSSE
PIÈCE D'OR.

191

Lerichepafin écarquille les yeux.

Il n'a jamais vu une pièce AUSSI GROSSE. Selon lui, elle doit valoir une fortune.

De toute évidence, il n'a jamais mis

les pieds au
Pas-Cher-Rama.

– **J'EN AI
PLEIN...**
ajoute Léon
en prenant soin
de mettre la pièce
sous le soleil pour
la faire briller.

« HUM...

pense l'homme
en se grattant
le menton. On
n'a jamais ASSEZ
D'AMIS RICHES.
D'ailleurs, ces
enfants arrivent

juste à point
sur l'île. J'avais
justement besoin
de goûteurs pour
mes nouveaux
colas aux larmes
de sirènes. »

— **ENTREZ**,
leur dit-il en leur
ouvrant la porte
de son château.

196

**Les enfants
le suivent.**

Clac ! La porte se
ferme derrière eux.

WoOOoW !

Ils se retrouvent
dans **une immense
salle**, avec de
gigantesques

197

FAUTEUILS, un ÉCRAN aussi grand que ceux qu'on trouve au cinéparc, une distributrice de gommes, un bar à bonbons ainsi que des MACHINES À POPCORN, À BARBOTINE et à crème glacée!

198

– Qu'est-ce qu'il y a là-dessous ? demande Lulu en pointant du doigt une **grosse boîte** posée dans un coin et dissimulée sous un grand drap noir.

– C'EST UNE SURPRISE !

Je vais vous montrer de quoi il s'agit dans quelques **minutes**.

Auparavant, je dois aller me changer. En ATTENDANT, vous pouvez mettre le film qui vous plaît.

200

– MERCI !
disent les filles
en prenant
place sur les
fauteuils.

Lerichepafin, qui
s'apprête à **monter**
dans l'ascenseur pour
aller à sa chambre,
se retourne :

– **MANGEZ et BUVEZ tout** ce qui vous plaît, mais gardez-vous une petite place pour la surprise ! **À TANTÔT !**

203

Mimi, Lulu et Léon, SOURIANT DE TOUTES LEURS DENTS, envoient la main à l'homme d'affaires.

DING ! Les portes de l'ascenseur se ferment.

Aussitôt qu'ils
se retrouvent seuls,
Mimi se tourne vers
les jumeaux :

– **ON L'A EU!**
Il croit vraiment
qu'on vient d'une
famille royale !

– **OUI**, répond
Lulu en replaçant

ses colliers. Comme
le dit l'expression :
**le poisson a mordu
au CALEÇON...**

Léon, qui vient
de se servir une
poignée de boules
au chocolat, grogne :

– On ne dit pas
que le poisson

a mordu au caleçon,
mais à l'hameçon !

CROUNCH !
CROUNCH !
CROUNCH !
MIAM !

– PFFF !
réplique sa sœur
en levant le nez.

208

En tout cas, toi,
tu mords dans
des cochonneries,
mais **tu sais très
bien que maman
NE VEUT PAS
QU'ON MANGE
N'IMPORTE QUOI
entre les repas...**

– Espèce de
porte-panier !

209

Tu ferais mieux
de ne pas raconter
ça à notre retour
à la maison, sinon...

Oh non ! Ils ne vont
pas recommencer
à se chicaner !

Mimi, qui vient
de soulever un pan

du drap recouvrant
la mystérieuse
boîte, interrompt
les jumeaux
en disant :

— **Hé ! C'est
une machine
DISTRIBUTRICE
de BOISSONS
GAZEUSES !**

Elle doit avoir
un RAPPORT
avec notre affaire.

— Élémentaire,
ma chère Mimi, lance
Lulu avec un clin
d'œil. Maintenant,
trouvons Bellanie !

— Fachile à dire...
On ne chait

212

même pas par
où commencher,
répond Léon,
la bouche pleine.

CROUNCH-CROUNCH !

Effectivement,
pour s'orienter
dans le château,
les détectives

en herbe **AURAIENT besoin d'un PLAN...**

– Ici ! s'exclame Lulu en ouvrant la porte du salon, rempli de rayons de bibliothèque.

À l'intérieur se trouve une **affiche LUMINEUSE,**

215

comme on en voit
à l'entrée des centres
commerciaux.

● ● ● ● ● ● ● ● ● ● ● ● ● ● ● ●

LAVE-AUTO
2e sous-sol

PISCINE
OLYMPIQUE
INTÉRIEURE
Rez-de-chaussée

SALLE DES DÉGUISEMENTS D'HALLOWEEN
33e étage

ROYAUME DU PÈRE NOËL
41e étage

BUFFET CHINOIS
13e étage

PARC D'ATTRACTIONS
19e étage

TOILETTES PUBLIQUES
9e étage

LABORATOIRE DE L'USINE DE COLAS
7e étage

218

– **BINGO !** crie Mimi en mettant le doigt sur le pictogramme représentant le laboratoire. C'est là que doit se trouver la sirène. Allons-y !

– **Pensez-vous qu'on POURRAIT**

d'abord faire un petit saut chez le PÈRE NOËL ? demande Léon. J'aimerais lui **COMMANDER MES CADEAUX** à l'avance pour être certain d'avoir les bons, cette année...

220

– **NON !**
répond Mimi.
Bellanie attend
d'être délivrée.

– C'EST VRAI, ÇA !
renchérit Lulu-la-
princesse-espionne
en vérifiant que
tous ses bijoux
sont en ordre.

222

Léon grimace,
un peu déçu.
Puis, il propose :

— **D'accord**, mais
commençons par
le commencement.
Trouvons un nom
à notre mission,
COMME DANS
LES FILMS.

GÉNIAL !

Le cerveau de Mimi
entre aussitôt
en ébullition.

– Qu'est-ce
que vous pensez
de « MISSION
BUBULLES » ?

– OUAIS !
répondent
les jumeaux
en chœur,
ce qui est
plutôt rare.

Léon s'élance
aussitôt vers
l'ascenseur.

– VENEZ !

– Il vaudrait mieux emprunter l'escalier, suggère Mimi.
Ce serait **PLUS DISCRET,** et on risquerait moins de se faire prendre par Lerichepafin.

227

– **T'es rusée comme un** CANARD, Mimi, lâche Lulu, admirative.

– **COMME UN RENARD.** On dit « rusé comme un renard », soupire Léon en

commençant
à gravir les escaliers.

Dix minutes
plus tard, les
amis atteignent
le septième étage.

– On aurait...
peut-être...
dû... prendre...
l'ascenseur...
finalement...

dit Mimi, à bout
de souffle.

– L'important...
c'est... qu'on
soit... rendus,
répond Lulu pour
l'encourager. Mais
où aller? Il y a plein
de portes, par ici...

— On n'a qu'à suivre le **bruit des pleurs**... réplique Léon, aux aguets. Écoutez !

Tendant l'oreille, ils perçoivent des SANGLOTS provenant du fond du corridor.

236

– BOUUUUUH ! BOUHHHHH !

LES ENFANTS

se précipitent dans cette direction, poussent une **porte** et se retrouvent dans un laboratoire rempli de chaudrons dégageant des

vapeurs parfumées,
de fioles contenant
des **sirops
multicolores**,
de machines
à faire de la **barbe
à papa**. Tout
au fond se dresse
un grand écran
de télé devant
lequel est placé
un bocal géant

rempli d'eau.
Dedans, il y a...

– BELLANIE !

– BoUUUuhhh !

Les trois espions
accourent auprès
de la sirène
prisonnière,

qui semble captivée
par les images
projetées à l'écran.

– **NE VOUS
EN FAITES
PAS!** tente
de la rassurer
Léon. Nous
sommes là pour
vous sauver!

— **Qui êtes-vous?** demande Bellanie, avant de renifler et de se remettre à **PLEURER de** **plus belle.**

SNIF!
SNIF!
BOUOUHHHHH!

– Nous sommes des amis de votre sœur, dit doucement Lulu. Nous sommes venus vous libérer.

– AH... AH... AH OUI? SNIIIIF! BOUHHH!

Une nuée de bulles quittent les yeux de la SIRÈNE et sont avalées par un aspirateur à larmes, qui est branché à un tuyau rouge rayé de blanc situé derrière le bocal. **Le boyau sort du laboratoire par un mur.**

– **C'est quoi, ça ?** demande Léon en désignant le tube.

Bellanie se retourne dans sa prison de verre.

– **ÇA ? C'est un tuyau branché**

244

à une **distributrice de BOISSONS gazeuses**, au salon. C'est Lerichepafin qui a fabriqué cette machine, qui lui sert à créer ses colas à base de larmes de sirènes. **OH! C'EST TROP TRISTE!**

246

– Quoi donc?
demande Mimi.

**La sirène tourne
à NOUVEAU
SUR ELLE-MÊME**
et pointe l'écran
de **télévision**
en retenant
difficilement
un sanglot.

— Eh bien, dans ce film, la sorcière offre à BLANCHE-NEIGE DU PAIN À L'AIL empoisonné au lieu d'une pomme. Donc, la princesse perd connaissance, mais le prince ne veut pas l'embrasser

pour la réveiller
parce qu'elle a trop
mauvaise haleine...
Ce qui fait qu'elle
reste endormie
et seule à tout
jamais. Même les
nains, ne pouvant
pas supporter son
odeur, la tiennent
à l'écart.

250

BOUH-OU-OUH !!!

Les trois sauveurs de sirènes échangent **UN REGARD catastrophé**. C'est scandaleux ! Pour faire pleurer Bellanie, Lerichepafin l'oblige à visionner

des films tristes
toute la journée !

En effet, à côté
de la télévision
sont étalés des
coffrets contenant
des ŒUVRES
aux titres qui
donnent envie de
pleurer, tels que :

La Belle au bois
dormant ronfle
comme un vieux
moteur ; Cendrillon
changée en citrouille ;
Raiponce a des poux
plein la tresse ;
La Petite Sirène
chante faux ;
Le Prince transformé
en grenouille
pour de bon ;
La Belle est bête.

QUELLE HORREUR !

– ÇA SUFFIT !
dit fermement Mimi
en éteignant la télé.
Nous allons trouver
un moyen de vous
faire sortir d'ici.

Sur ce, les **amis** se mettent à explorer les lieux...

— **Qu'est-ce que vous diriez de la faire SORTIR PAR LE TUYAU des toilettes ?** demande Léon.

– ÇA NE VA PAS, NON ! ? ! réplique sa sœur. C'est dégueu ! BEURK ! Des fois, on dirait que tu as une cervelle de taureau !

– Une cervelle de moineau, Lulu.

J'ai une cervelle de moineau, répond distraitement son frère en refermant le COUVERCLE de la cuvette.

— **Hé !** Ce n'est pas moi qui l'ai dit !

POUAH-HA-HA !

258

Quand il réalise
ce qu'il vient de dire
à son propre sujet,
le garçon grogne.

– ARRRRGH !
GRRR !

Du fond du
laboratoire, **la voix
de Mimi retentit,**

coupant court
à cette nouvelle
QUERELLE.

– HÉ ! J'AI
TROUVÉ !

L'apprentie agente
secrète vient
rejoindre ses amis
en poussant une
baignoire sur

260

261

roulettes. Elle est remplie d'eau tiède et de mousse pour le bain parfumée au **CUPCAKE À LA VANILLE.** Il s'agit sans nul doute **possible** d'une expérience de Lerichepafin visant à créer un nouveau savon moussant...

– On fait entrer
Bellanie dedans,
et le tour est joué !

– BIEN PENSÉ !
approuvent les
jumeaux, excités.

– Dépêchez-vous !
les avertit Bellanie.
Lerichepafin

pourrait arriver
d'une seconde
à l'autre !

Oui, mais comment
s'y prendre pour
**VIDER LE
BOCAL ?**

— Vous n'avez qu'à
enlever le bouchon,
indique la sirène.

Je vais sauter dans
la baignoire.

Pendant que
les filles poussent
la baignoire devant
le bocal, Léon

266

grimpe sur un petit **BANC** pour être en mesure d'ouvrir la voie à Bellanie.

Soudain, des bruits incongrus les stoppent net.

ProoOOOoout!
Beurrrrrrrp!

– QU'EST-CE QUE C'EST?

demande Lulu.

– J'ai PÉTÉ ET ROTÉ dans l'eau pour faire une petite surprise à Lerichepafin. Ça lui apprendra à vouloir **exploiter** les sirènes ! répond Bellanie avec un clin d'œil.

Reprouuuut-prout !

Un TOURBILLON de bulles ENVAHIT LE BOCAL.

Les trois amis
éclatent de rire.

POP! BANG! Léon
retire le bouchon
du bocal et le laisse
tomber sur le sol.

— Vous pouvez y
aller, dit le garçon.

Sans plus attendre,
Bellanie se ramasse
sur elle-même
et bondit hors
de sa prison.

– **C'est bon !**
dit Mimi quand
la sirène est
bien installée

dans L'EAU
MOUSSEUSE.
Maintenant,
passons à la
deuxième étape
de notre mission :
l'évacuation.

– On s'y prend
comment ?
demande Léon.

272

— Lulu et moi,
on va descendre
par l'ascenseur et
rejoindre Lerichepafin
au salon, répond
la jeune fille d'un
air professionnel.
On va **trouver
le moyen de
le faire sortir
et de l'entraîner**
loin du château.

274

Quant à vous, attendez **CINQ MINUTES**, puis prenez l'ascenseur à votre tour. À ce moment-là, la voie devrait être libre. Alors, vous sortirez et vous vous dirigerez le plus rapidement possible vers la forêt, par le chemin pavé.

Lulu et Bellanie
hochent la tête.
**Elles sont d'accord
avec Mimi.**

– C'est compris.
Bonne chance !
lance Léon.

– BONNE
CHANCE !

CHAPITRE 7
BEUUUURK !

— Enfin, vous revoilà ! s'exclame le kidnappeur de sirènes en voyant réapparaître les filles. **Où étiez-vous passées ?**

— On était aux **TOILETTES**, au neuvième étage,

279

répond Mimi avec un air innocent.

L'HOMME a troqué sa robe de chambre pour un short en nylon et une chemise avec des imprimés de requins. « **C'EST DRÔLE**, songe

281

Lulu en observant simultanément l'inventeur et **les imprimés**. Lerichepafin ressemble dangereusement à un squale. »

— **Où est votre AMI ?** demande l'homme d'affaires en souriant de toutes ses dents, ce qui accentue sa ressemblance avec cette dangereuse créature marine.

Mimi et Lulu échangent UN REGARD NERVEUX.

– Il est dans les **TOILETTES** des gars, répond Lulu. Il a dit qu'il viendrait nous rejoindre dans quelques minutes. En attendant, on pourrait peut-être aller se promener dehors. **IL FAIT TELLEMENT BEAU !**

284

— D'accord, répond l'homme, qui a du mal à contenir son **IMPATIENCE**. Mais avant, je veux vous montrer quelque chose. C'est la **SURPRISE** dont je vous parlais à votre arrivée ! Comme votre ami

est absent, je referai
ma démonstration
pour lui tantôt.
**Je suis TELLEMENT
excité à l'idée
de vous présenter
mon INVENTION**
que je ne peux
plus attendre.
Voici donc...

L'inventeur tire **SUR LE DRAP NOIR**, dévoilant une machine distributrice couverte de boutons lumineux et pourvue d'un tuyau rouge rayé de blanc branché à une prise murale.

287

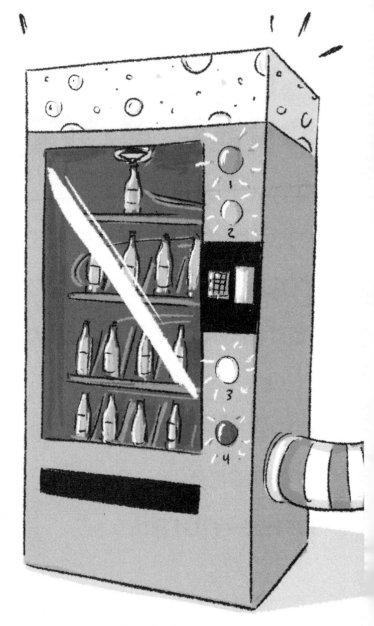

288

Les deux
agentes secrètes
reconnaissent tout
de suite le boyau
relié au BOCAL
dans lequel était
enfermée Bellanie.

— Cette distributrice,
continue l'inventeur,
fier de lui, n'est que
le modèle réduit

d'une immense
machine qui
va révolutionner
le monde de la
boisson gazeuse
et me rendre encore
plus riche que
je le suis déjà !

applaudissent les filles, qui jettent de temps à autre des regards en direction de l'ascenseur.

Le temps presse. Léon et Bellanie sont sur le point de surgir dans le salon.

Mimi et Lulu doivent
à tout prix attirer
Lerichepafin
à l'extérieur.

Mais celui-ci ne
veut rien entendre.
Il tient absolument
à faire goûter son
cola à ses invitées...

— Non, merci, refuse poliment Lulu.

— Non, merci, dit Mimi.

Le kidnappeur-fabricant DE BOISSONS gazéifiées insiste.

– **Voyons, les filles !** C'est super bon. Vous devriez Y GOÛTER... C'est un ingrédient secret qui donne à mes boissons leurs **bulles légères et leur SAVEUR** spéciale...

294

sluUUUrp !

L'homme aspire
un long trait de cola
à l'aide d'une paille.

Tout à coup,
il GRIMACE
et devient
blanc, puis vert.

295

– POUAH !
C'est donc bien
mauvais ! Ça goûte...
ça goûte...

Pendant quelques
SECONDES,
Lerichepafin analyse
cette **SAVEUR** qui
le fait frissonner.
« Cette boisson

297

goûte les vieux
**OIGNONS
ET LA CROTTE
DE POISSON !**
BUUUURP !
POUAH !
C'est abominable ! »

Il se retient
**DIFFICILEMENT
DE VOMIR.**

298

Soudain, les portes
de l'ascenseur
s'ouvrent sur
Léon et Bellanie.

Pour Mimi, c'est
le temps de passer
à l'action.

— TOUT LE MONDE DEHORS! ET QUE ÇA SAUTE!

crie la jeune fille avant de se mettre à courir vers la porte d'entrée, suivie de Lulu, qui tient sa couronne à deux mains, et de Léon, qui pousse la baignoire dans

300

laquelle patauge
la sirène. Cette
dernière s'accroche
aux robinets pour
ne pas passer
par-dessus bord.

SPLISH!
SPLASH!
SPLOUF!

302

De son côté, Lerichepafin mâche désespérément une **BOULE DE GOMME** à la menthe pour masquer les saveurs de pet et de ROT DE SIRÈNE qui s'accrochent de toutes leurs forces à ses papilles.

303

Soudain, il réalise que ses jeunes invités lui ont joué un vilain tour...

– **HÉ! REVENEZ ICI TOUT DE SUITE**, petits vauriens!

OH, OH !

Les apprentis SUPERHÉROS et leur nouvelle amie RÉUSSIRONT-ILS À ÉCHAPPER AU MÉCHANT HOMME D'AFFAIRES ?

CHAPITRE 8

UN VRAI
SAUVE-QUI-PEUT !

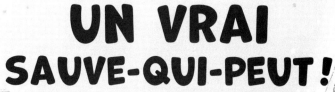

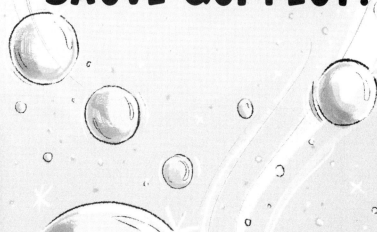

— **Plus vite ! Plus VIIIIIITE !**

crie Bellanie alors qu'ils s'engagent dans l'allée pavée menant à la plage. Je ne veux plus **JAMAIS** me retrouver dans un bocal !

— Ne vous inquiétez pas, la rassure Mimi, qui court à côté de la baignoire. Lerichepafin ne réussira pas à nous rattraper. **C'EST PROMIS !**

La troupe s'enfonce dans la petite forêt de palmiers qui

sépare le château
DE LA PLAGE.
Bientôt, les fuyards
aperçoivent une
PANCARTE sur
laquelle on peut lire :

« VOUS QUITTEZ
LE CHÂTEAU
BIEN VITE ! Vérifiez
que vous n'avez

rien oublié, car
nous gardons LES
OBJETS PERDUS ».

Lulu s'arrête.

– QU'EST-CE
QUE TU FAIS ?
demande Mimi,
PANIQUÉE.

— Je veux prendre
le temps de compter
mes **BRACELETS,**
mes **COLLIERS**
et mes **BAGUES.**
Tu as lu ce
qui est écrit ?
Je n'ai pas envie
de laisser des bijoux
à Lerichepafin !
Tu devrais faire
comme moi.

314

— **Ce n'est vraiment pas le moment !** COURS ! lui crie son amie en la prenant par un bras.

LA FUITE DES JEUNES et de la sirène reprend de plus belle.

315

Quelques mètres plus loin, ils se trouvent devant une nouvelle affiche, électronique, cette fois, sur laquelle on peut lire :

« Avez-vous aimé VOTRE SÉJOUR AU CHÂTEAU ?

Votre opinion COMPTE pour nous. Aussi, nous vous INVITONS à répondre à un petit SONDAGE qui ne prendra que quelques minutes de votre temps... »

317

— Pensez-vous
qu'on devrait ?
demande Lulu.

— **NooOOOon** !
crient Mimi et Léon
sans s'arrêter
de courir.

Ils vont sortir
de la forêt quand

318

ils aperçoivent une troisième affiche :

« AVANT DE PARTIR, vous devez PAYER. Insérez une pièce dans la fente prévue à cet effet. »

ET BANG !

Une barrière se
ferme devant eux.

– QU'EST-CE QU'ON FAIT ? On n'a pas
un sou ! s'exclame
Mimi en tournant
la tête du côté de
leur poursuivant.

321

OH ! Lerichepafin
se rapproche !

— **Je pense que
j'ai ce qu'il faut !**
dit Léon en fouillant
dans une poche de
son maillot de bain.

Le garçon insère
ensuite une pièce

en plastique dans
la machine reliée
à la barrière... qui,
à leur plus grande
surprise, se lève.

Les enfants
S'EMPRESSENT
de passer de l'autre
côté. Soudain,
la machine dans

laquelle ils ont mis
la prétendue pièce
d'or se met à crier :

« C'EST
UN FAUX
SOU! C'EST
UN FAUX
SOU!»

324

Et, juste au moment où Lerichepafin va franchir la barrière, celle-ci se détraque.

BANG !

La lourde barre de bois PEINTE en noir et jaune tombe sur la tête de l'inventeur et l'assomme.

326

– **Grouahhhh !**

Criant de douleur
et de rage, l'homme
masse son crâne,
sur lequel **pousse
une belle grosse
PRUNE.**

Tout en riant
malgré la gravité
de la situation, les

enfants poursuivent leur course vers la plage. Derrière eux, Lerichepafin, qui s'est relevé, crie encore :

— ATTENDEZ QUE JE VOUS ATTRAPE ! Je vais **tous** vous mettre dans des bocaux !

328

Heureusement pour les jeunes agents secrets et la sirène, la mer ne se trouve qu'à quelques pas. Tout à coup, Perla sort de l'eau, entourée de ses amis dauphins.

– Bellanie, ma sœur !

– **PERLA !**

Quand elle juge qu'elle est suffisamment près des vagues, la SIRÈNE SAUTE de la baignoire.

SPLOUSH !

330

Tandis que Bellanie nage vers sa sœur, les enfants **courent aussi VITE** qu'ils le peuvent pour entrer dans l'eau et échapper au propriétaire du château. Mais ce dernier, qui a réussi à franchir la barrière et à

331

s'approcher d'eux
en courant à toute
vitesse, tend le bras
et attrape Léon,
qui hurle d'effroi.

– **Ouahhhhh!**

– Ne t'en fais pas,
Léon! crie Perla
avant d'enfiler
ses castagnettes.

CLAC-CLAC-CLAC- CLAC-CLAC-CLAC!

Aussitôt, tous les CRABES présents sur cette partie de l'île quittent leurs cachettes et se lancent à l'assaut de Lerichepafin.

333

334

Quand ce dernier comprend ce qui est en train de lui arriver, il ne peut plus se **SAUVER**; les crabes l'ont déjà épinglé. L'un d'entre eux menace même de lui pincer le nez. **CLAC-CLAC !**

— Monsieur Lerichepafin, dit Perla avec sévérité, si vous voulez que mes amis vous **relâchent**, **VOUS DEVEZ PROMETTRE** de ne plus vous en prendre à aucune sirène, ni à aucun

animal vivant dans
l'eau ou sur la terre !

– GRRRR !

L'homme tente
de se dégager,
mais les crabes
le tiennent bien
serré. Par ailleurs,
des pinces claquent
de chaque côté

337

de ses oreilles...
et c'est ce qui finit
par le convaincre.

– **C'est promis!**
ARRÊTEZ! Je
vous en supplie!
Plus jamais je ne
tenterai de chasser,
d'emprisonner
ou d'exploiter
qui que ce soit...

338

— Promettez-vous
aussi de ne plus
JAMAIS TENTER
de fabriquer et
de vendre des
BOISSONS
GAZEUSES
AUX LARMES
DE SIRÈNES ?

— **GrrⅠrrouaah !**

339

340

CLAC-CLAC-CLAC !

– **Je promets !**
Je promets !

– Tant mieux, dit
Perla en lui faisant
les gros yeux.
Et n'oubliez pas
ceci : je vais vous
avoir à l'œil !

Se tournant vers
les crabes, la sirène
les remercie pour
leur collaboration
avant de ranger ses
castagnettes.

Tandis que les
crustacés retournent
à leurs occupations
quotidiennes,
laissant Lerichepafin

342

seul **AVEC SA PRUNE AU MILIEU DE LA PLAGE,** Perla s'adresse aux enfants :

— Il faut y aller, car tes parents, Mimi, sont sur le point de se réveiller...

343

Se souvenant du **tour de MAGIE** qui endort, Léon tente sa chance :

— Pensez-vous que vous pourriez me montrer comment faire pour endormir mes parents ? **CE SERAIT PRATIQUE, IL ME SEMBLE...**

344

PERLA ÉCLATE DE RIRE.

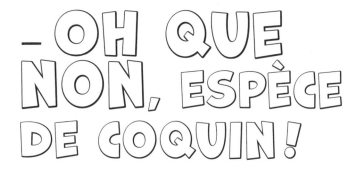

– OH QUE NON, ESPÈCE DE COQUIN !

Puis elle donne le signal du départ aux dauphins.

ET C'EST REPARTI !

CRRR ! HI-HI ! WAOUUUUH !

CHAPITRE 9
LE PLUS MERVEILLEUX DES ANNIVERSAIRES

— **C'est bon de pouvoir nager LIBREMENT dans l'eau salée !** s'exclame Bellanie quand toute la bande se retrouve à nouveau près de la plage du chalet de Mimi. **Merci, chers amis !**

Je n'oublierai jamais
ce que vous avez
fait pour moi !

Trois larmes de joie
coulent sur les joues
de la sirène avant
de se transformer
en belles grosses
billes brillantes.
WOW !

351

Les jeunes n'ont jamais assisté à un tour aussi extraordinaire. Ils en ont le souffle coupé.

– Sous **l'effet du soleil** et du sel marin, les larmes de joie des sirènes

352

se transforment
en billes porte-
bonheur, explique-
t-elle en donnant
une sphère à
chacun des enfants.
**Mais tout ça doit
rester SECRET.**

– PROMIS,
soufflent les trois
jeunes aventuriers.

353

Autour des **sirènes,**
les **DAUPHINS**
bondissent
et s'ébrouent.

HIC-HIC-
CRRRR-
HI-HI-HI !

chantent-ils tout
en éclaboussant
les enfants.

354

Perla les remercie
et les salue avant
de traduire :

— Ils disent que
vous serez toujours
les bienvenus
à Villedesvagues.

— OH ! MERCI !

Les enfants sont très émus.

Perla sourit et fouille dans son petit sac. Elle en sort **cinq MAGNIFIQUES COLLIERS.**

— Il y en a un pour chacun de nous, explique-t-elle.

Ce sont des colliers d'amitié. Je les ai **FABRIQUÉS** en me disant qu'un jour, je rencontrerais des personnes exceptionnelles avec qui je voudrais les PARTAGER. Ce jour est arrivé. Désormais, nous sommes les meilleurs

357

358

amis du monde,
pour toujours.

– **POUR
TOUJOURS**,
répètent les trois
amis en enfilant
chacun leur collier.

– Merci pour tout.
Vous avez sauvé le
royaume des sirènes

de Villedesvagues,
dit gravement Perla.

— **Nous ne vous oublierons JAMAIS**, déclare à son tour Bellanie.

Tout à coup, sous le parasol, Sophie et Nathan se réveillent et s'étirent.

– MIMIIIII, LULUUUUU, LEOOOON ! C'est l'heure du goûter !

– ON ARRIIIIIVE ! crie Mimi, qui SE RETOURNE avec l'intention de demander

aux sirènes si
elle et ses amis
auront l'occasion
de les revoir un jour.

OH! ELLES ONT DISPARU!

— **C'était juste trop, trop génial!** lance Léon en sortant de l'eau. En tout cas, j'ai hâte de goûter à ton **GÂTEAU**. Cette aventure m'a creusé l'appétit...

— Je n'aurais jamais **pensé** vivre une telle histoire... ajoute Lulu, qui regarde sa bille avec ravissement.

– C'est le plus beau jour **de ma vie !** s'exclame Mimi.

Nathan et Sophie se joignent au groupe. Et, en chœur, tout le monde se met **À CHANTER** :

Ma chère Mimi, c'est à ton tour...

364

GLOSSAIRE

Accourir : arriver
en courant

Désaltérer : rafraîchir,
couper la soif

Écarquiller : ouvrir grand
(les yeux)

En détresse (être) :
en danger

Étonné : surpris

Incongrus : bizarres

Ravissement : grande joie

Ronchonner : grogner

Squale : requin

Dominique de Loppinot

Mini Toon

La nuit des patates zombies

RICHARD PETIT

Mini Toon

Mais où il est, ce dragon ?

CATHERINE ROUSSEL

Mini Toon

Les matantes de l'espace

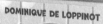

DOMINIQUE DE LOPPINOT

Mini Toon

Des pirates dans ma baignoire

Julie Royer

Mini Toon

Les sirènes pleurent des bulles

CINDY ROY

Mini Toon

CENT DRILLONS À LA POSTE !